CAPTAIN AMERICA + CABLE | WOLVERINE + HULK | BLACK WIDOW + ROGUE | IRON MAN + KITTY PRYDE | BLACK PANTHER + STORM | HAWKEYE + GAMBIT

SPIDER-MAN + BEAST | CAPTAIN AMERICA + QUENTIN QUIRE | IRON FIST + DOOP | LOKI + MISTER SINISTER | WOLVERINE + CAPTAIN MARVEL | THING + GAMBIT

W9-BAF-424

DEC 17 2013

# A+X =AWESOME

| WRITERS | PENCILERS | INKERS |
|---|---|---|
| DAN SLOTT, JEPH LOEB, CHRIS BACHALO, PETER DAVID, JASON AARON, KAARE ANDREWS, JASON LATOUR, KATHRYN IMMONEN, KIERON GILLEN & MIKE COSTA | RON GARNEY, DALE KEOWN, CHRIS BACHALO, MIKE DEL MUNDO, PASQUAL FERRY, BILLY TAN, DAVID LÓPEZ, DAVID LAFUENTE, JOE BENNETT, GIUSEPPE CAMUNCOLI & STEFANO CASELLI | DANNY MIKI, CAM SMITH, MARK MORALES, TIM TOWNSEND, MIKE DEL MUNDO, PASQUAL FERRY, BILLY TAN, KAARE ANDREWS, ALVARO LÓPEZ, DAVID LAFUENTE, MICHELE BENEVENTO & STEFANO CASELLI |

COLOR ARTISTS: WIL QUINTANA, FRANK D'ARMATA, CHRIS BACHALO, BRIAN REBER, JIM CHARALAMPIDIS, LEE LOUGHRIDGE, JIM CAMPBELL, DAN BROWN & ANDRES MOSSA

LETTERERS: VC'S CLAYTON COWLES WITH COMICRAFT'S ALBERT DESCHESNE (#1)

COVER ART: DALE KEOWN & MORRY HOLLOWELL (#1), CHRIS BACHALO & TIM TOWNSEND (#2), PASQUAL FERRY & DAVID CURIEL (#3), KAARE ANDREWS (#4), DAVID LAFUENTE & JIM CHARALAMPIDIS (#5), AND GIUSEPPE CAMUNCOLI & RAIN BEREDO (#6)

ASSOCIATE EDITOR: JORDAN D. WHITE    EDITOR: NICK LOWE

WITH ASSISTANT EDITOR: JENNIFER M. SMITH (#6)    EDITOR: JEANINE SCHAEFER (#6)

COLLECTION EDITOR: JENNIFER GRÜNWALD    ASSISTANT EDITORS: ALEX STARBUCK & NELSON RIBEIRO
EDITOR, SPECIAL PROJECTS: MARK D. BEAZLEY    SENIOR EDITOR, SPECIAL PROJECTS: JEFF YOUNGQUIST
SVP OF PRINT & DIGITAL PUBLISHING SALES: DAVID GABRIEL    BOOK DESIGNER: RODOLFO MURAGUCHI

EDITOR IN CHIEF: AXEL ALONSO    CHIEF CREATIVE OFFICER: JOE QUESADA
PUBLISHER: DAN BUCKLEY    EXECUTIVE PRODUCER: ALAN FINE

A+X VOL. 1: = AWESOME. Contains material originally published in magazine form as A+X #1-6. First printing 2013. ISBN# 978-0-7851-6674-0. Published by MARVEL WORLDWIDE, INC., a subsidiary of MARVEL ENTERTAINMENT, LLC. OFFICE OF PUBLICATION: 135 West 50th Street, New York, NY 10020. Copyright © 2012 and 2013 Marvel Characters, Inc. All rights reserved. All characters featured in this issue and the distinctive names and likenesses thereof, and all related indicia are trademarks of Marvel Characters, Inc. No similarity between any of the names, characters, persons, and/or institutions in this magazine with those of any living or dead person or institution is intended, and any such similarity which may exist is purely coincidental. **Printed in the U.S.A.** ALAN FINE, EVP - Office of the President, Marvel Worldwide, Inc. and EVP & CMO Marvel Characters B.V.; DAN BUCKLEY, Publisher & President - Print, Animation & Digital Divisions; JOE QUESADA, Chief Creative Officer; TOM BREVOORT, SVP of Publishing; DAVID BOGART, SVP of Operations & Procurement, Publishing; C.B. CEBULSKI, SVP of Creator & Content Development; DAVID GABRIEL, SVP of Print & Digital Publishing Sales; JIM O'KEEFE, VP of Operations & Logistics; DAN CARR, Executive Director of Publishing Technology; SUSAN CRESPI, Editorial Operations Manager; ALEX MORALES, Publishing Operations Manager; STAN LEE, Chairman Emeritus. For information regarding advertising in Marvel Comics or on Marvel.com, please contact Niza Disla, Director of Marvel Partnerships, at ndisla@marvel.com. For Marvel subscription inquiries, please call 800-217-9158. **Manufactured between 4/3/2013 and 5/6/2013 by QUAD/GRAPHICS, VERSAILLES, KY, USA.**

10 9 8 7 6 5 4 3 2 1

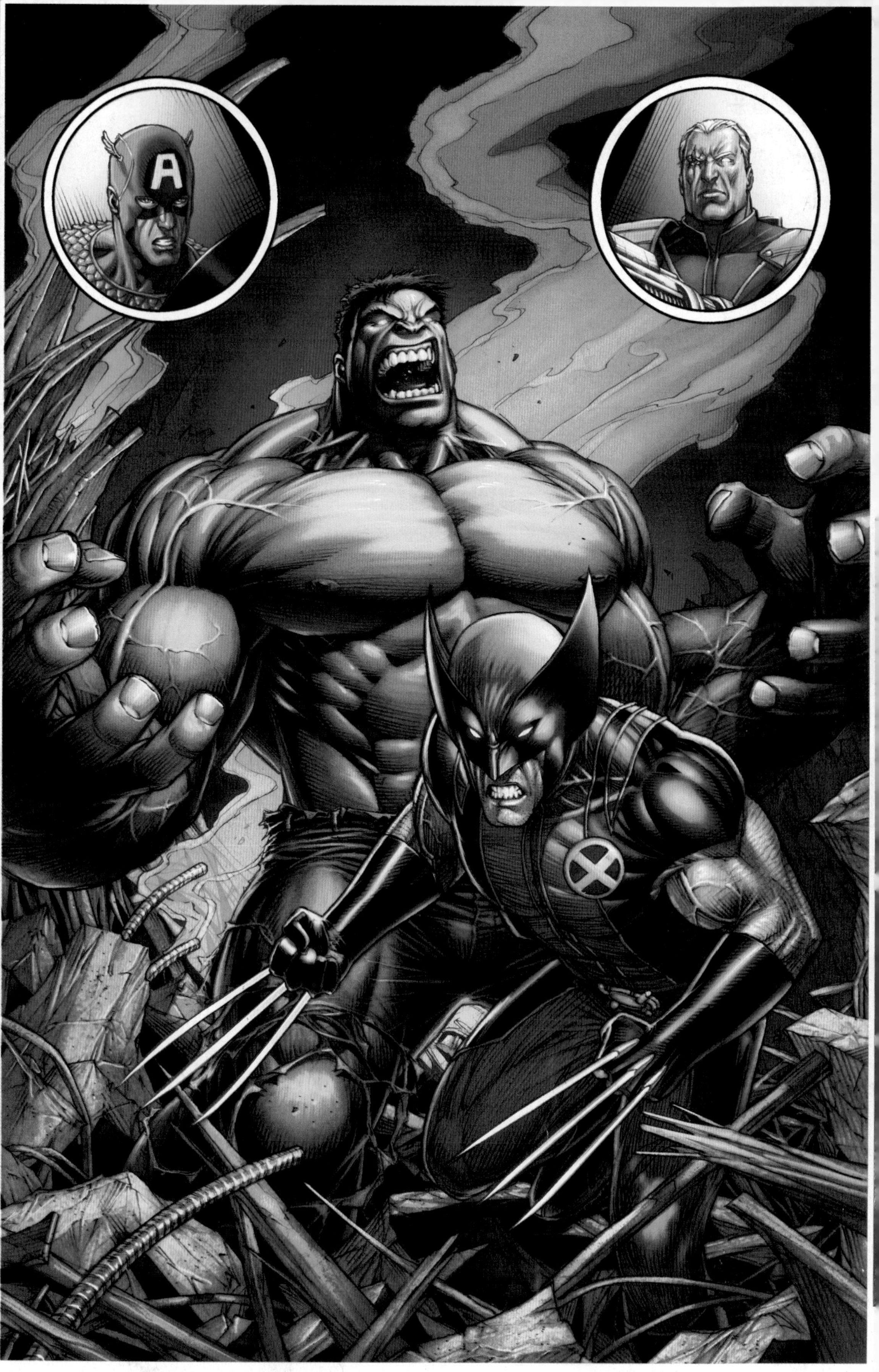

**A + X = 1**

Q: Hello, there! What comic book is this?
A: This is A+X, the comic where we add one AVENGER plus one X-MAN and get ONE MILLION AWESOMES worth of TEAM-UP ACTION!

Q: Oh, is this sort of like that AVX thing I heard about?
A: NO WAY! That was Avengers VERSUS X-Men! This is totally after that, when they've put their differences aside in favor of being BEST PALS working together to BEAT the PUDDING out of BAD GUYS!

Q: OK, so this has nothing to do with the end of AVX 12 with the Phoenix Force and the--?
A: Nope! Forget all that and just jump in with BOTH FEET for TWO TITANIC TALES of HERCULEAN HEROISM combating VENTURESOME VILLAINY.

Q: So, who's in this issue?
A: First story has CAPTAIN AMERICA, America's premier SUPER-SOLDIER from WORLD WAR TWO teaming up with CABLE, a TIME-JUMPING mutant soldier of fortune with CYBORG PARTS. You can only IMAGINE how much they have in COMMON!

Q: What about the second story?
A: That one's got HULK and WOLVERINE. You know Hulk, right? Big GREEN guy who gets ANGRY and SMASHES THINGS. Wolverine is a little CANADIAN guy who gets ANGRY and SLASHES THINGS (with his metal claws).

Q: So, where do these stories take place in each character's continuity?
A: STOP THINKING SO MUCH! It fits where it fits! It's enough to know that these stories ROCK! Now, GET READING!

# CAPTAIN AMERICA + CABLE

| DAN SLOTT | RON GARNEY | DANNY MIKI | CAM SMITH | MARK MORALES | WIL QUINTANA | VC'S CLAYTON COWLES |
|---|---|---|---|---|---|---|
| WRITER | PENCILER | INKERS | | | COLORIST | LETTERER |

# THE INCREDIBLE HULK + WOLVERINE

| JEPH LOEB | DALE KEOWN | DANNY MIKI | FRANK D'ARMATA | COMICRAFT'S ALBERT DESCHESNE |
|---|---|---|---|---|
| WRITER | PENCILER | INKER | COLORIST | LETTERER |

| JORDAN D. WHITE | NICK LOWE | AXEL ALONSO | JOE QUESADA | DAN BUCKLEY | ALAN FINE |
|---|---|---|---|---|---|
| ASSISTANT EDITOR | EDITOR | EDITOR IN CHIEF | CHIEF CREATIVE OFFICER | PUBLISHER | EXECUTIVE PRODUCER |

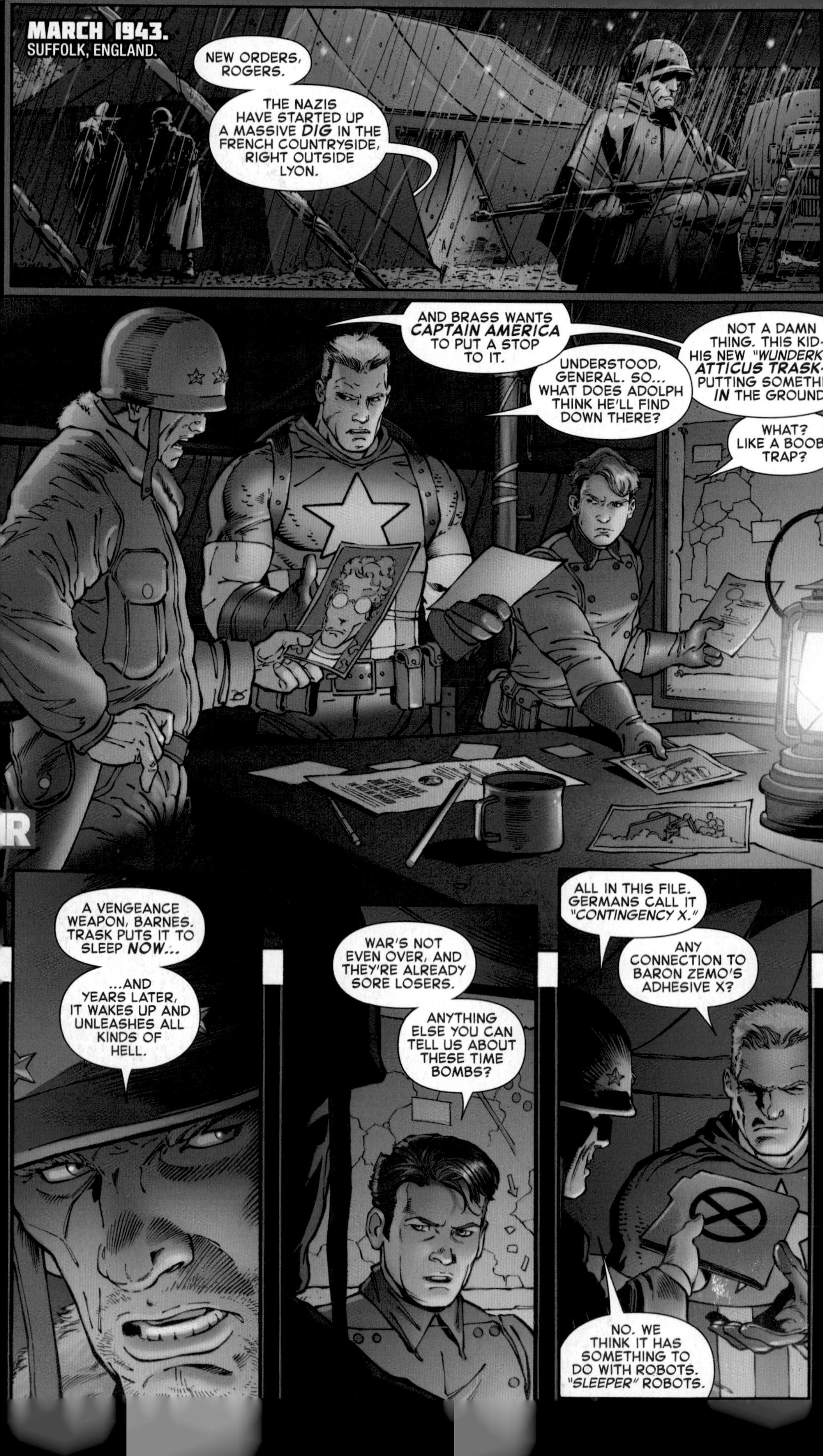
MARCH 1943.
SUFFOLK, ENGLAND.
NEW ORDERS, ROGERS.
THE NAZIS HAVE STARTED UP A MASSIVE DIG IN THE FRENCH COUNTRYSIDE, RIGHT OUTSIDE LYON.
AND BRASS WANTS CAPTAIN AMERICA TO PUT A STOP TO IT.
UNDERSTOOD, GENERAL. SO... WHAT DOES ADOLPH THINK HE'LL FIND DOWN THERE?
NOT A DAMN THING. THIS KID-- HIS NEW "WUNDERKIND," ATTICUS TRASK--IS PUTTING SOMETHING IN THE GROUND.
WHAT? LIKE A BOOBY TRAP?
A VENGEANCE WEAPON, BARNES. TRASK PUTS IT TO SLEEP NOW...
...AND YEARS LATER, IT WAKES UP AND UNLEASHES ALL KINDS OF HELL.
WAR'S NOT EVEN OVER, AND THEY'RE ALREADY SORE LOSERS.
ANYTHING ELSE YOU CAN TELL US ABOUT THESE TIME BOMBS?
ALL IN THIS FILE. GERMANS CALL IT "CONTINGENCY X."
ANY CONNECTION TO BARON ZEMO'S ADHESIVE X?
NO. WE THINK IT HAS SOMETHING TO DO WITH ROBOTS. "SLEEPER" ROBOTS.

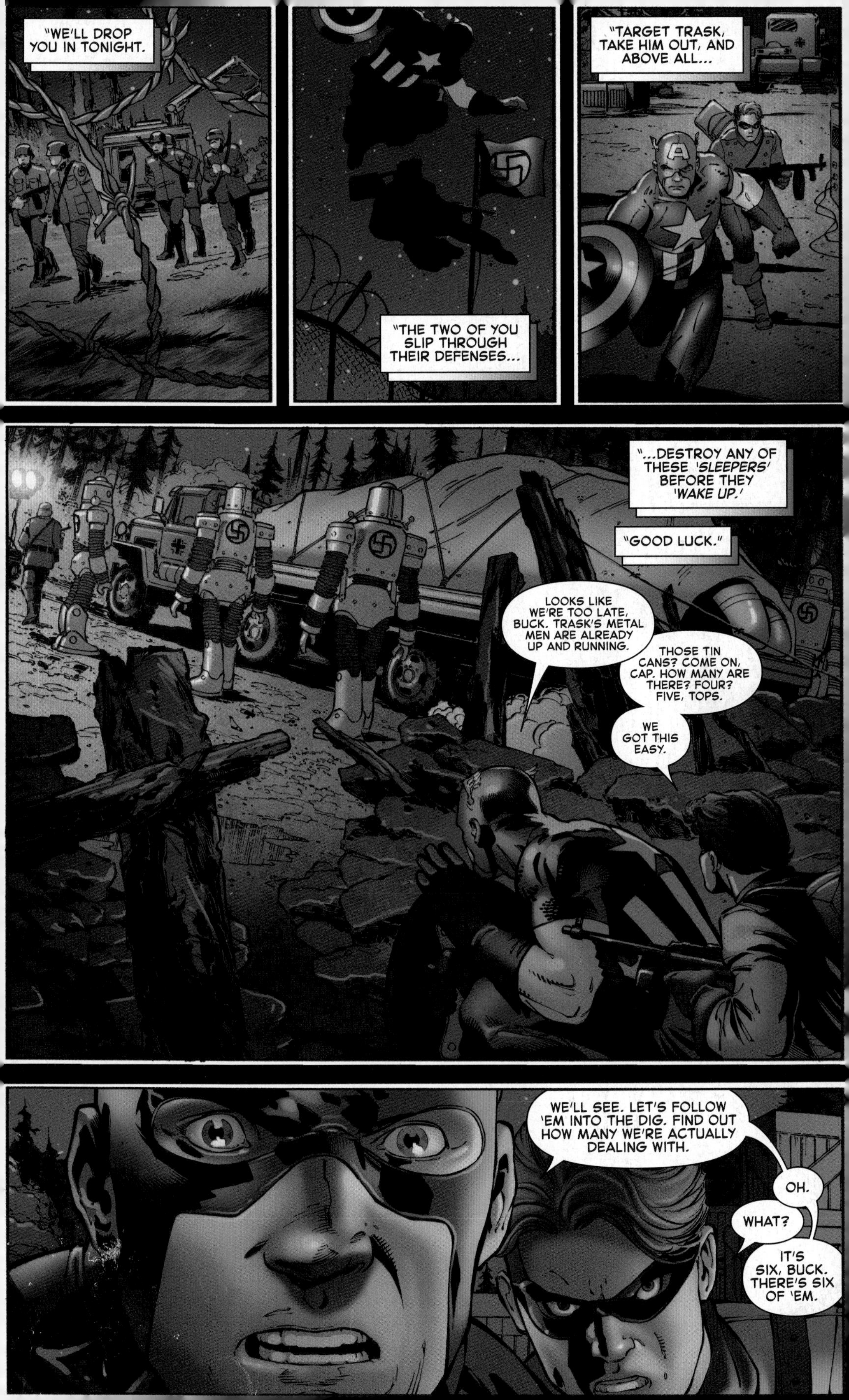
"WE'LL DROP YOU IN TONIGHT.
"THE TWO OF YOU SLIP THROUGH THEIR DEFENSES...
"TARGET TRASK, TAKE HIM OUT, AND ABOVE ALL...
"...DESTROY ANY OF THESE 'SLEEPERS' BEFORE THEY 'WAKE UP.'
"GOOD LUCK."
LOOKS LIKE WE'RE TOO LATE, BUCK. TRASK'S METAL MEN ARE ALREADY UP AND RUNNING.
THOSE TIN CANS? COME ON, CAP. HOW MANY ARE THERE? FOUR? FIVE, TOPS.
WE GOT THIS EASY.
WE'LL SEE. LET'S FOLLOW 'EM INTO THE DIG. FIND OUT HOW MANY WE'RE ACTUALLY DEALING WITH.
OH.
WHAT?
IT'S SIX, BUCK. THERE'S SIX OF 'EM.

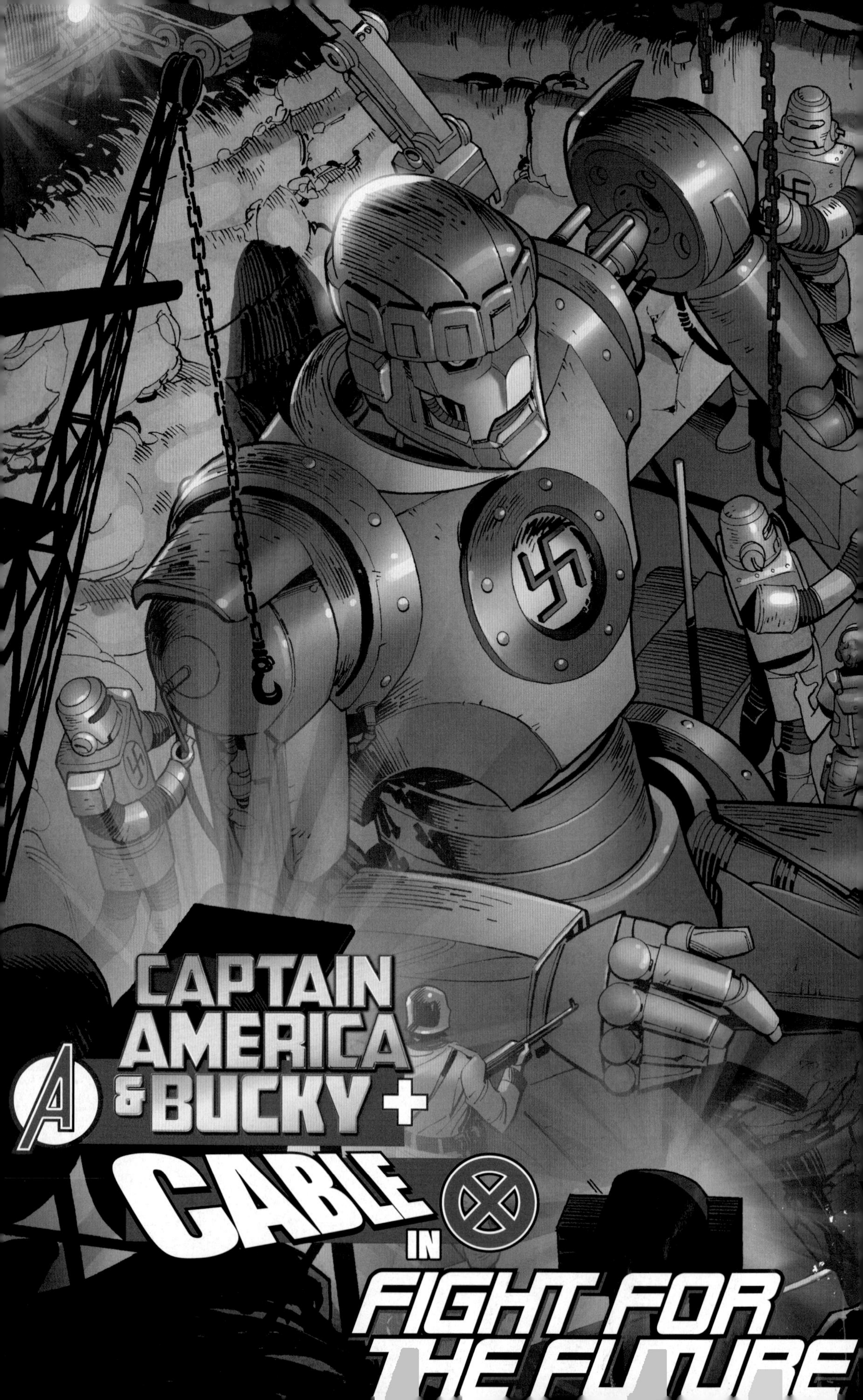

CAPTAIN AMERICA & BUCKY +
CABLE
IN
FIGHT FOR THE FUTURE

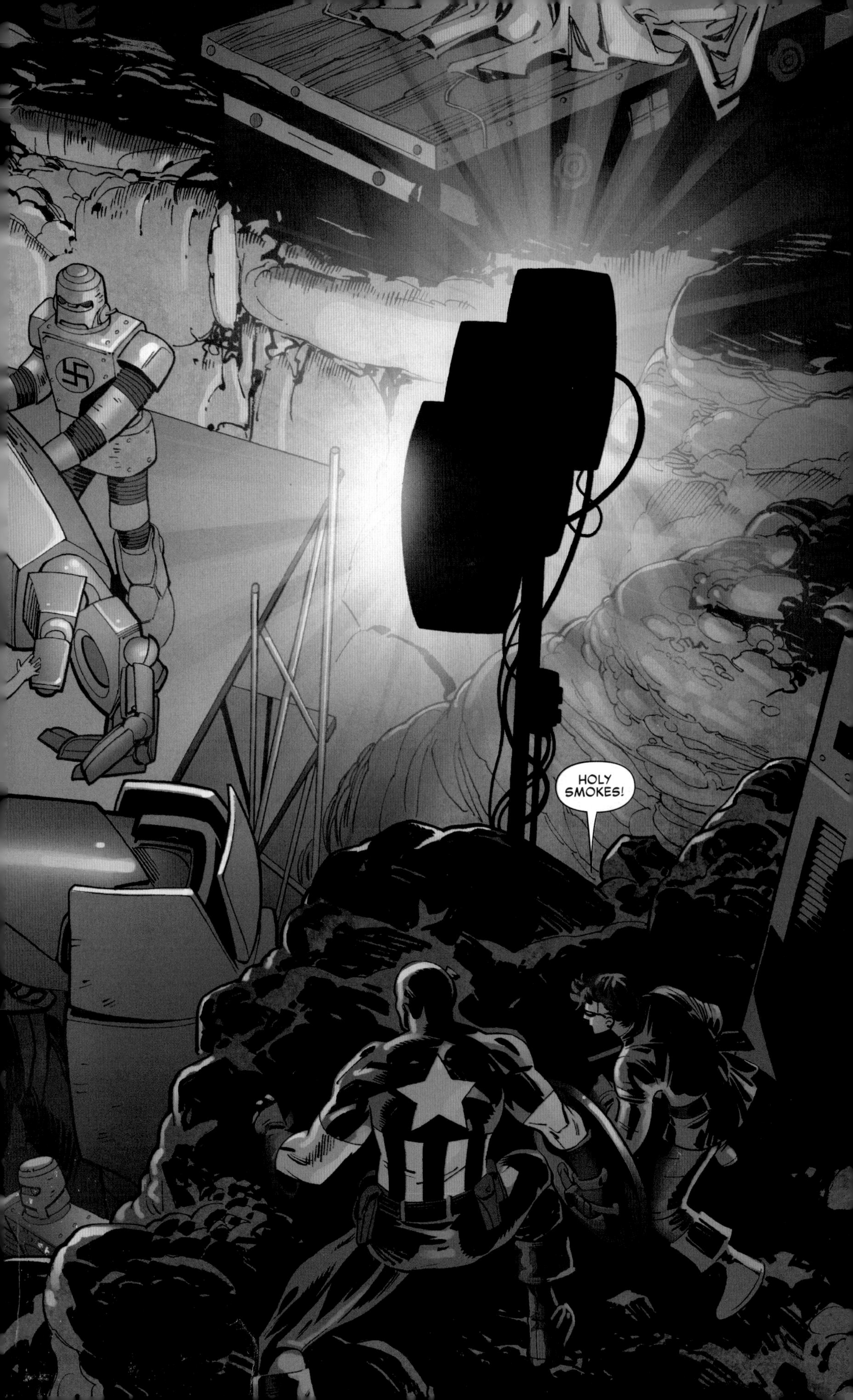
HOLY SMOKES!

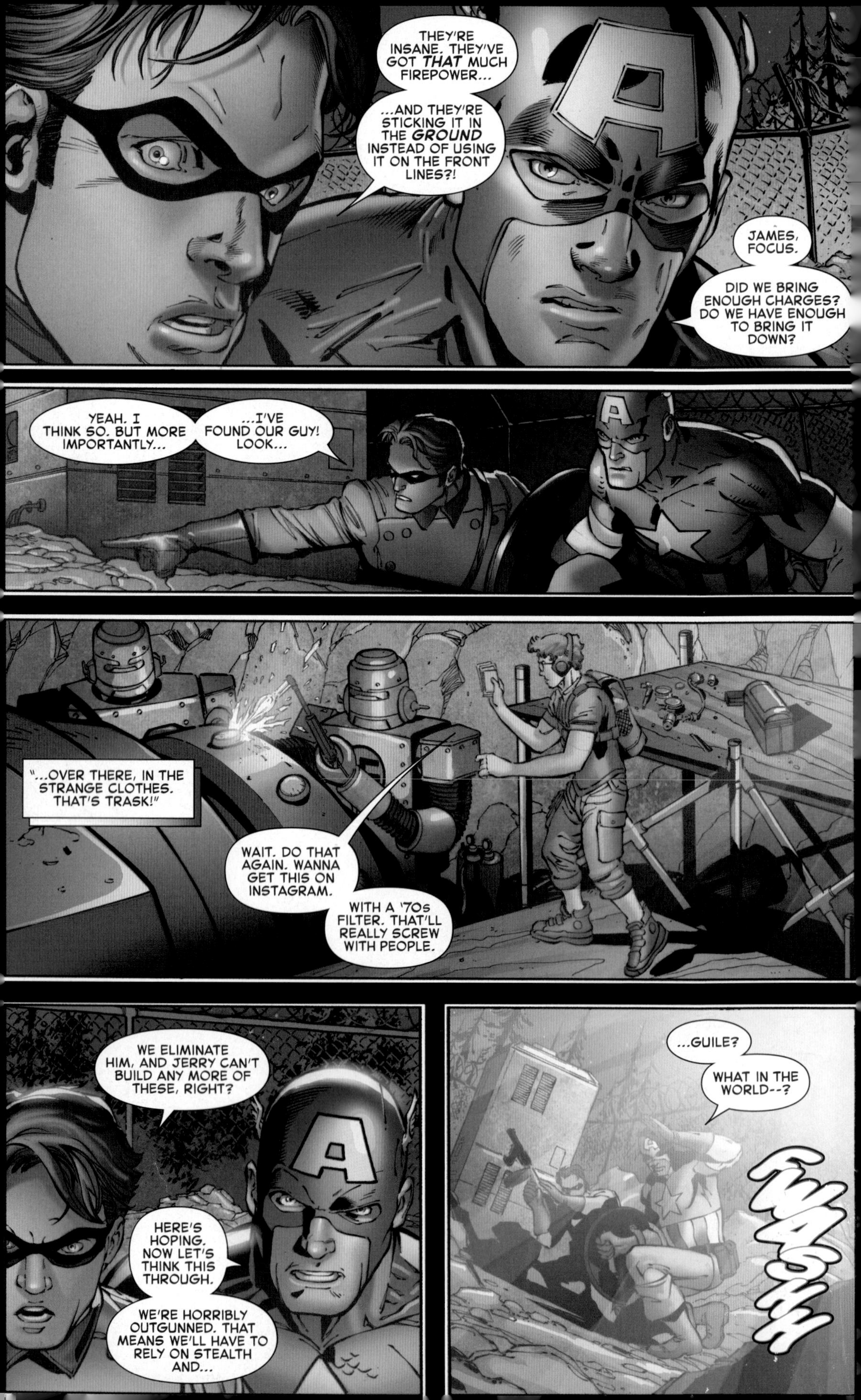
THEY'RE INSANE. THEY'VE GOT THAT MUCH FIREPOWER...
...AND THEY'RE STICKING IT IN THE GROUND INSTEAD OF USING IT ON THE FRONT LINES?!
JAMES, FOCUS.
DID WE BRING ENOUGH CHARGES? DO WE HAVE ENOUGH TO BRING IT DOWN?
YEAH. I THINK SO. BUT MORE IMPORTANTLY...
...I'VE FOUND OUR GUY! LOOK...
"...OVER THERE, IN THE STRANGE CLOTHES. THAT'S TRASK!"
WAIT. DO THAT AGAIN. WANNA GET THIS ON INSTAGRAM.
WITH A '70s FILTER. THAT'LL REALLY SCREW WITH PEOPLE.
WE ELIMINATE HIM, AND JERRY CAN'T BUILD ANY MORE OF THESE, RIGHT?
HERE'S HOPING. NOW LET'S THINK THIS THROUGH.
WE'RE HORRIBLY OUTGUNNED. THAT MEANS WE'LL HAVE TO RELY ON STEALTH AND...
...GUILE?
WHAT IN THE WORLD--?
FWASHH

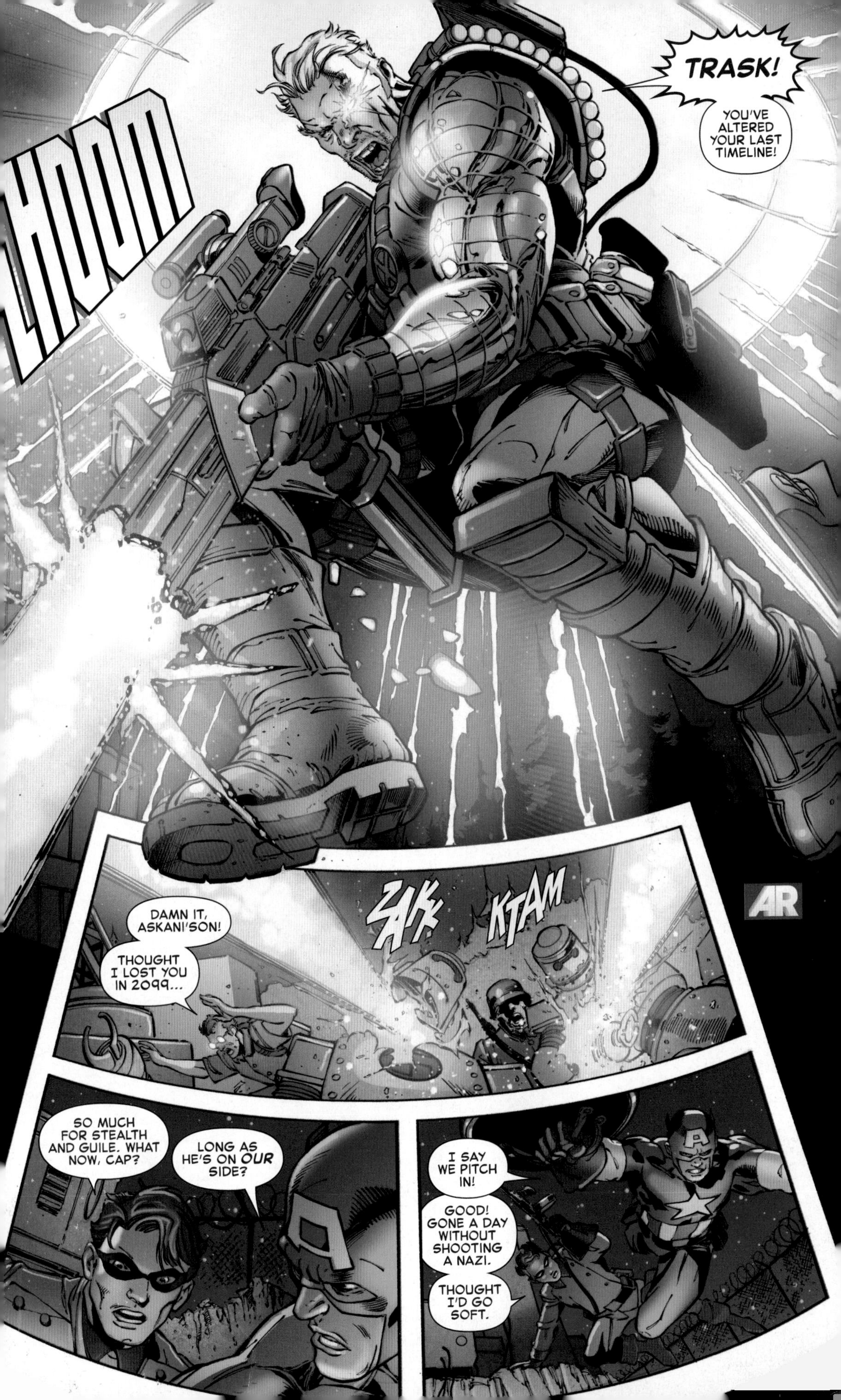

CHOOM
TRASK!
YOU'VE ALTERED YOUR LAST TIMELINE!
ZAK
KTAM
DAMN IT, ASKANI'SON!
THOUGHT I LOST YOU IN 2099...
SO MUCH FOR STEALTH AND GUILE. WHAT NOW, CAP?
LONG AS HE'S ON OUR SIDE?
I SAY WE PITCH IN!
GOOD! GONE A DAY WITHOUT SHOOTING A NAZI.
THOUGHT I'D GO SOFT.

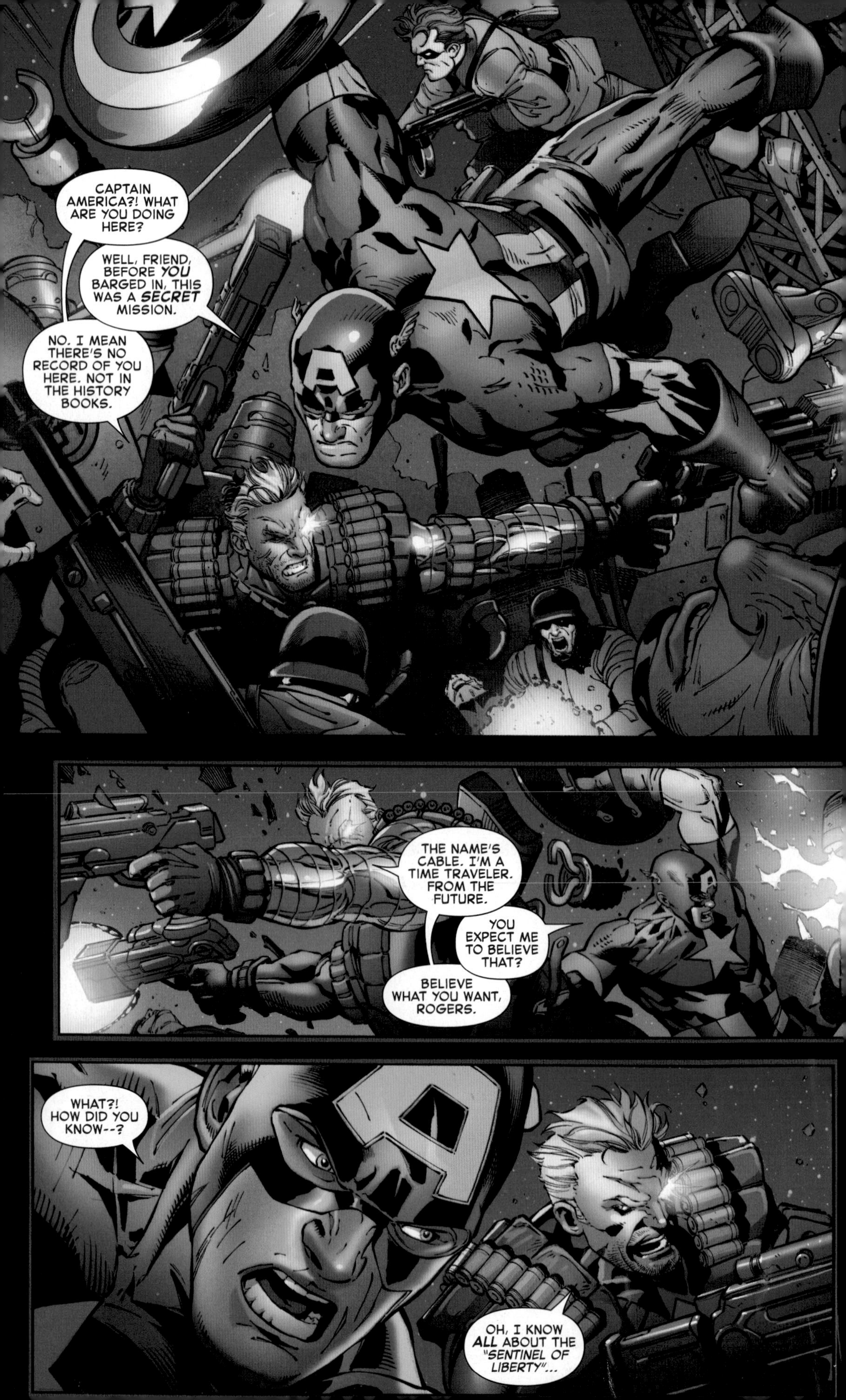
CAPTAIN AMERICA?! WHAT ARE YOU DOING HERE?
WELL, FRIEND, BEFORE YOU BARGED IN, THIS WAS A SECRET MISSION.
NO. I MEAN THERE'S NO RECORD OF YOU HERE. NOT IN THE HISTORY BOOKS.
THE NAME'S CABLE. I'M A TIME TRAVELER. FROM THE FUTURE.
YOU EXPECT ME TO BELIEVE THAT?
BELIEVE WHAT YOU WANT, ROGERS.
WHAT?! HOW DID YOU KNOW--?
OH, I KNOW ALL ABOUT THE "SENTINEL OF LIBERTY"...

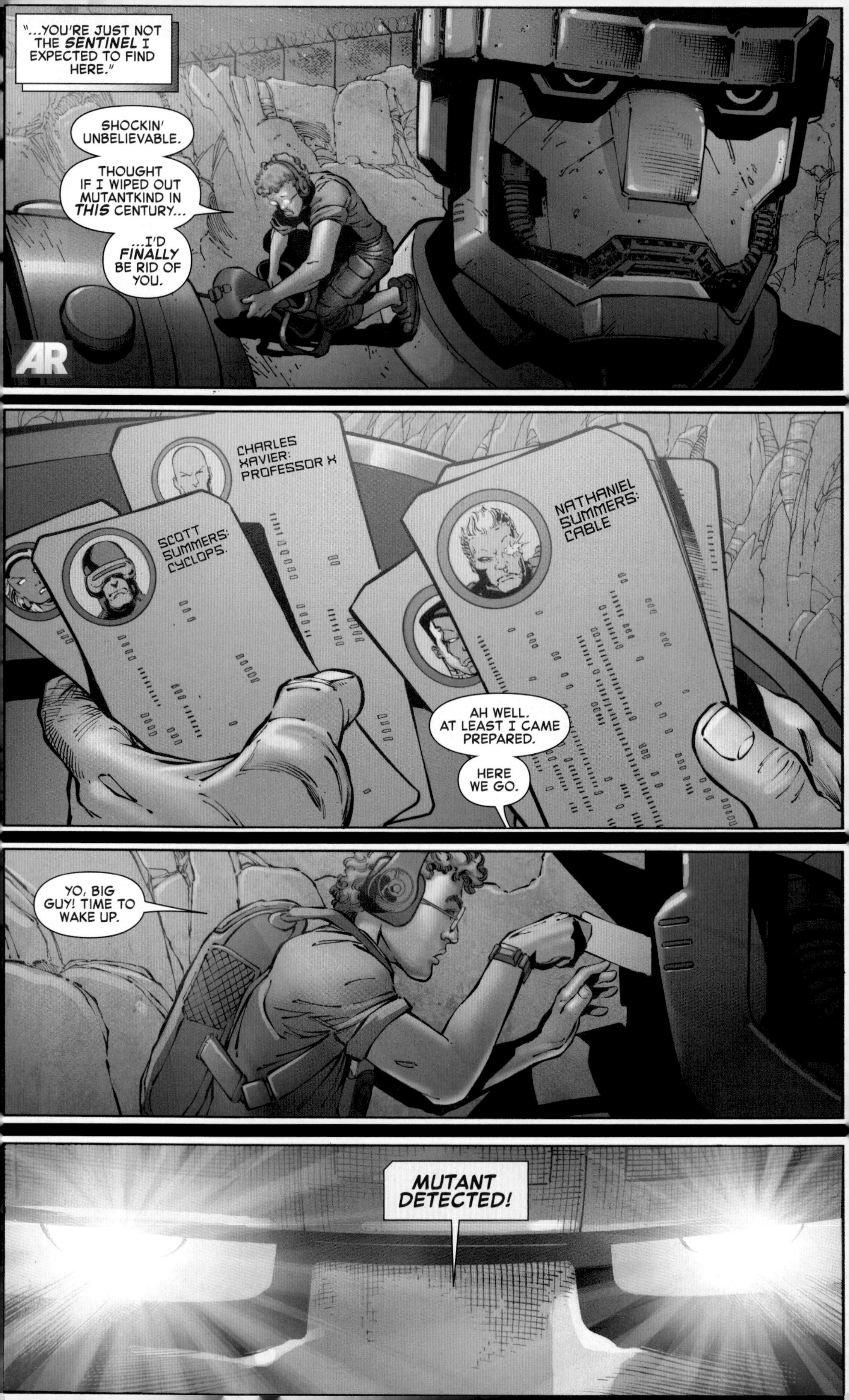
"...YOU'RE JUST NOT THE SENTINEL I EXPECTED TO FIND HERE."
SHOCKIN' UNBELIEVABLE.
THOUGHT IF I WIPED OUT MUTANTKIND IN THIS CENTURY...
...I'D FINALLY BE RID OF YOU.
CHARLES XAVIER: PROFESSOR X
SCOTT SUMMERS: CYCLOPS.
NATHANIEL SUMMERS: CABLE
AH WELL. AT LEAST I CAME PREPARED.
HERE WE GO.
YO, BIG GUY! TIME TO WAKE UP.
MUTANT DETECTED!

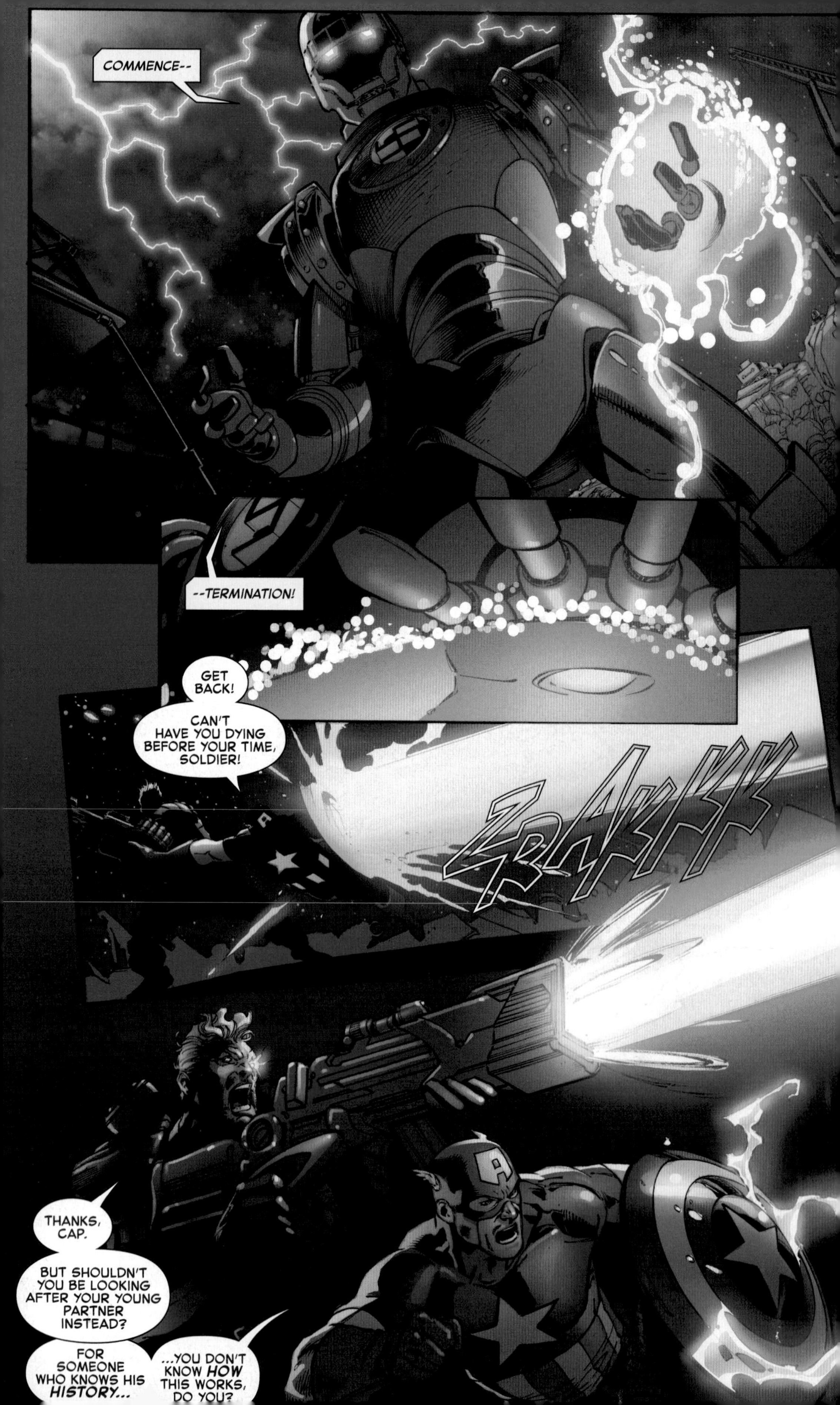
COMMENCE--
--TERMINATION!
GET BACK!
CAN'T HAVE YOU DYING BEFORE YOUR TIME, SOLDIER!
ZRAKKK
THANKS, CAP.
BUT SHOULDN'T YOU BE LOOKING AFTER YOUR YOUNG PARTNER INSTEAD?
FOR SOMEONE WHO KNOWS HIS HISTORY...
...YOU DON'T KNOW HOW THIS WORKS, DO YOU?

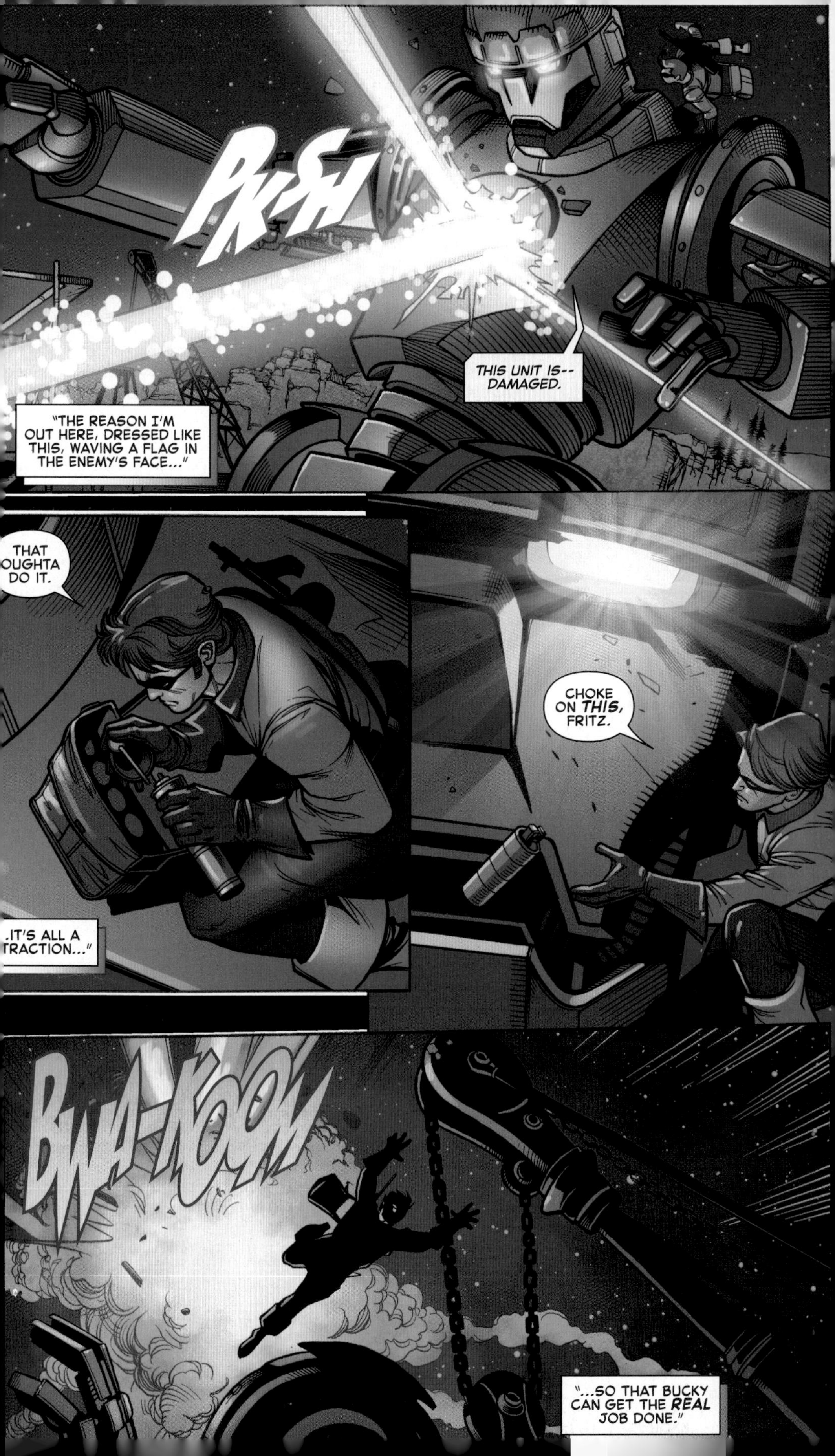
PKSH
THIS UNIT IS--
DAMAGED.
"THE REASON I'M OUT HERE, DRESSED LIKE THIS, WAVING A FLAG IN THE ENEMY'S FACE..."
THAT OUGHTA DO IT.
.IT'S ALL A TRACTION..."
CHOKE ON THIS, FRITZ.
BWA-KOOM
"...SO THAT BUCKY CAN GET THE REAL JOB DONE."

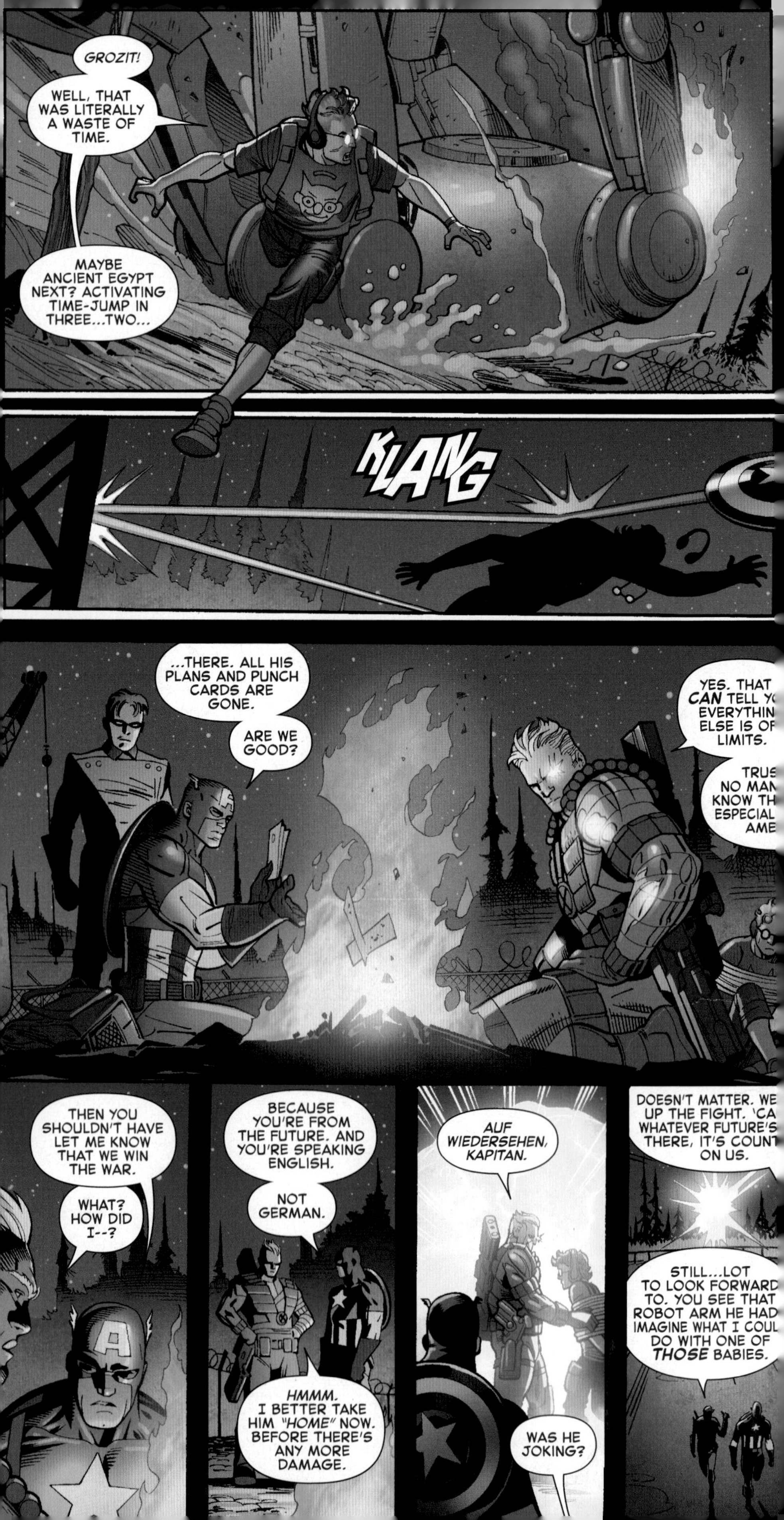
GROZIT!
WELL, THAT WAS LITERALLY A WASTE OF TIME.
MAYBE ANCIENT EGYPT NEXT? ACTIVATING TIME-JUMP IN THREE...TWO...
KLANG
...THERE. ALL HIS PLANS AND PUNCH CARDS ARE GONE.
ARE WE GOOD?
YES. THAT CAN TELL YO EVERYTHIN ELSE IS OF LIMITS.
TRUS NO MAN KNOW TH ESPECIAL AME
THEN YOU SHOULDN'T HAVE LET ME KNOW THAT WE WIN THE WAR.
WHAT? HOW DID I--?
BECAUSE YOU'RE FROM THE FUTURE. AND YOU'RE SPEAKING ENGLISH.
NOT GERMAN.
HMMM. I BETTER TAKE HIM "HOME" NOW. BEFORE THERE'S ANY MORE DAMAGE.
AUF WIEDERSEHEN, KAPITAN.
WAS HE JOKING?
DOESN'T MATTER. WE UP THE FIGHT. 'CA WHATEVER FUTURE'S THERE, IT'S COUNT ON US.
STILL...LOT TO LOOK FORWARD TO. YOU SEE THAT ROBOT ARM HE HAD IMAGINE WHAT I COUL DO WITH ONE OF THOSE BABIES.

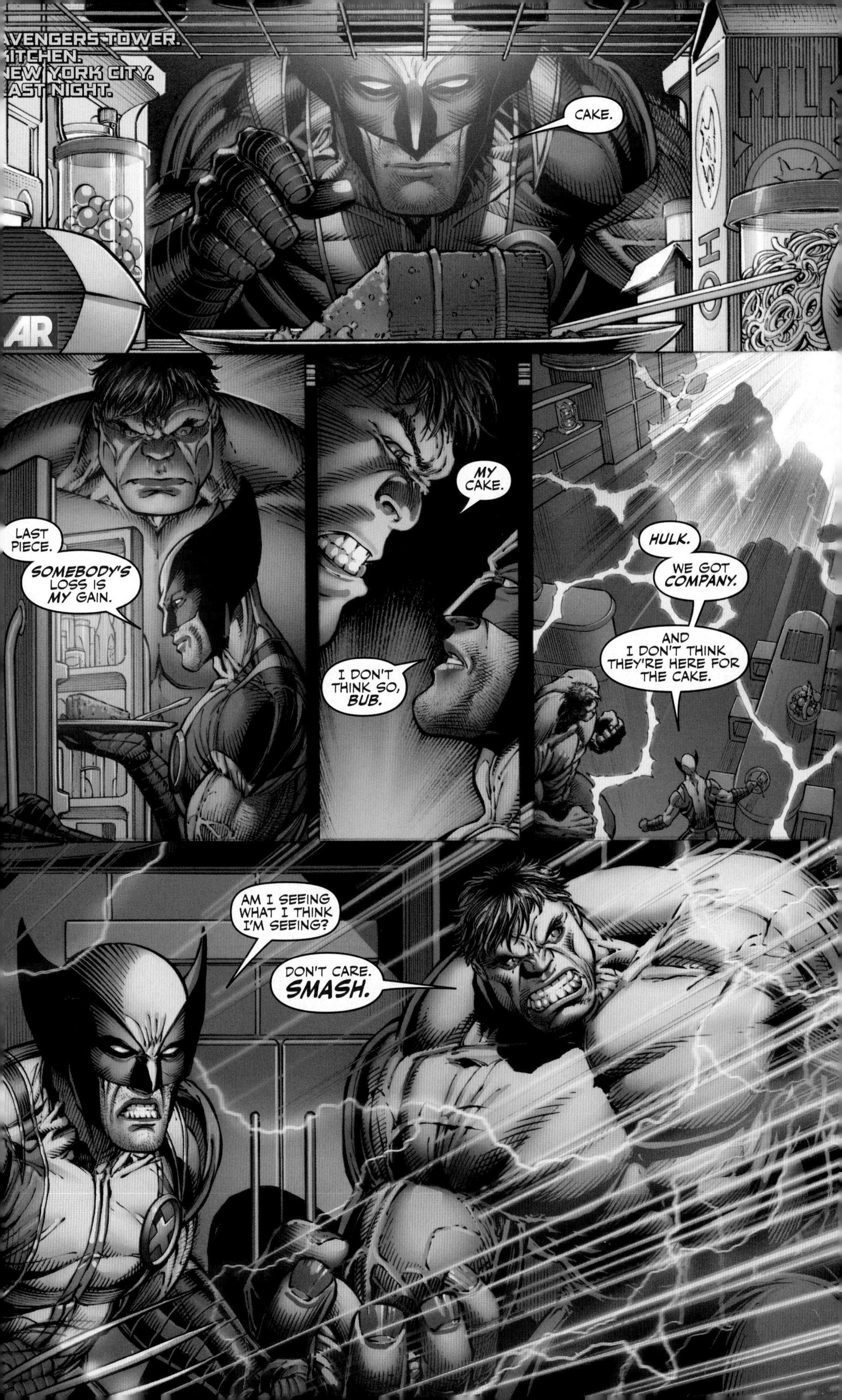

AVENGERS TOWER. KITCHEN. NEW YORK CITY. LAST NIGHT.
CAKE.
MILK
LAST PIECE.
SOMEBODY'S LOSS IS MY GAIN.
MY CAKE.
I DON'T THINK SO, BUB.
HULK.
WE GOT COMPANY.
AND I DON'T THINK THEY'RE HERE FOR THE CAKE.
AM I SEEING WHAT I THINK I'M SEEING?
DON'T CARE. SMASH.

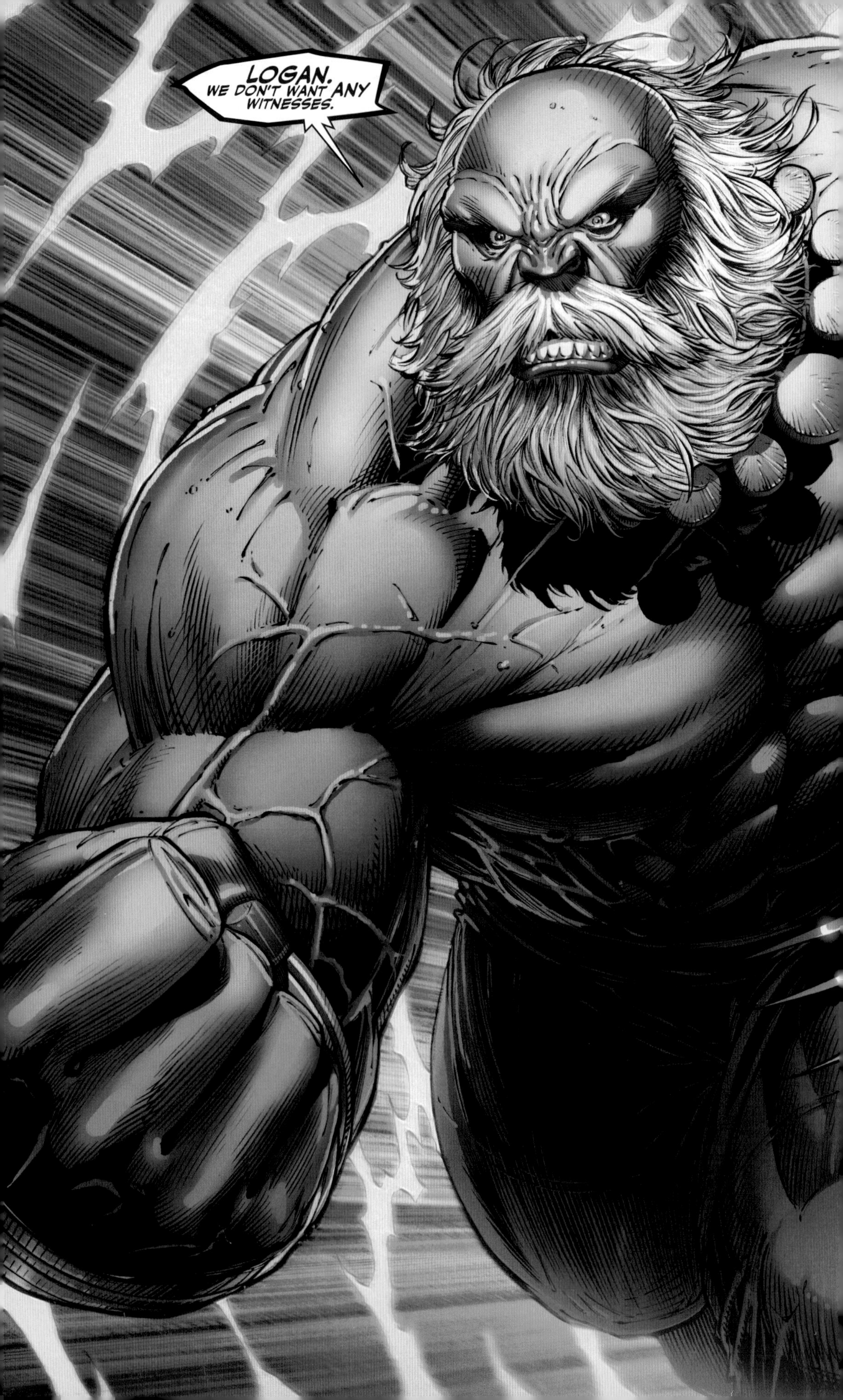
LOGAN. WE DON'T WANT ANY WITNESSES.

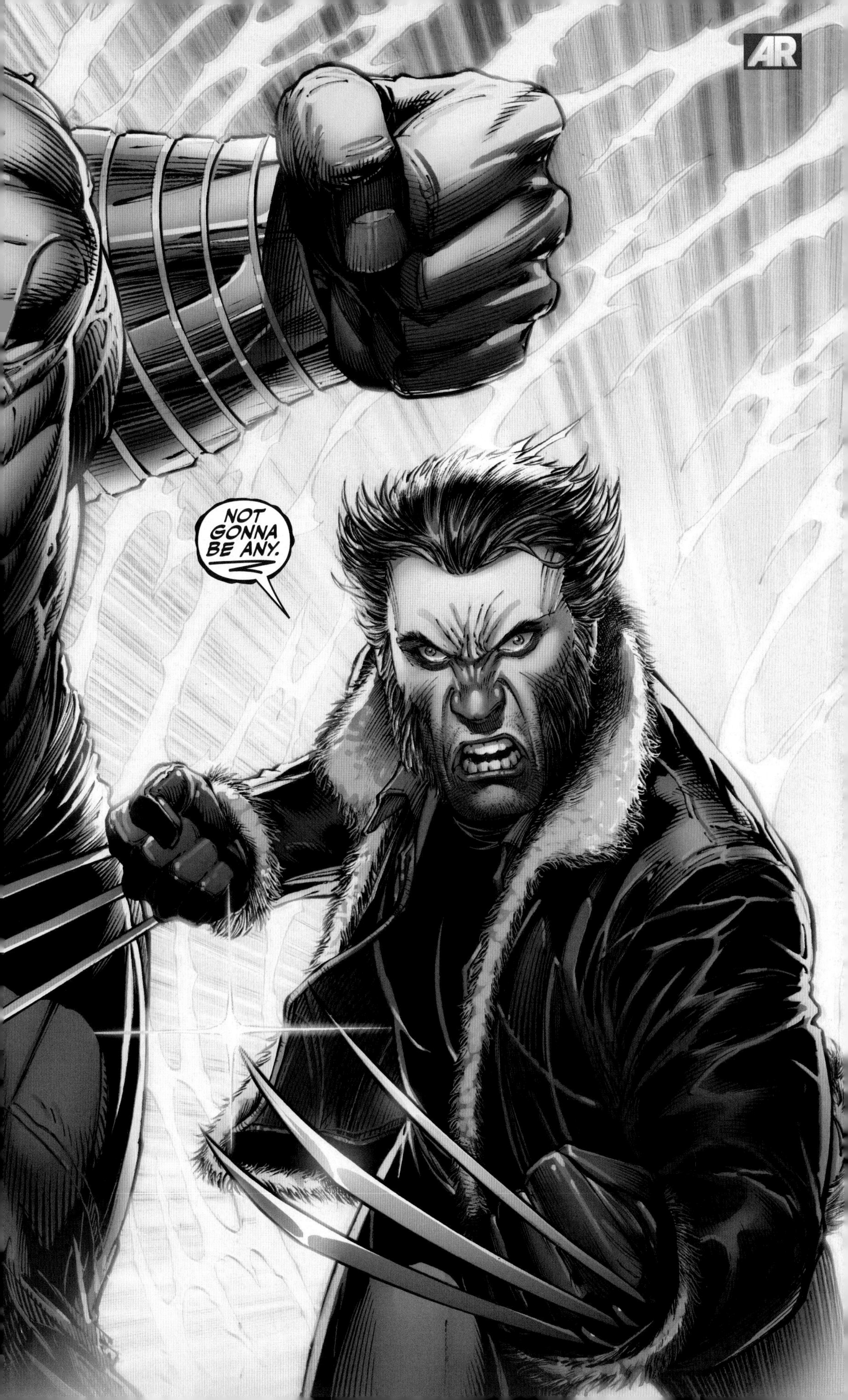
NOT GONNA BE ANY.

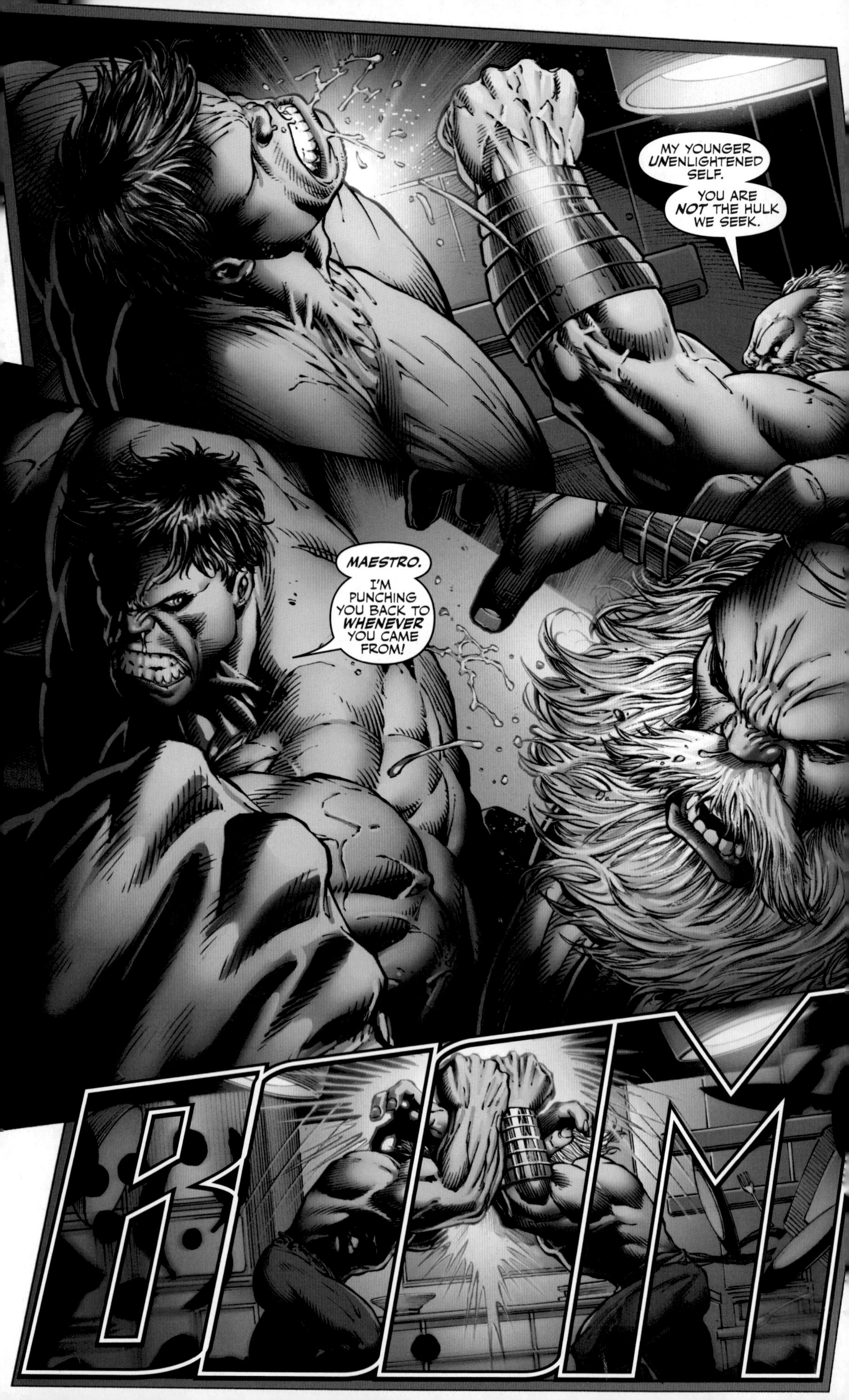
MY YOUNGER UNENLIGHTENED SELF.
YOU ARE NOT THE HULK WE SEEK.
MAESTRO.
I'M PUNCHING YOU BACK TO WHENEVER YOU CAME FROM!

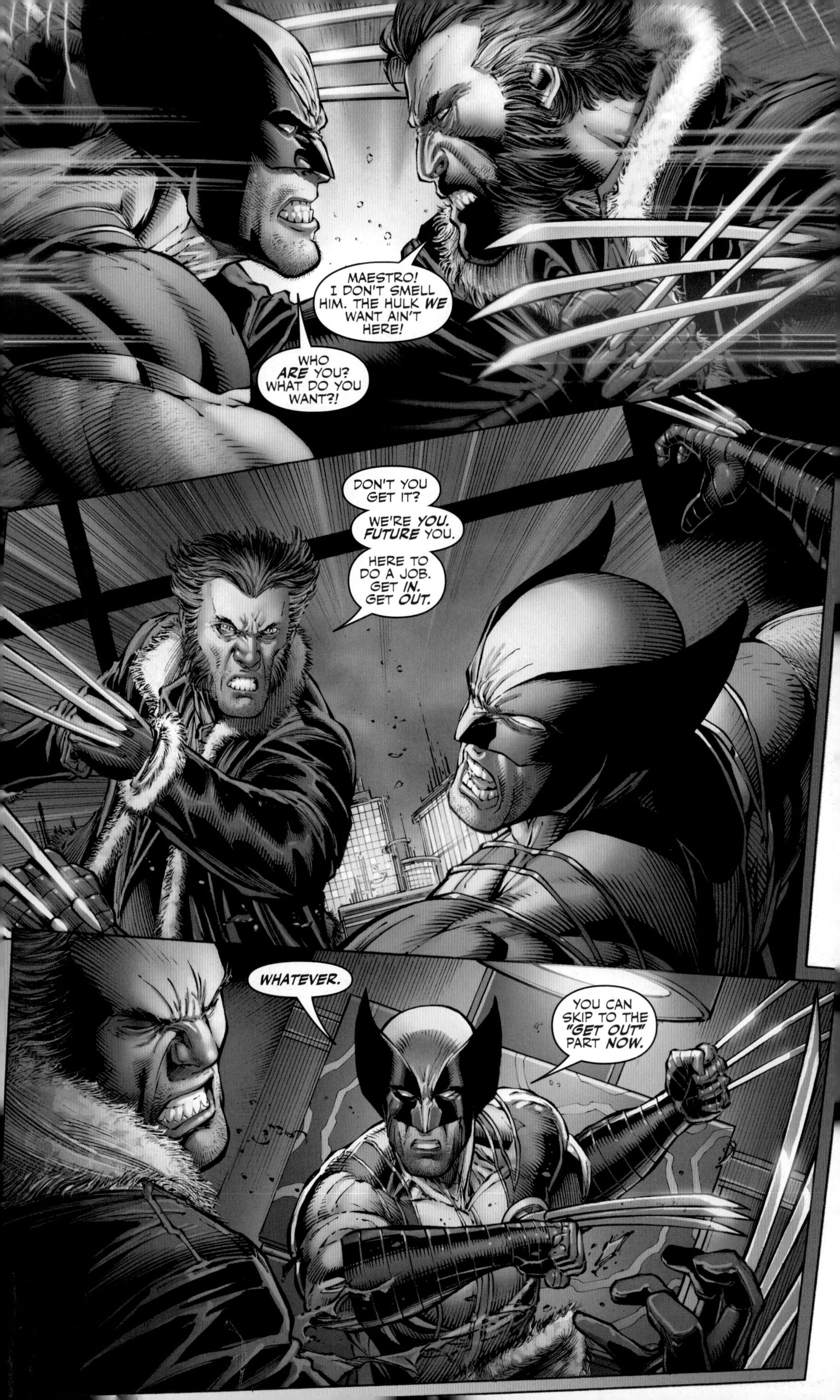
MAESTRO! I DON'T SMELL HIM. THE HULK WE WANT AIN'T HERE!
WHO ARE YOU? WHAT DO YOU WANT?!
DON'T YOU GET IT?
WE'RE YOU. FUTURE YOU.
HERE TO DO A JOB. GET IN. GET OUT.
WHATEVER.
YOU CAN SKIP TO THE "GET OUT" PART NOW.

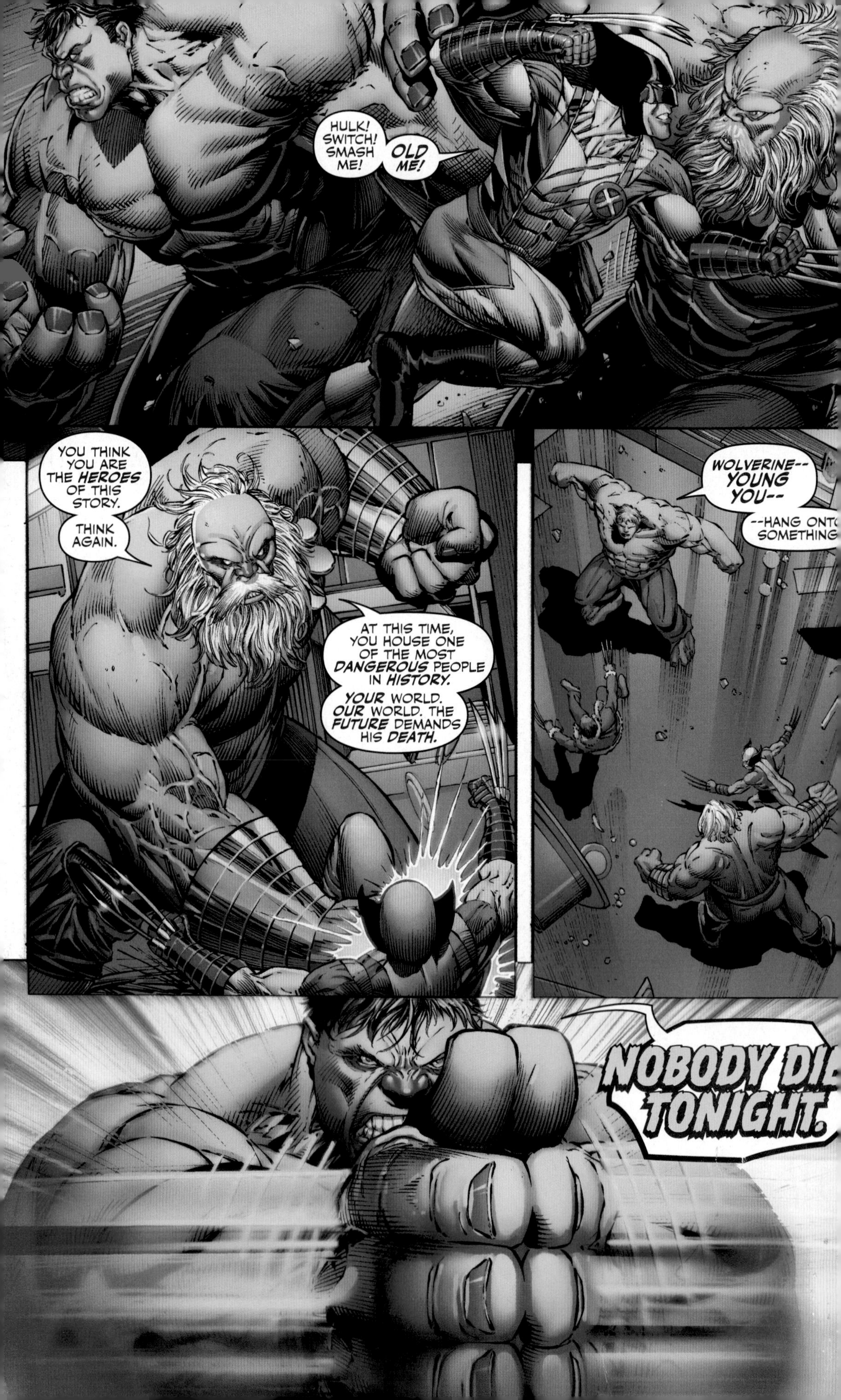
HULK! SWITCH! SMASH ME!
OLD ME!
YOU THINK YOU ARE THE HEROES OF THIS STORY.
THINK AGAIN.
AT THIS TIME, YOU HOUSE ONE OF THE MOST DANGEROUS PEOPLE IN HISTORY.
YOUR WORLD. OUR WORLD. THE FUTURE DEMANDS HIS DEATH.
WOLVERINE-- YOUNG YOU--
--HANG ONTO SOMETHING
NOBODY DIE TONIGHT.

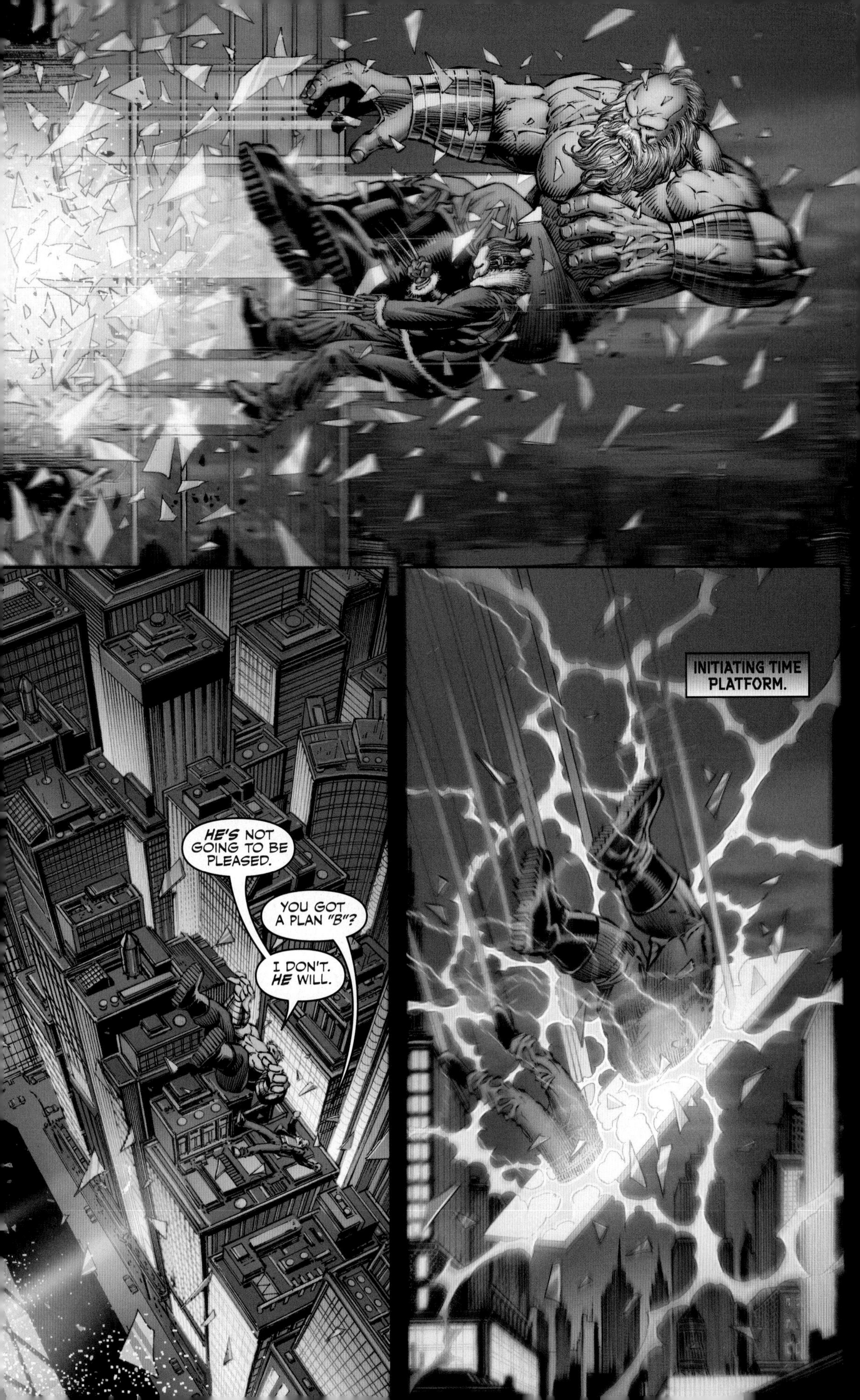
HE'S NOT GOING TO BE PLEASED.
YOU GOT A PLAN "B"?
I DON'T. HE WILL.
INITIATING TIME PLATFORM.

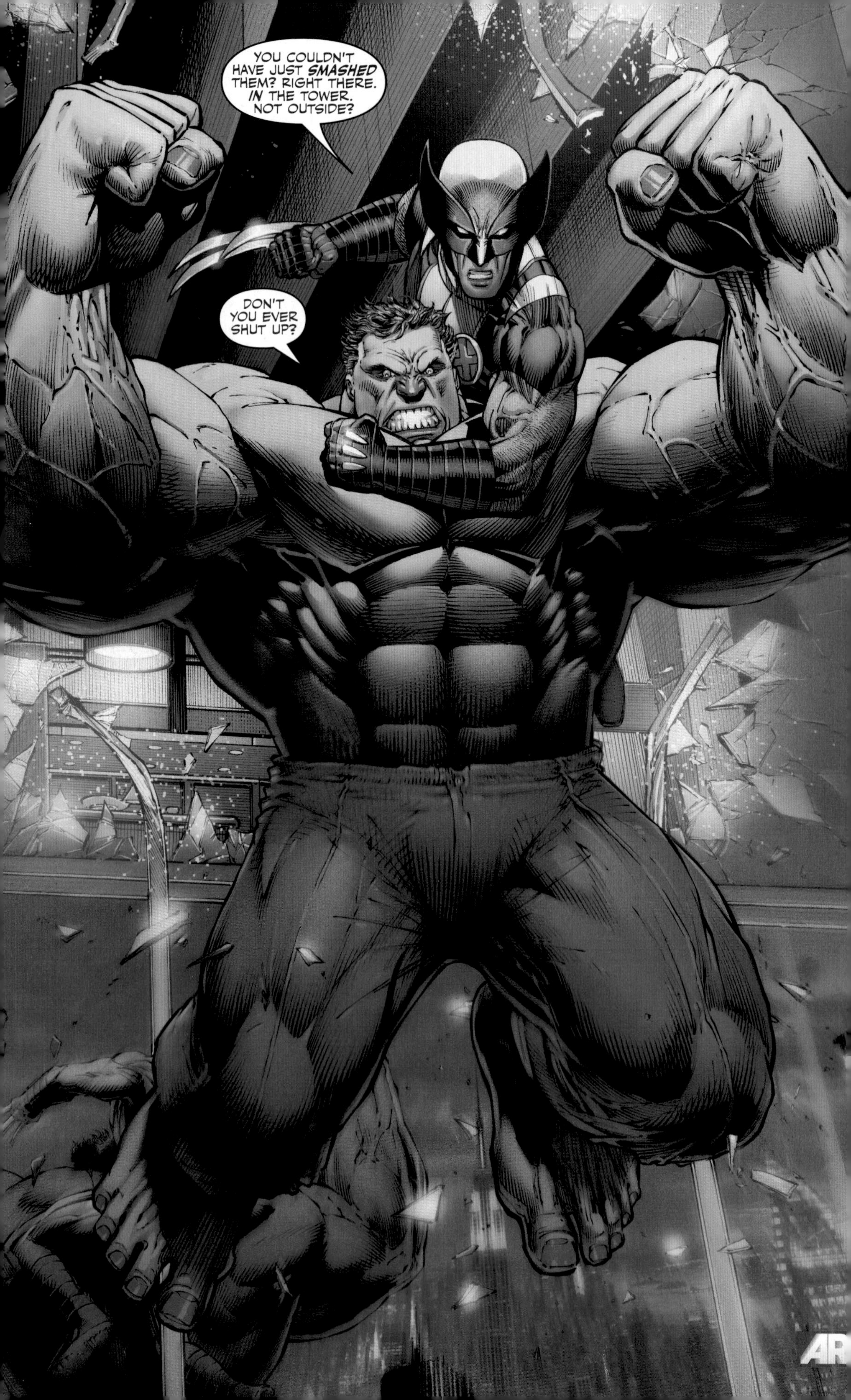
YOU COULDN'T HAVE JUST SMASHED THEM? RIGHT THERE. IN THE TOWER. NOT OUTSIDE?
DON'T YOU EVER SHUT UP?

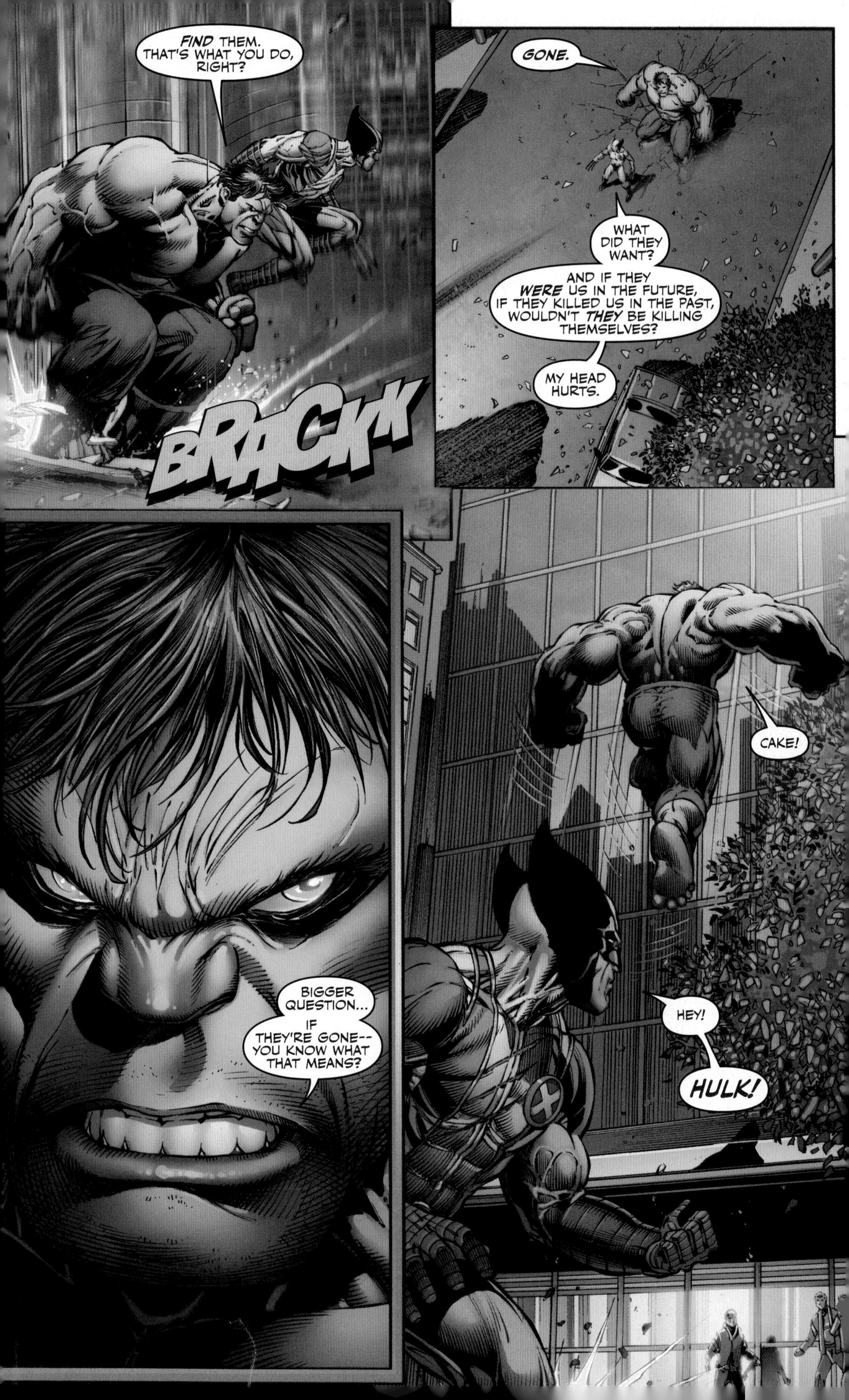
FIND THEM. THAT'S WHAT YOU DO, RIGHT?
BRACKK
GONE.
WHAT DID THEY WANT?
AND IF THEY WERE US IN THE FUTURE, IF THEY KILLED US IN THE PAST, WOULDN'T THEY BE KILLING THEMSELVES?
MY HEAD HURTS.
BIGGER QUESTION...
IF THEY'RE GONE-- YOU KNOW WHAT THAT MEANS?
CAKE!
HEY!
HULK!

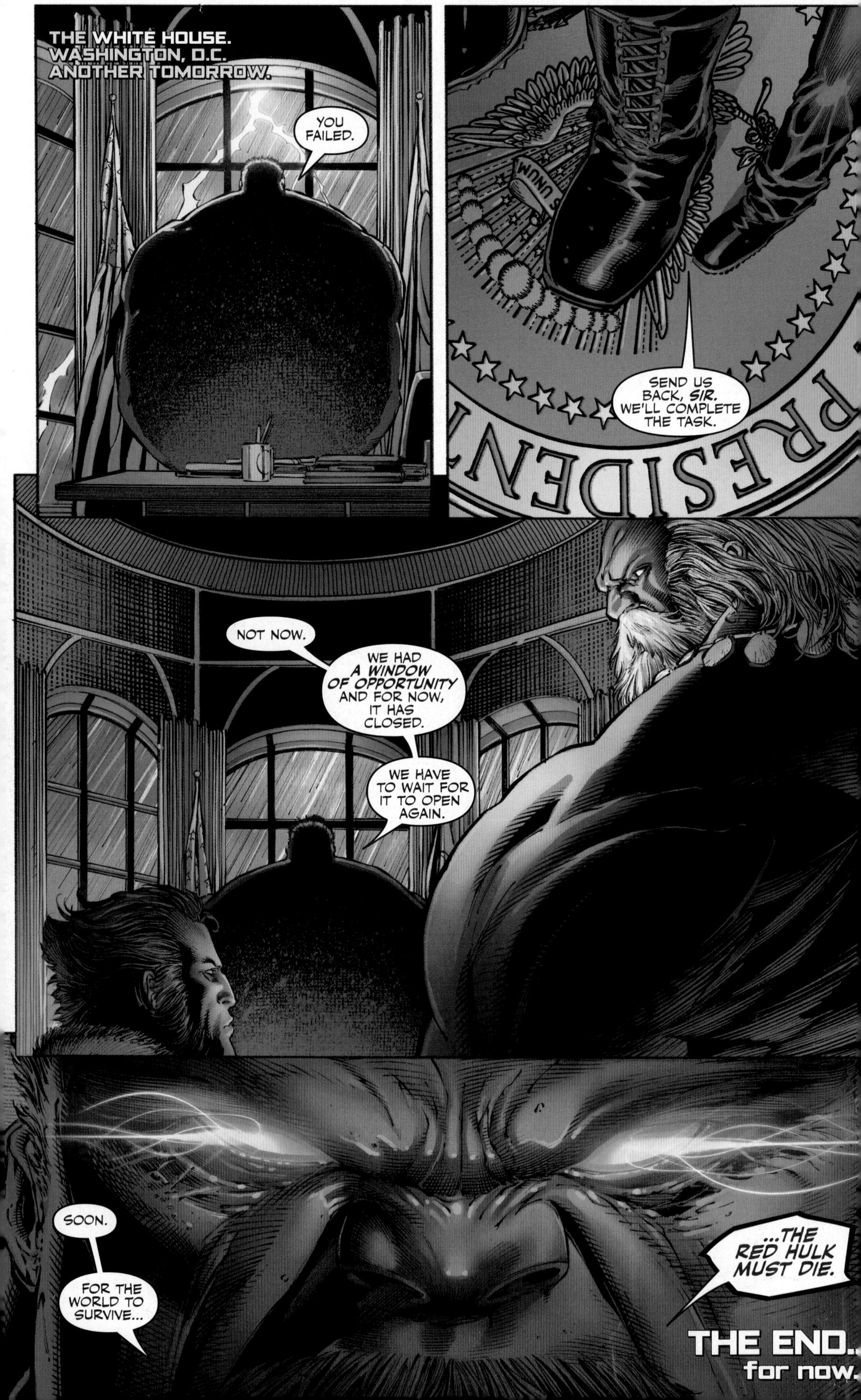
THE WHITE HOUSE. WASHINGTON, D.C. ANOTHER TOMORROW.
YOU FAILED.
SEND US BACK, SIR. WE'LL COMPLETE THE TASK.
PRESIDENT
NOT NOW.
WE HAD A WINDOW OF OPPORTUNITY AND FOR NOW, IT HAS CLOSED.
WE HAVE TO WAIT FOR IT TO OPEN AGAIN.
SOON.
FOR THE WORLD TO SURVIVE...
...THE RED HULK MUST DIE.
THE END... for now.

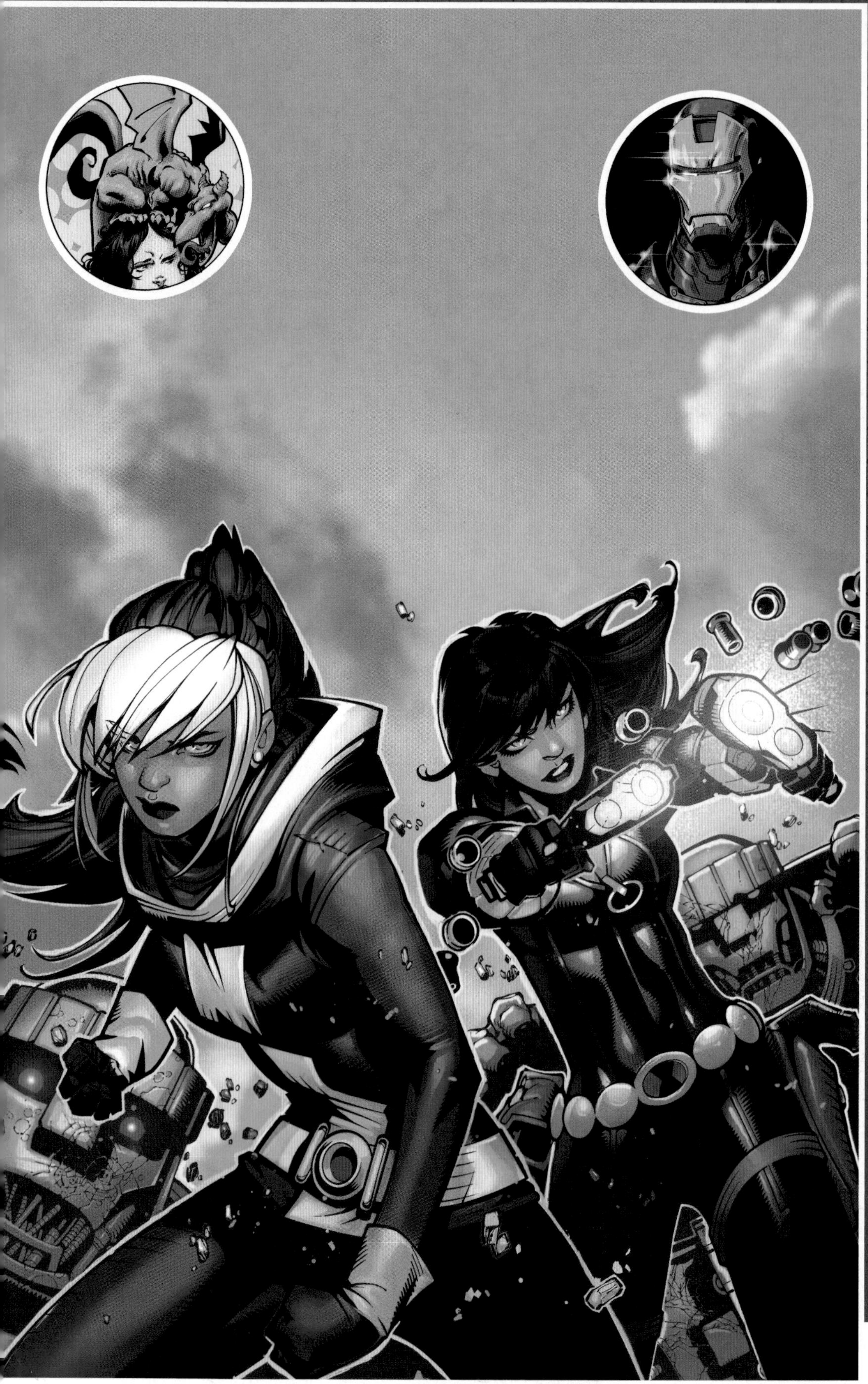

# A + X = 2

Q: This is [illegible] com[illegible] book, right? What comic book is this?
A: This? Why, this is A+X #2, the comic where we do an even NEWER kind of math...SUPERMATH. One AVENGER plus one X-MAN divided by an evil villain!

Q: What does that equal?
A: IT EQUALS FUN, BRO! If you can find a comic more packed to the gills with heroes teaming to TROUNCE some dudes, YOU BUY IT! But then still buy this one, too.

Q: Oh, this is one of those MARVEL NOW! books, right? From that reboo--
A: DO NOT SAY THE R-WORD! MARVEL NOW! isn't any kind of boot, re- or otherwise! And anyway, who cares about that? The only B
you should be worrying about is the one our HEROES are giving to villains' FACES!

Q: What heroes do you mean?
A: First up, we got BLACK WIDOW (you know, the redhead spy from that AVENGERS movie) teaming up with ROGUE (you know, the power-stealer with the white streak in her hair from them X-MEN movies)! But these ladies ain't talking hair--they're BUSTIN' HEADS!

Q: And what's in the second story?
A: In that one we've got KITTY PRYDE, a super-smart lady X-MAN, teaming up with IRON MAN, a super-smart playboy AVENG
And, SPOILERS! They're gonna fight ALIENS!

Q: That sounds like a lot of fun!
A: YOU'RE TELLING ME?!?

# A+X

## BLACK WIDOW + ROGUE

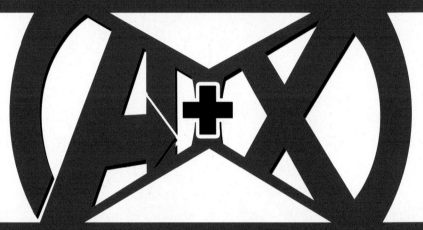

CHRIS BACHALO — WRITER/PENCILER/COLORIST
TIM TOWNSEND — INKER
VC'S CLAYTON COWLES — LETTERER

## IRON MAN + KITTY PRYDE

PETER DAVID — WRITER
MIKE DEL MUNDO — ARTIST
VC'S CLAYTON COWLES — LETTERER

JORDAN D. WHITE — ASSISTANT EDITOR
NICK LOWE — EDITOR
AXEL ALONSO — EDITOR IN CHIEF
JOE QUESADA — CHIEF CREATIVE OFFICER
DAN BUCKLEY — PUBLISHER
ALAN FINE — EXECUTIVE PRODUCER

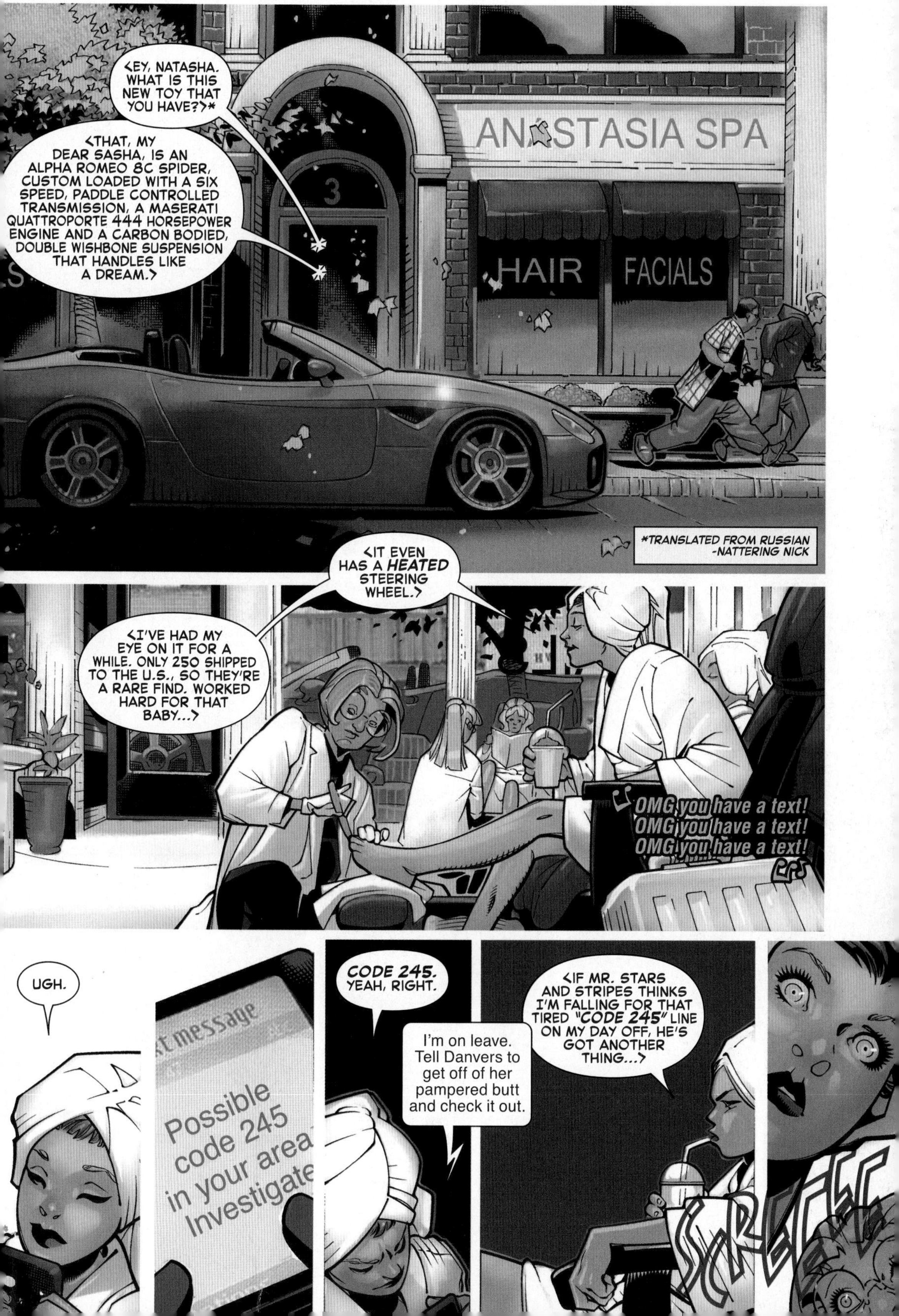

<EY, NATASHA. WHAT IS THIS NEW TOY THAT YOU HAVE?>*
<THAT, MY DEAR SASHA, IS AN ALPHA ROMEO 8C SPIDER, CUSTOM LOADED WITH A SIX SPEED, PADDLE CONTROLLED TRANSMISSION, A MASERATI QUATTROPORTE 444 HORSEPOWER ENGINE AND A CARBON BODIED, DOUBLE WISHBONE SUSPENSION THAT HANDLES LIKE A DREAM.>
ANASTASIA SPA
HAIR
FACIALS
*TRANSLATED FROM RUSSIAN -NATTERING NICK
<IT EVEN HAS A HEATED STEERING WHEEL.>
<I'VE HAD MY EYE ON IT FOR A WHILE. ONLY 250 SHIPPED TO THE U.S., SO THEY'RE A RARE FIND. WORKED HARD FOR THAT BABY...>
OMG you have a text! OMG you have a text! OMG you have a text!
UGH.
Possible code 245 in your area Investigate
CODE 245. YEAH, RIGHT.
I'm on leave. Tell Danvers to get off of her pampered butt and check it out.
<IF MR. STARS AND STRIPES THINKS I'M FALLING FOR THAT TIRED "CODE 245" LINE ON MY DAY OFF, HE'S GOT ANOTHER THING...>

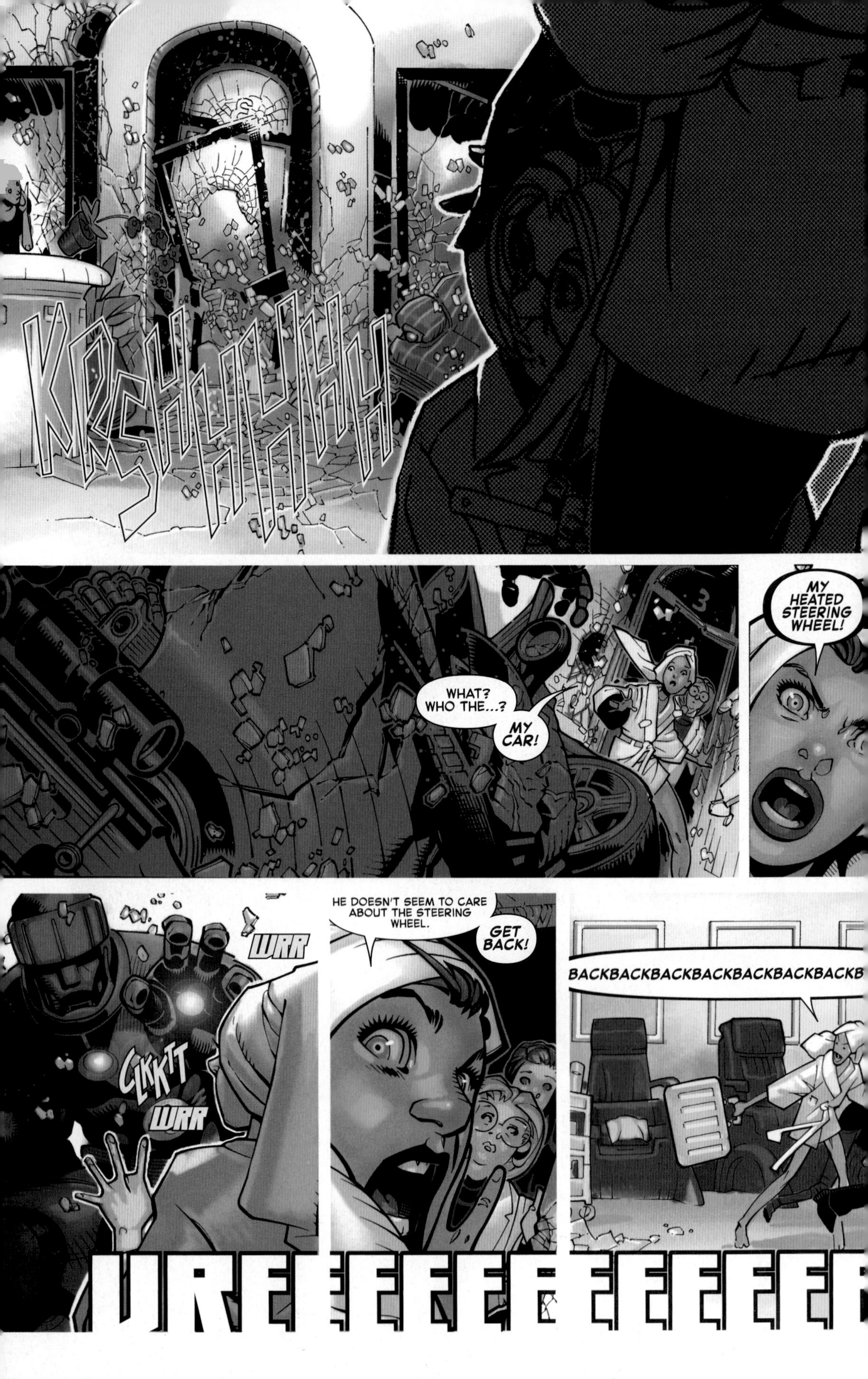
KRSHHHHHH
WHAT? WHO THE...?
MY CAR!
MY HEATED STEERING WHEEL!
WRR
CLKKTT
WRR
HE DOESN'T SEEM TO CARE ABOUT THE STEERING WHEEL.
GET BACK!
BACKBACKBACKBACKBACKBACKBACKB
WREEEEEEEEEEE

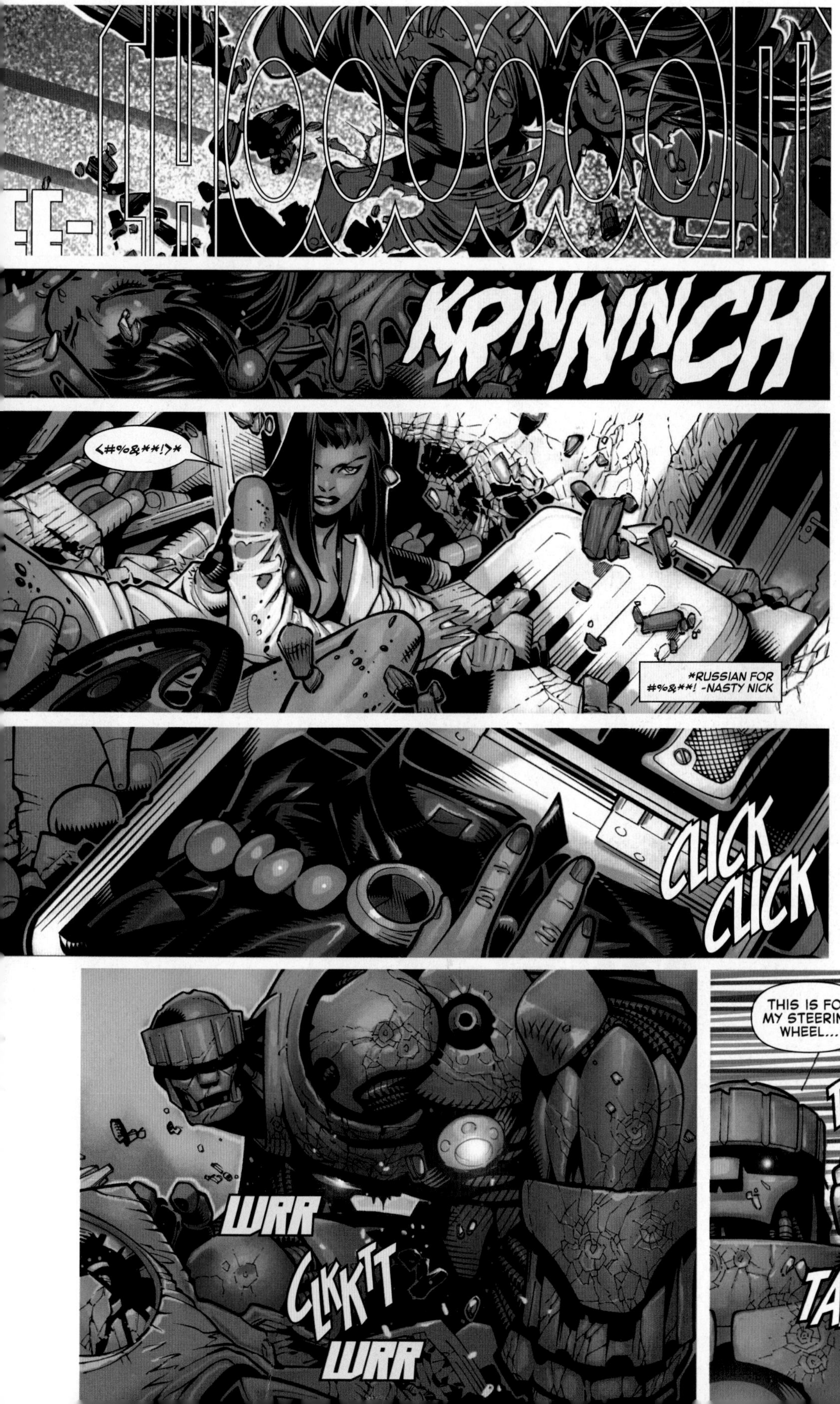
KRNNNCH
<#%&**!>*
*RUSSIAN FOR #%&**! -NASTY NICK
CLICK
CLICK
WRR
CLKKTT
WRR
THIS IS FOR MY STEERING WHEEL...
TIK
TAK

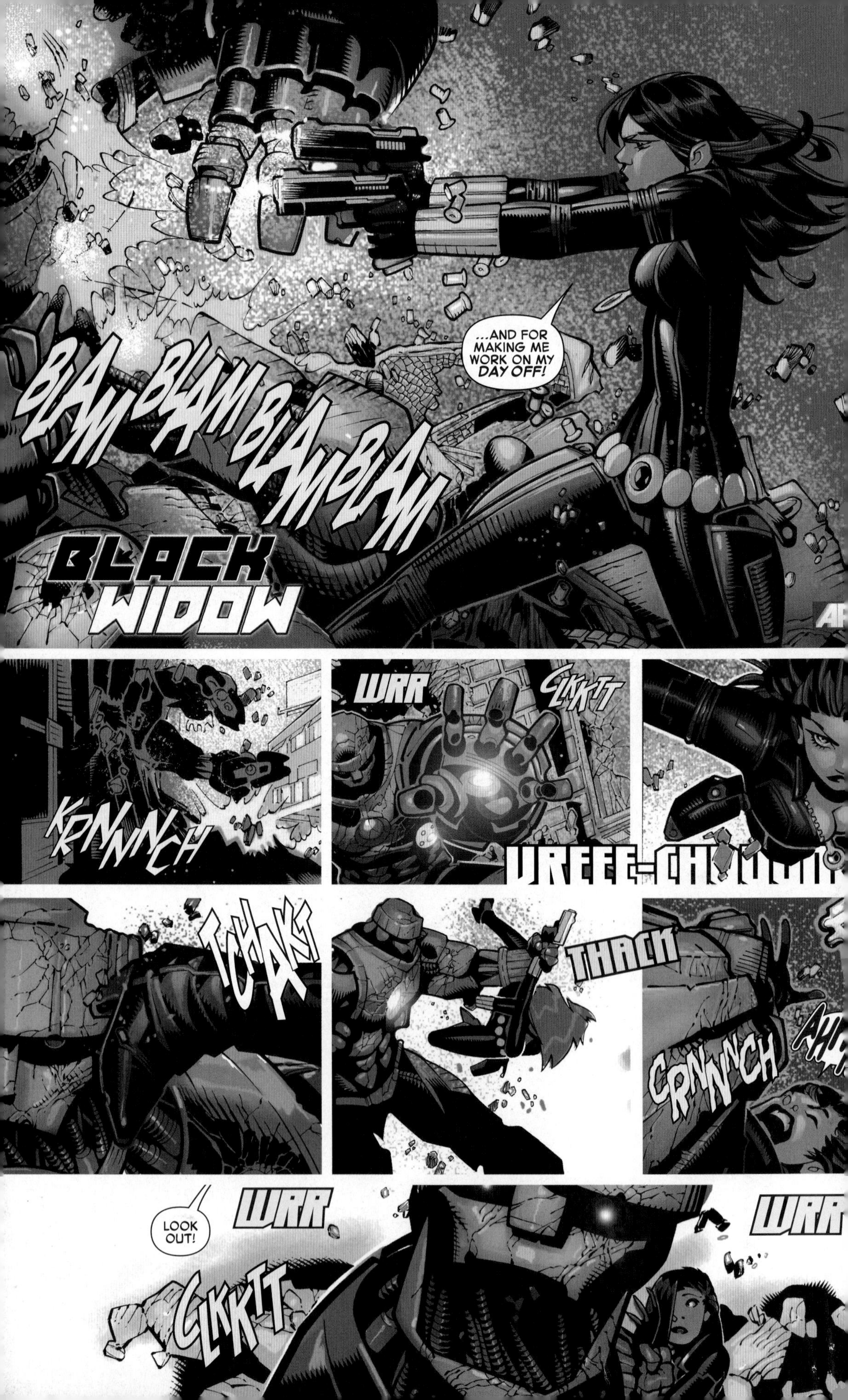
BLAM BLAM BLAM BLAM
...AND FOR MAKING ME WORK ON MY DAY OFF!
BLACK WIDOW
KRNNNCH
WRR
CLKKTT
UREEE-CH
TCHAKT
THACK
CRNNCH
LOOK OUT!
WRR
WRR
CLKKTT

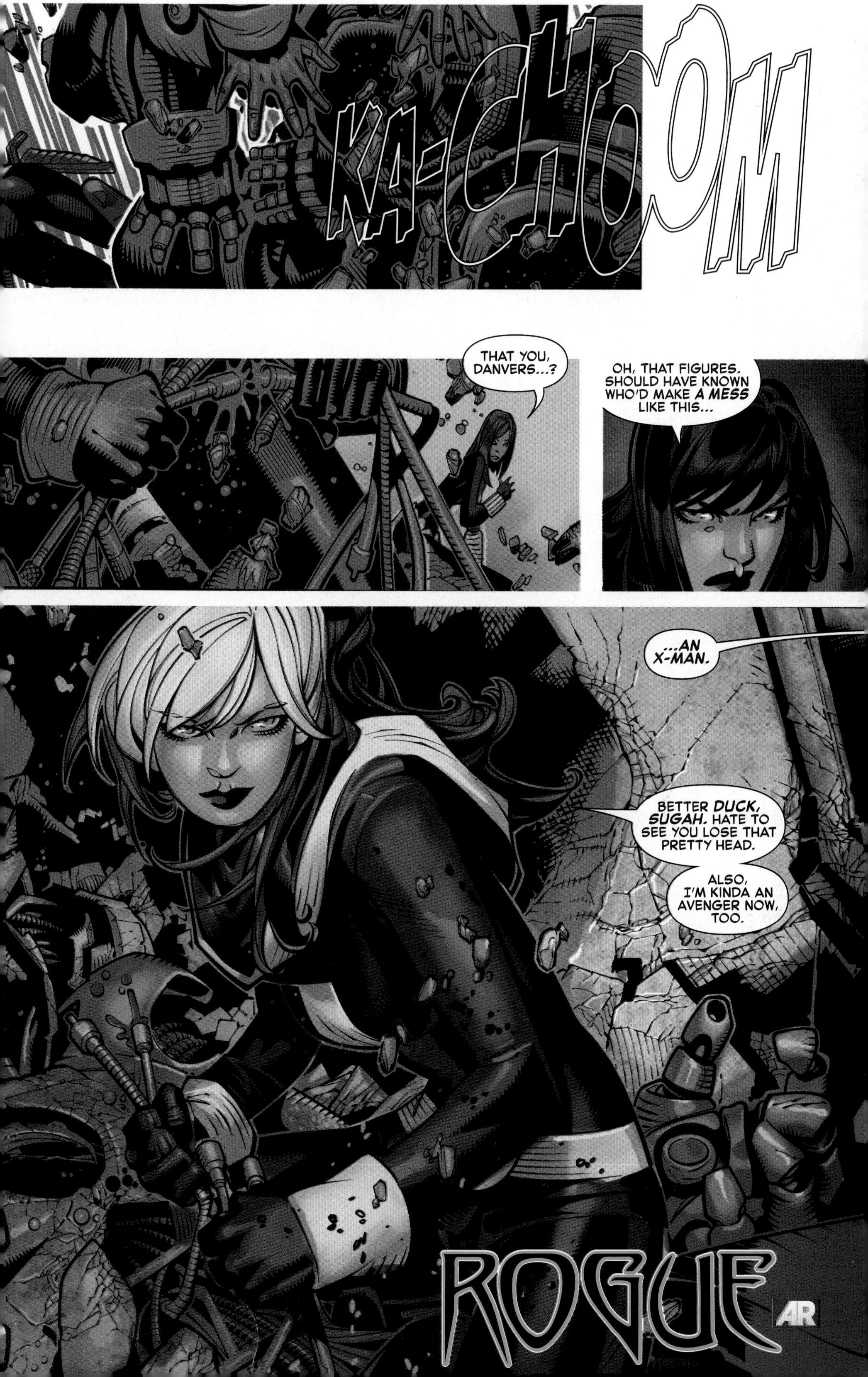
KA-CHOOM
THAT YOU, DANVERS...?
OH, THAT FIGURES. SHOULD HAVE KNOWN WHO'D MAKE A MESS LIKE THIS...
...AN X-MAN.
BETTER DUCK, SUGAH. HATE TO SEE YOU LOSE THAT PRETTY HEAD.
ALSO, I'M KINDA AN AVENGER NOW, TOO.
ROGUE
AR

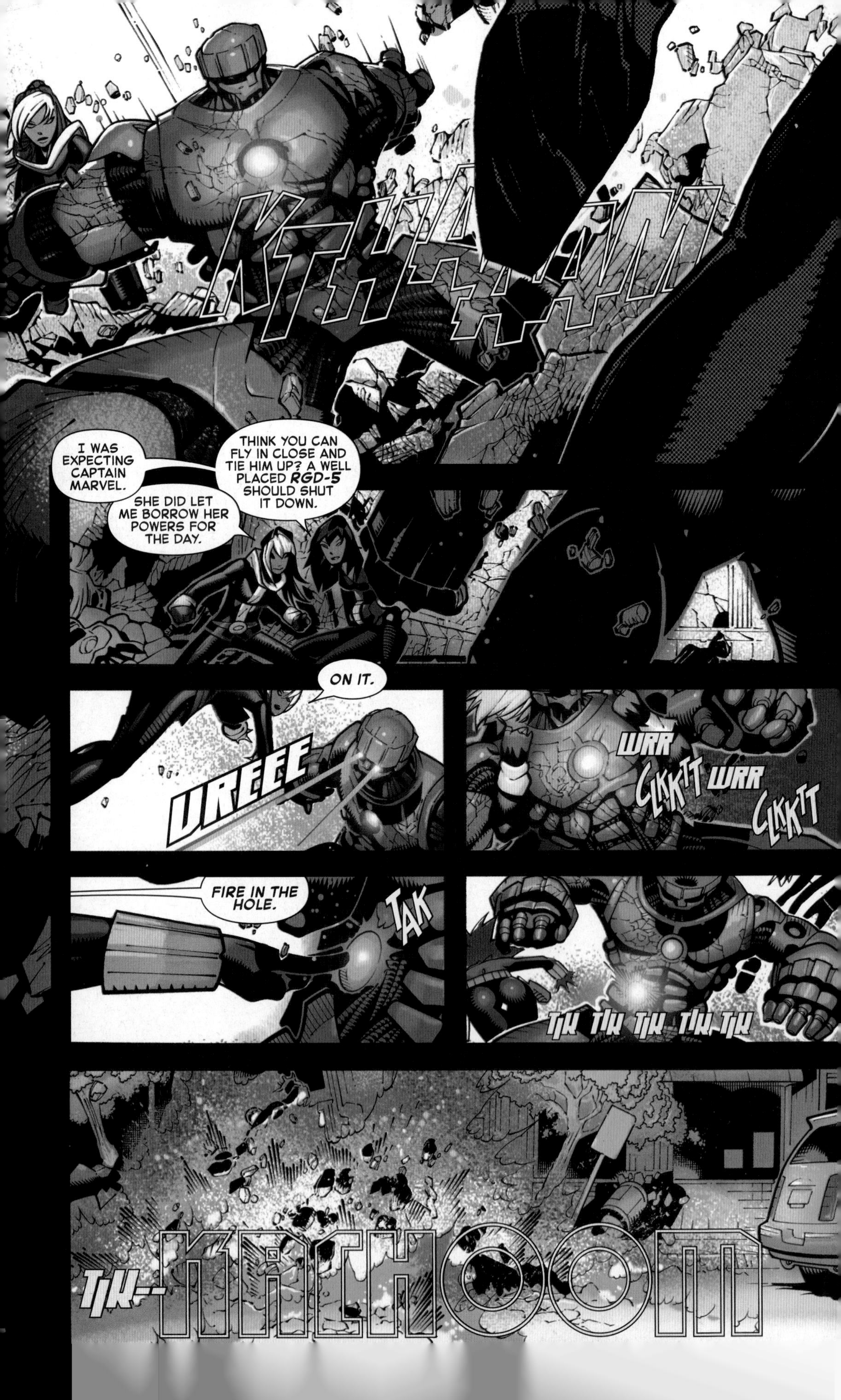

KTHAAAM
I WAS EXPECTING CAPTAIN MARVEL.
SHE DID LET ME BORROW HER POWERS FOR THE DAY.
THINK YOU CAN FLY IN CLOSE AND TIE HIM UP? A WELL PLACED RGD-5 SHOULD SHUT IT DOWN.
ON IT.
UREEE
WRR
CLKKTT WRR
CLKKTT
FIRE IN THE HOLE.
TAK
TIK TIK TIK TIK TIK
TIK--KRACHOOM

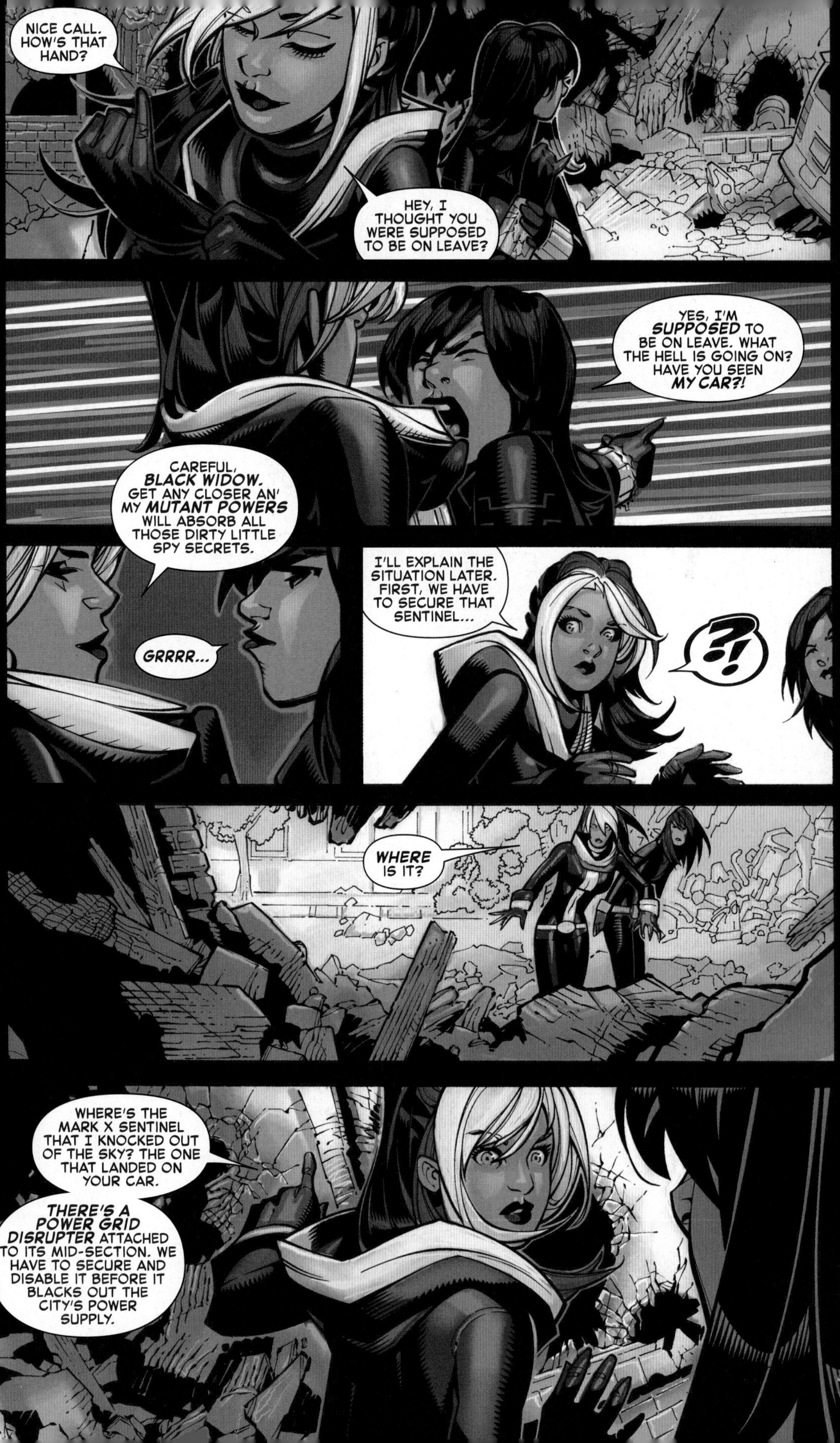
NICE CALL. HOW'S THAT HAND?
HEY, I THOUGHT YOU WERE SUPPOSED TO BE ON LEAVE?
YES, I'M SUPPOSED TO BE ON LEAVE. WHAT THE HELL IS GOING ON? HAVE YOU SEEN MY CAR?!
CAREFUL, BLACK WIDOW. GET ANY CLOSER AN' MY MUTANT POWERS WILL ABSORB ALL THOSE DIRTY LITTLE SPY SECRETS.
GRRRR...
I'LL EXPLAIN THE SITUATION LATER. FIRST, WE HAVE TO SECURE THAT SENTINEL...
?!
WHERE IS IT?
WHERE'S THE MARK X SENTINEL THAT I KNOCKED OUT OF THE SKY? THE ONE THAT LANDED ON YOUR CAR.
THERE'S A POWER GRID DISRUPTER ATTACHED TO ITS MID-SECTION. WE HAVE TO SECURE AND DISABLE IT BEFORE IT BLACKS OUT THE CITY'S POWER SUPPLY.

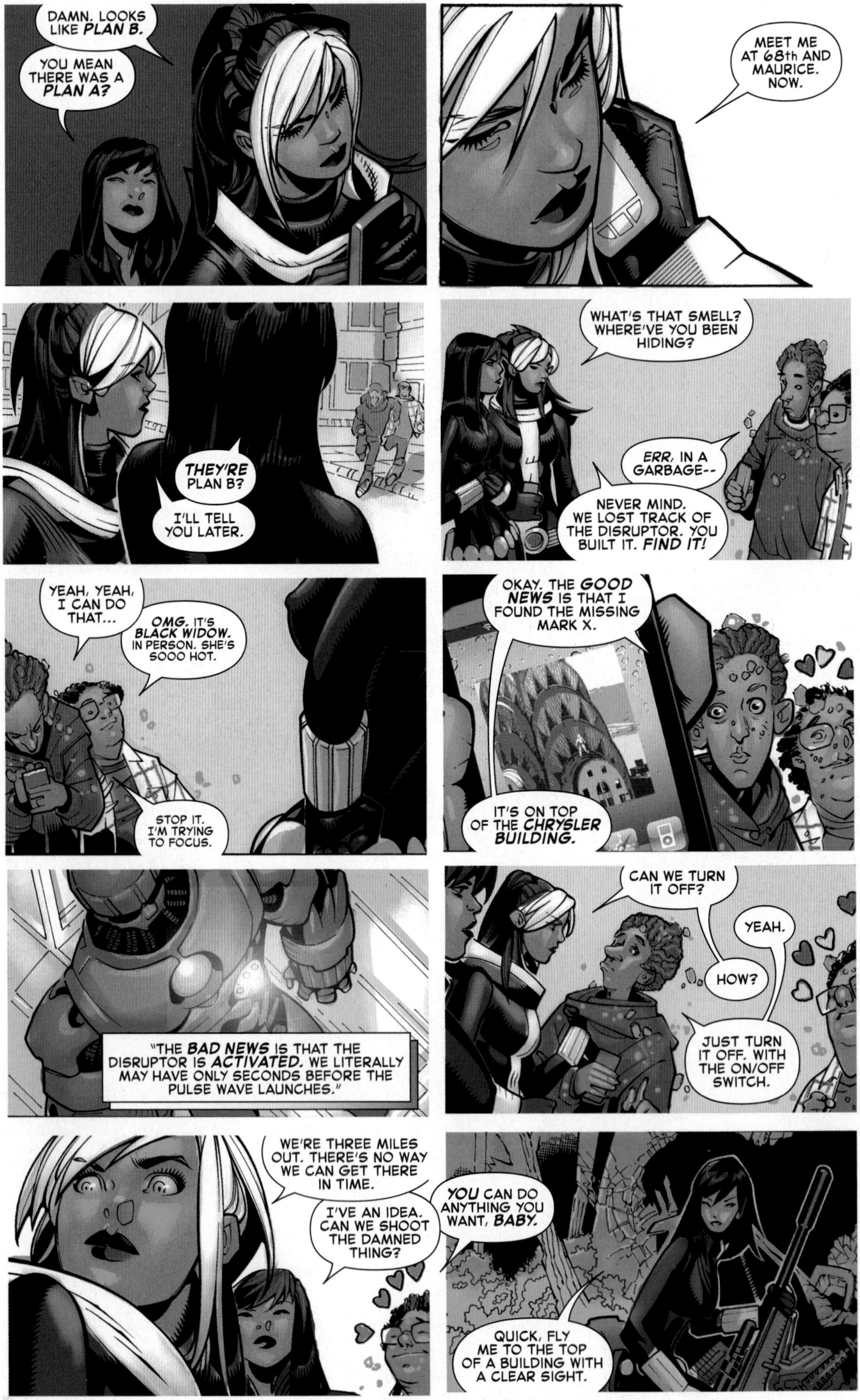
DAMN. LOOKS LIKE PLAN B.
YOU MEAN THERE WAS A PLAN A?
MEET ME AT 68th AND MAURICE. NOW.
THEY'RE PLAN B?
I'LL TELL YOU LATER.
WHAT'S THAT SMELL? WHERE'VE YOU BEEN HIDING?
ERR, IN A GARBAGE--
NEVER MIND. WE LOST TRACK OF THE DISRUPTOR. YOU BUILT IT. FIND IT!
YEAH, YEAH, I CAN DO THAT...
OMG. IT'S BLACK WIDOW. IN PERSON. SHE'S SOOO HOT.
STOP IT. I'M TRYING TO FOCUS.
OKAY. THE GOOD NEWS IS THAT I FOUND THE MISSING MARK X.
IT'S ON TOP OF THE CHRYSLER BUILDING.
"THE BAD NEWS IS THAT THE DISRUPTOR IS ACTIVATED. WE LITERALLY MAY HAVE ONLY SECONDS BEFORE THE PULSE WAVE LAUNCHES."
CAN WE TURN IT OFF?
YEAH.
HOW?
JUST TURN IT OFF. WITH THE ON/OFF SWITCH.
WE'RE THREE MILES OUT. THERE'S NO WAY WE CAN GET THERE IN TIME.
I'VE AN IDEA. CAN WE SHOOT THE DAMNED THING?
YOU CAN DO ANYTHING YOU WANT, BABY.
QUICK, FLY ME TO THE TOP OF A BUILDING WITH A CLEAR SIGHT.

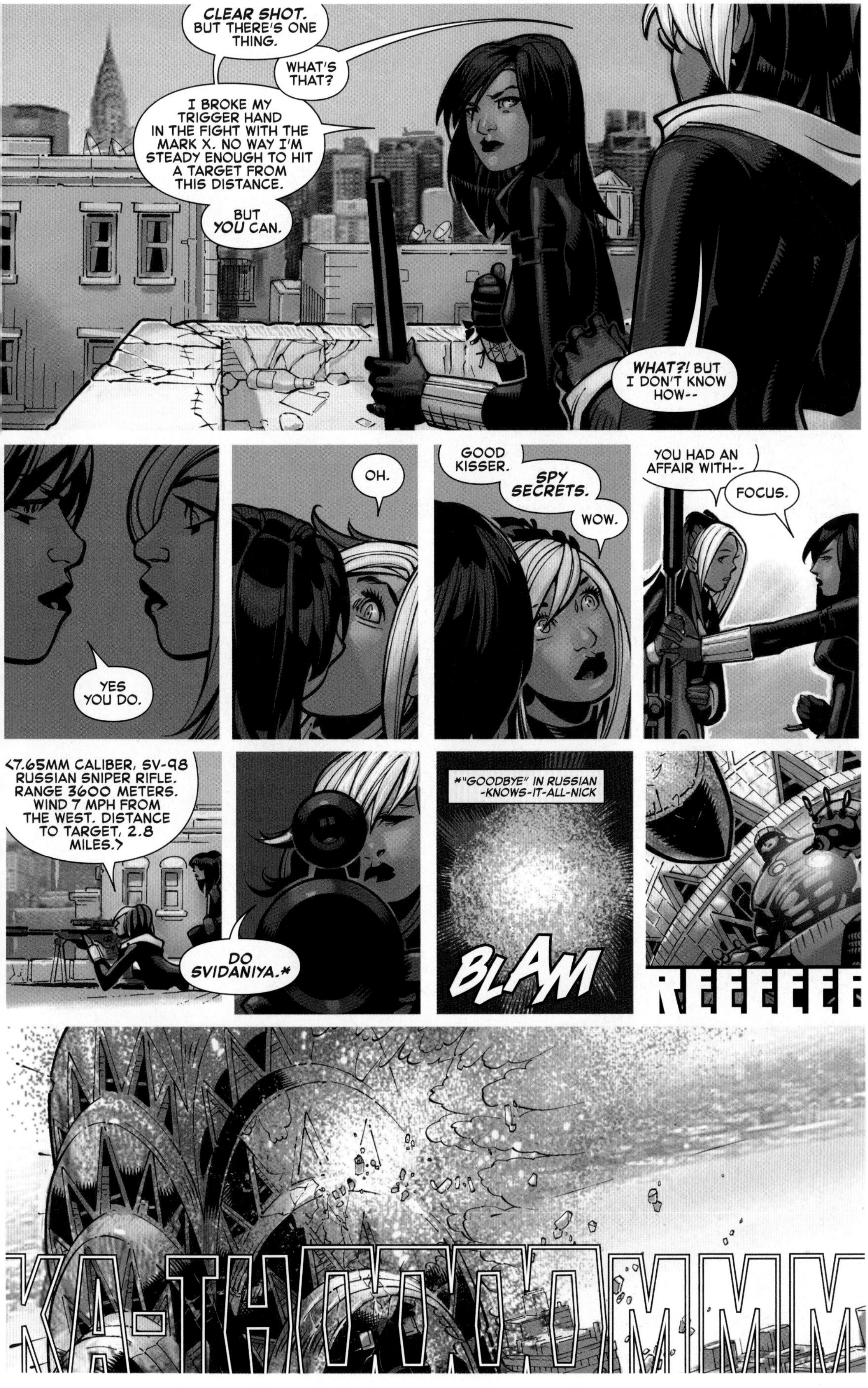
CLEAR SHOT. BUT THERE'S ONE THING.
WHAT'S THAT?
I BROKE MY TRIGGER HAND IN THE FIGHT WITH THE MARK X. NO WAY I'M STEADY ENOUGH TO HIT A TARGET FROM THIS DISTANCE.
BUT YOU CAN.
WHAT?! BUT I DON'T KNOW HOW--
YES YOU DO.
OH.
GOOD KISSER.
SPY SECRETS.
WOW.
YOU HAD AN AFFAIR WITH--
FOCUS.
<7.65MM CALIBER, SV-98 RUSSIAN SNIPER RIFLE. RANGE 3600 METERS. WIND 7 MPH FROM THE WEST. DISTANCE TO TARGET, 2.8 MILES.>
DO SVIDANIYA.*
*"GOODBYE" IN RUSSIAN -KNOWS-IT-ALL-NICK
BLAM
REEEEEE
KA-THOOOOOMMM

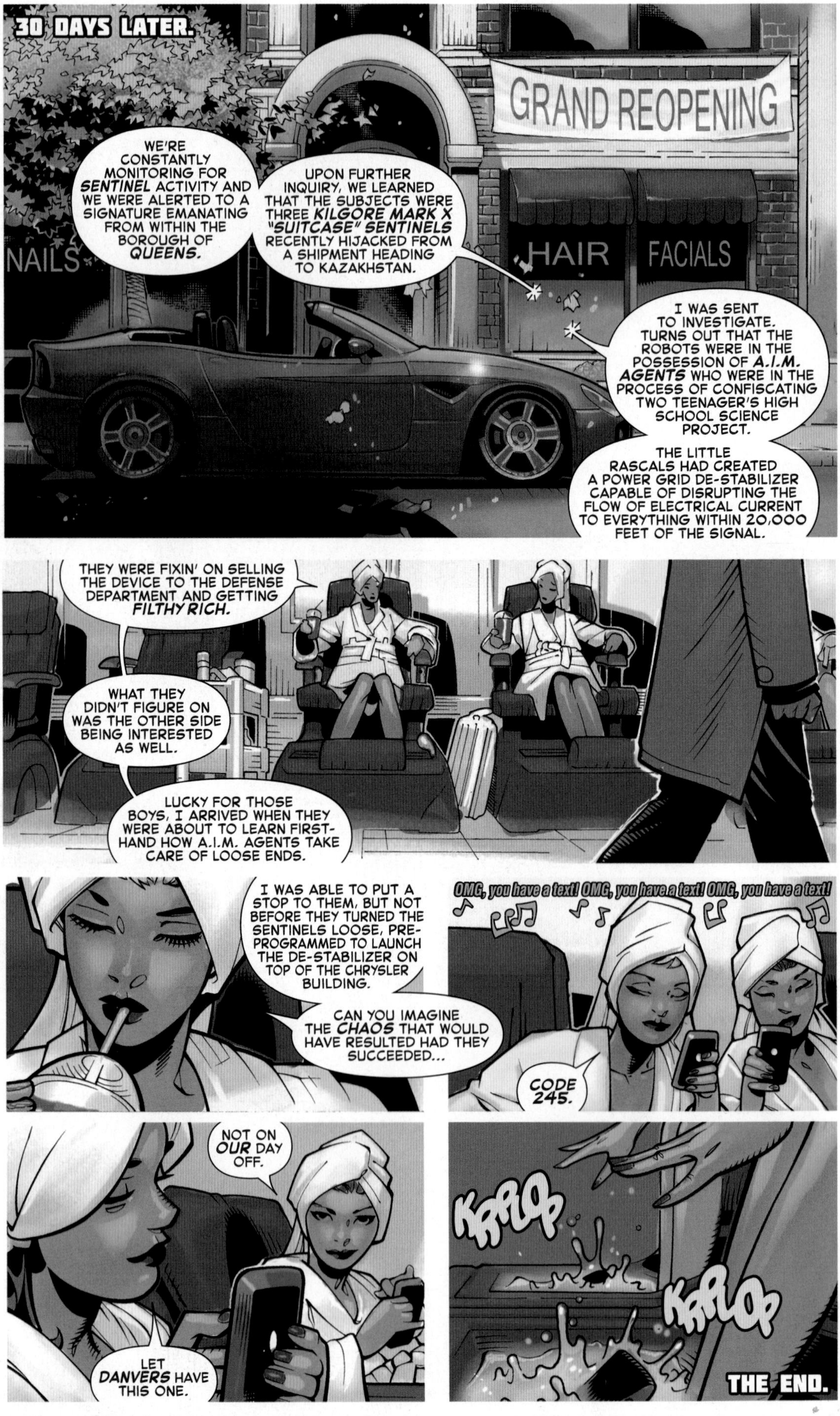
30 DAYS LATER.
GRAND REOPENING
WE'RE CONSTANTLY MONITORING FOR SENTINEL ACTIVITY AND WE WERE ALERTED TO A SIGNATURE EMANATING FROM WITHIN THE BOROUGH OF QUEENS.
UPON FURTHER INQUIRY, WE LEARNED THAT THE SUBJECTS WERE THREE KILGORE MARK X "SUITCASE" SENTINELS RECENTLY HIJACKED FROM A SHIPMENT HEADING TO KAZAKHSTAN.
NAILS
HAIR
FACIALS
I WAS SENT TO INVESTIGATE. TURNS OUT THAT THE ROBOTS WERE IN THE POSSESSION OF A.I.M. AGENTS WHO WERE IN THE PROCESS OF CONFISCATING TWO TEENAGER'S HIGH SCHOOL SCIENCE PROJECT.
THE LITTLE RASCALS HAD CREATED A POWER GRID DE-STABILIZER CAPABLE OF DISRUPTING THE FLOW OF ELECTRICAL CURRENT TO EVERYTHING WITHIN 20,000 FEET OF THE SIGNAL.
THEY WERE FIXIN' ON SELLING THE DEVICE TO THE DEFENSE DEPARTMENT AND GETTING FILTHY RICH.
WHAT THEY DIDN'T FIGURE ON WAS THE OTHER SIDE BEING INTERESTED AS WELL.
LUCKY FOR THOSE BOYS, I ARRIVED WHEN THEY WERE ABOUT TO LEARN FIRST-HAND HOW A.I.M. AGENTS TAKE CARE OF LOOSE ENDS.
I WAS ABLE TO PUT A STOP TO THEM, BUT NOT BEFORE THEY TURNED THE SENTINELS LOOSE, PRE-PROGRAMMED TO LAUNCH THE DE-STABILIZER ON TOP OF THE CHRYSLER BUILDING.
CAN YOU IMAGINE THE CHAOS THAT WOULD HAVE RESULTED HAD THEY SUCCEEDED...
OMG, you have a text! OMG, you have a text! OMG, you have a text!
CODE 245.
NOT ON OUR DAY OFF.
LET DANVERS HAVE THIS ONE.
KRPLOP
KRPLOP
THE END.

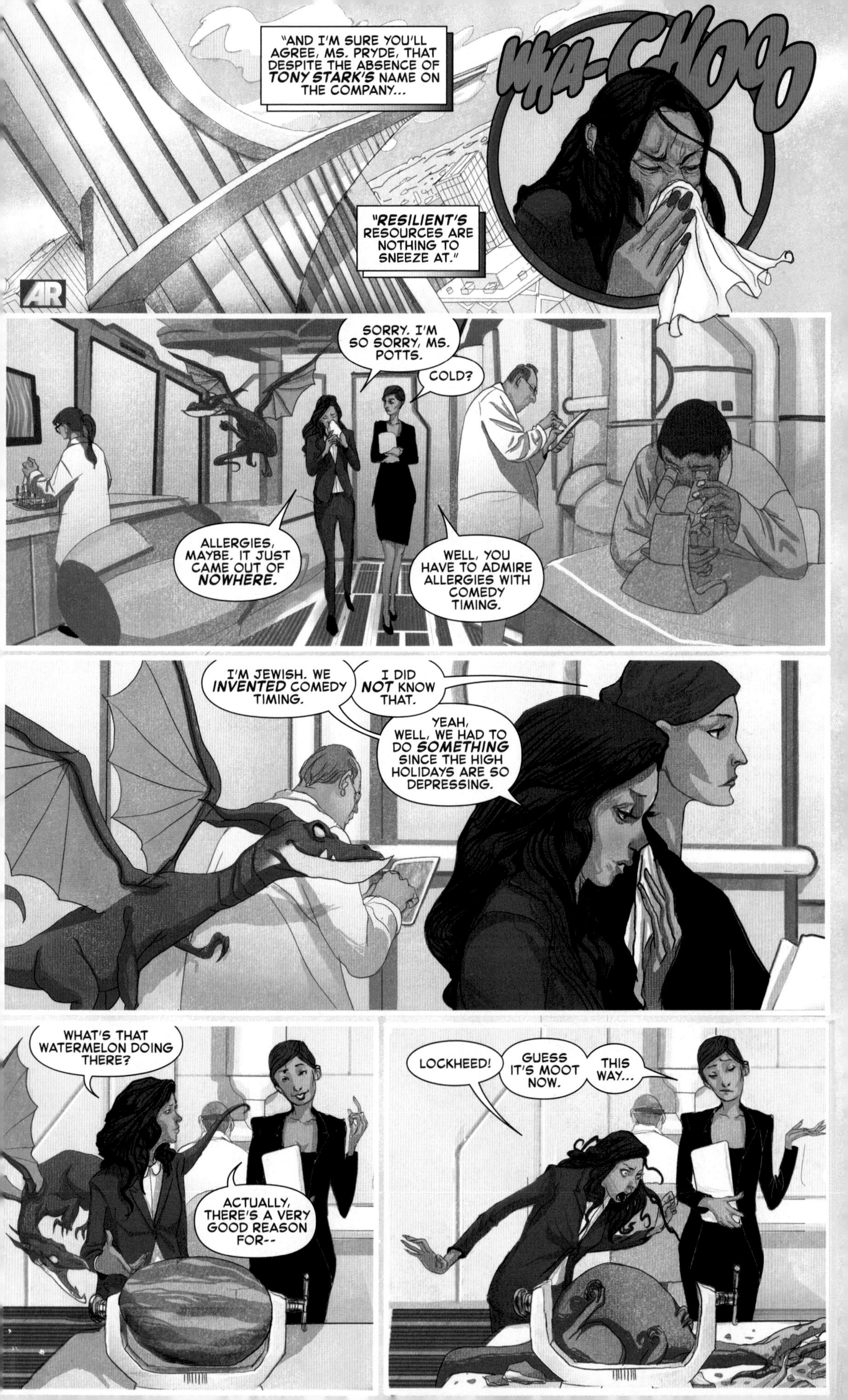
"AND I'M SURE YOU'LL AGREE, MS. PRYDE, THAT DESPITE THE ABSENCE OF TONY STARK'S NAME ON THE COMPANY...
WHA-CHOOO
"RESILIENT'S RESOURCES ARE NOTHING TO SNEEZE AT."
AR
SORRY. I'M SO SORRY, MS. POTTS.
COLD?
ALLERGIES, MAYBE. IT JUST CAME OUT OF NOWHERE.
WELL, YOU HAVE TO ADMIRE ALLERGIES WITH COMEDY TIMING.
I'M JEWISH. WE INVENTED COMEDY TIMING.
I DID NOT KNOW THAT.
YEAH, WELL, WE HAD TO DO SOMETHING SINCE THE HIGH HOLIDAYS ARE SO DEPRESSING.
WHAT'S THAT WATERMELON DOING THERE?
ACTUALLY, THERE'S A VERY GOOD REASON FOR--
LOCKHEED!
GUESS IT'S MOOT NOW.
THIS WAY...

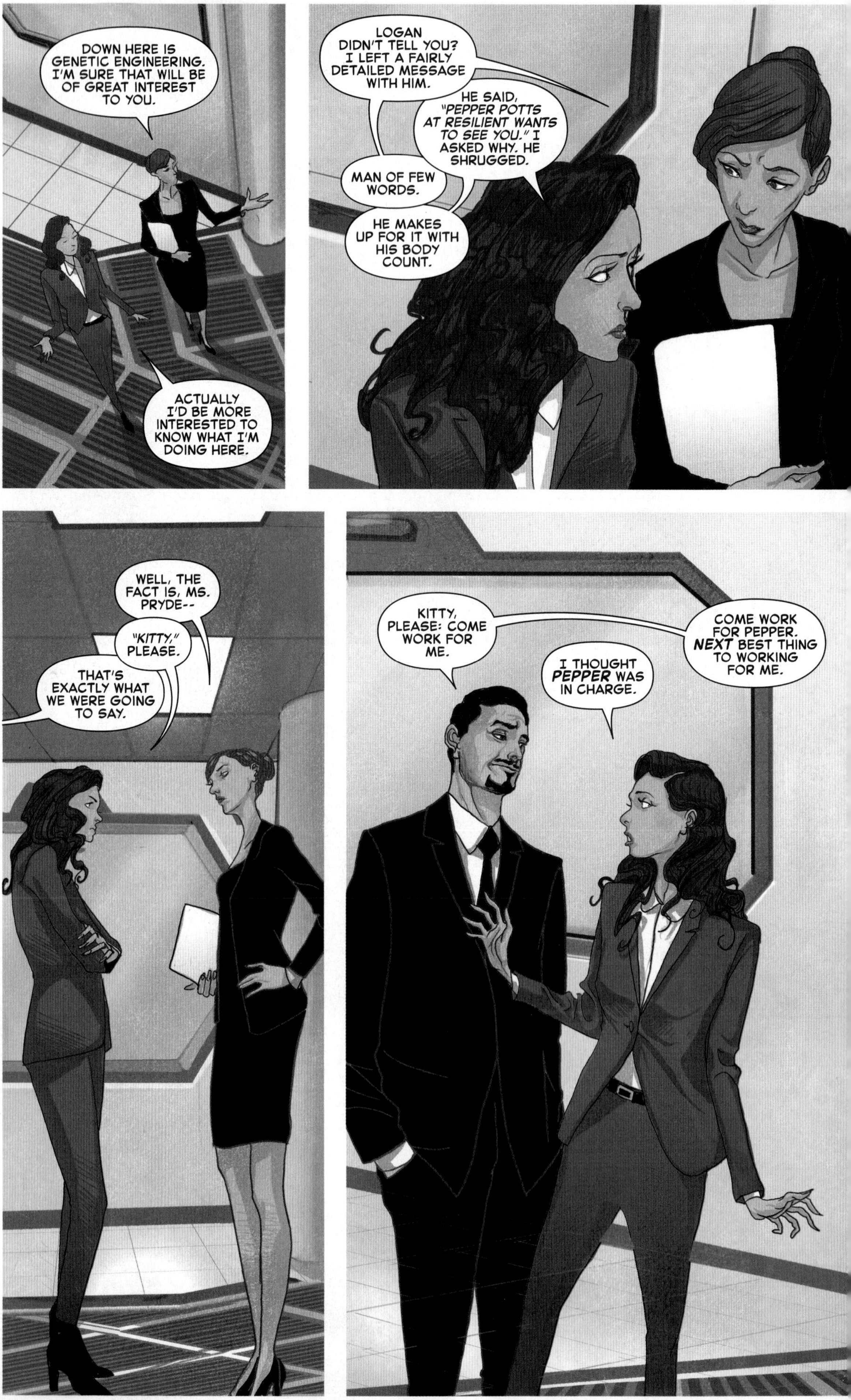
DOWN HERE IS GENETIC ENGINEERING. I'M SURE THAT WILL BE OF GREAT INTEREST TO YOU.
ACTUALLY I'D BE MORE INTERESTED TO KNOW WHAT I'M DOING HERE.
LOGAN DIDN'T TELL YOU? I LEFT A FAIRLY DETAILED MESSAGE WITH HIM.
HE SAID, "PEPPER POTTS AT RESILIENT WANTS TO SEE YOU." I ASKED WHY. HE SHRUGGED.
MAN OF FEW WORDS.
HE MAKES UP FOR IT WITH HIS BODY COUNT.
WELL, THE FACT IS, MS. PRYDE--
"KITTY," PLEASE.
THAT'S EXACTLY WHAT WE WERE GOING TO SAY.
KITTY, PLEASE: COME WORK FOR ME.
COME WORK FOR PEPPER. NEXT BEST THING TO WORKING FOR ME.
I THOUGHT PEPPER WAS IN CHARGE.

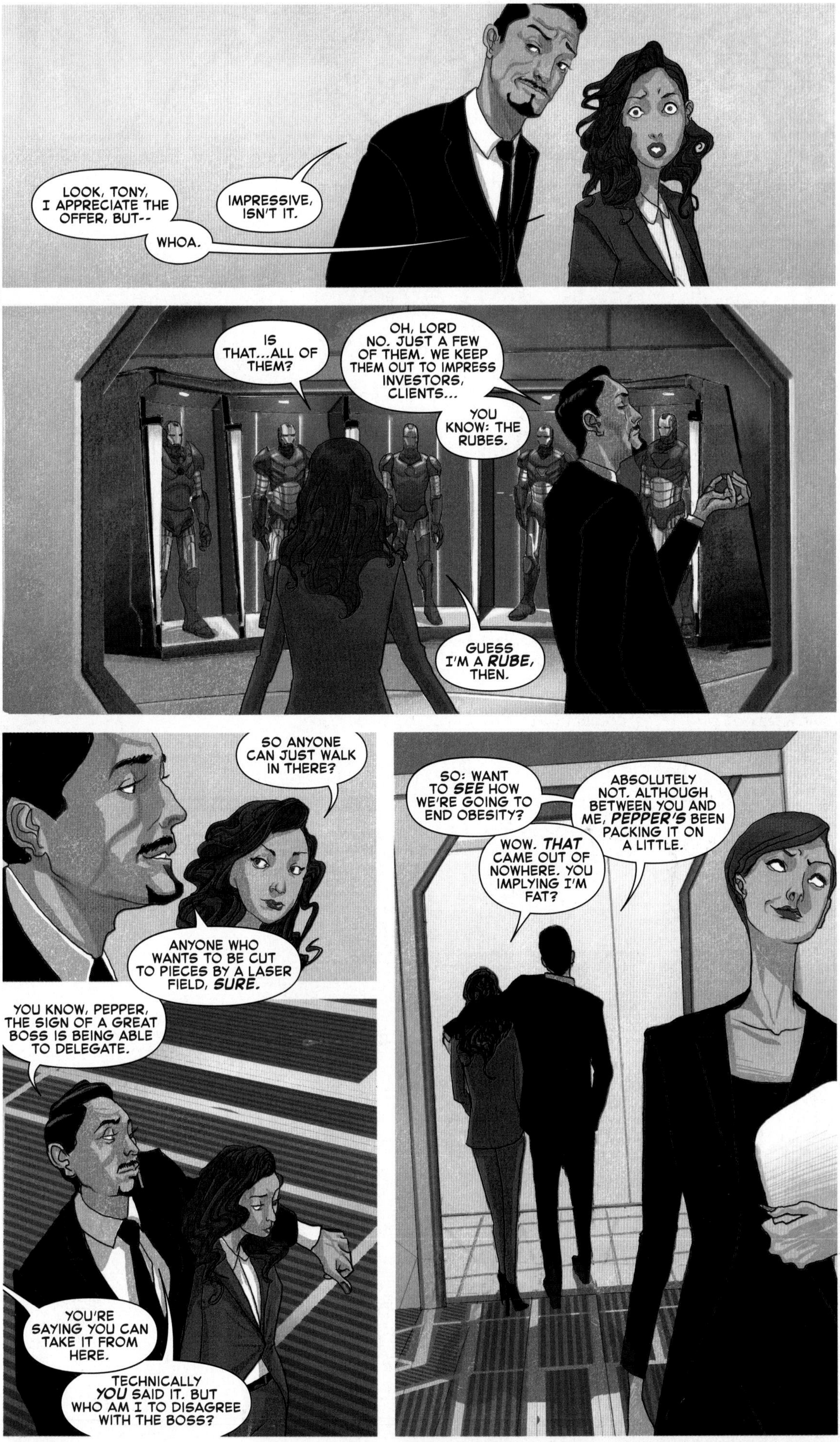
LOOK, TONY, I APPRECIATE THE OFFER, BUT--
WHOA.
IMPRESSIVE, ISN'T IT.
IS THAT...ALL OF THEM?
OH, LORD NO. JUST A FEW OF THEM. WE KEEP THEM OUT TO IMPRESS INVESTORS, CLIENTS...
YOU KNOW: THE RUBES.
GUESS I'M A **RUBE**, THEN.
SO ANYONE CAN JUST WALK IN THERE?
ANYONE WHO WANTS TO BE CUT TO PIECES BY A LASER FIELD, **SURE.**
YOU KNOW, PEPPER, THE SIGN OF A GREAT BOSS IS BEING ABLE TO DELEGATE.
YOU'RE SAYING YOU CAN TAKE IT FROM HERE.
TECHNICALLY **YOU** SAID IT. BUT WHO AM I TO DISAGREE WITH THE BOSS?
SO: WANT TO **SEE** HOW WE'RE GOING TO END OBESITY?
WOW. **THAT** CAME OUT OF NOWHERE. YOU IMPLYING I'M FAT?
ABSOLUTELY NOT. ALTHOUGH BETWEEN YOU AND ME, **PEPPER'S** BEEN PACKING IT ON A LITTLE.

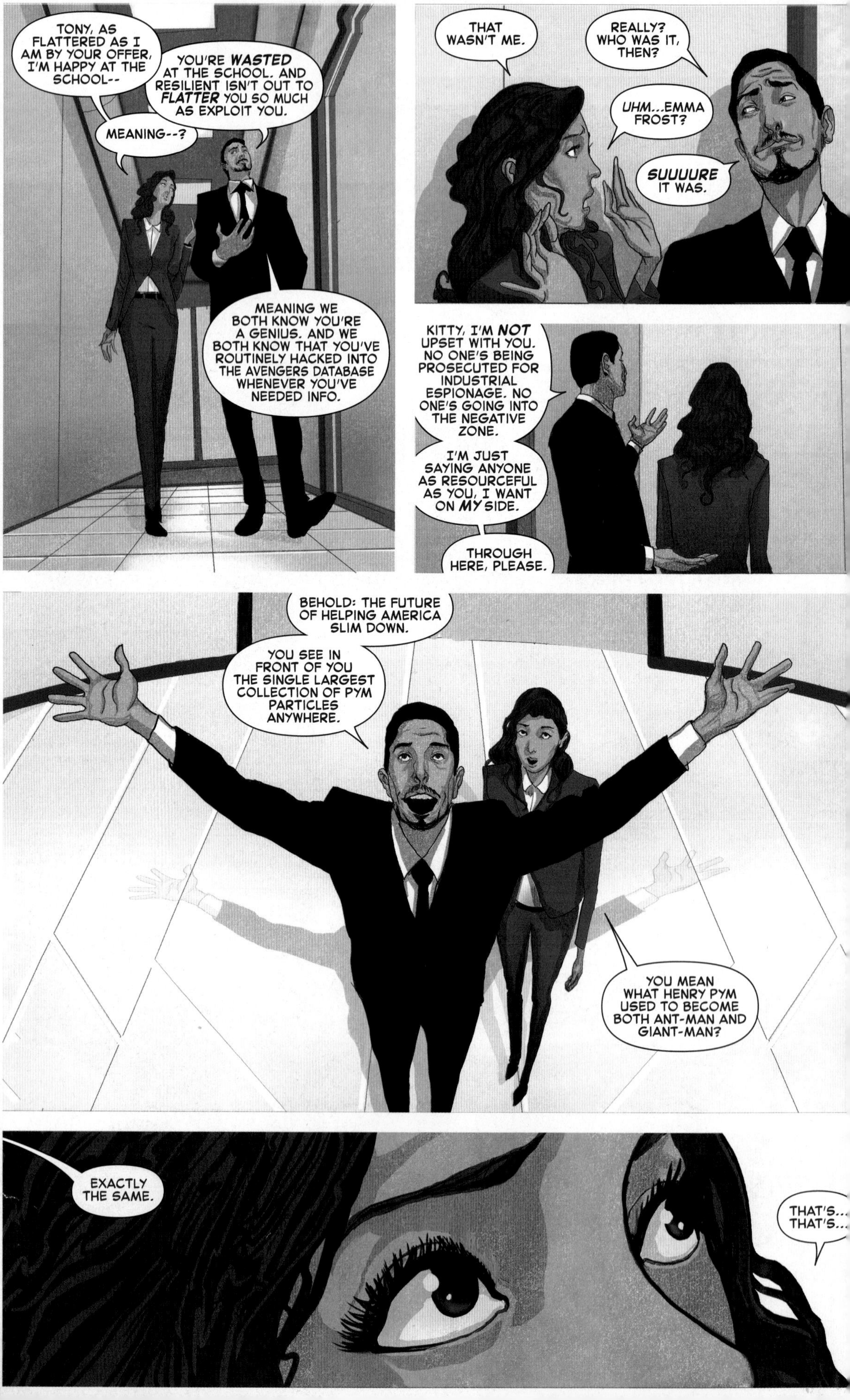
TONY, AS FLATTERED AS I AM BY YOUR OFFER, I'M HAPPY AT THE SCHOOL--
YOU'RE WASTED AT THE SCHOOL. AND RESILIENT ISN'T OUT TO FLATTER YOU SO MUCH AS EXPLOIT YOU.
MEANING--?
MEANING WE BOTH KNOW YOU'RE A GENIUS. AND WE BOTH KNOW THAT YOU'VE ROUTINELY HACKED INTO THE AVENGERS DATABASE WHENEVER YOU'VE NEEDED INFO.
THAT WASN'T ME.
REALLY? WHO WAS IT, THEN?
UHM...EMMA FROST?
SUUUURE IT WAS.
KITTY, I'M NOT UPSET WITH YOU. NO ONE'S BEING PROSECUTED FOR INDUSTRIAL ESPIONAGE. NO ONE'S GOING INTO THE NEGATIVE ZONE.
I'M JUST SAYING ANYONE AS RESOURCEFUL AS YOU, I WANT ON MY SIDE.
THROUGH HERE, PLEASE.
BEHOLD: THE FUTURE OF HELPING AMERICA SLIM DOWN.
YOU SEE IN FRONT OF YOU THE SINGLE LARGEST COLLECTION OF PYM PARTICLES ANYWHERE.
YOU MEAN WHAT HENRY PYM USED TO BECOME BOTH ANT-MAN AND GIANT-MAN?
EXACTLY THE SAME.
THAT'S... THAT'S...

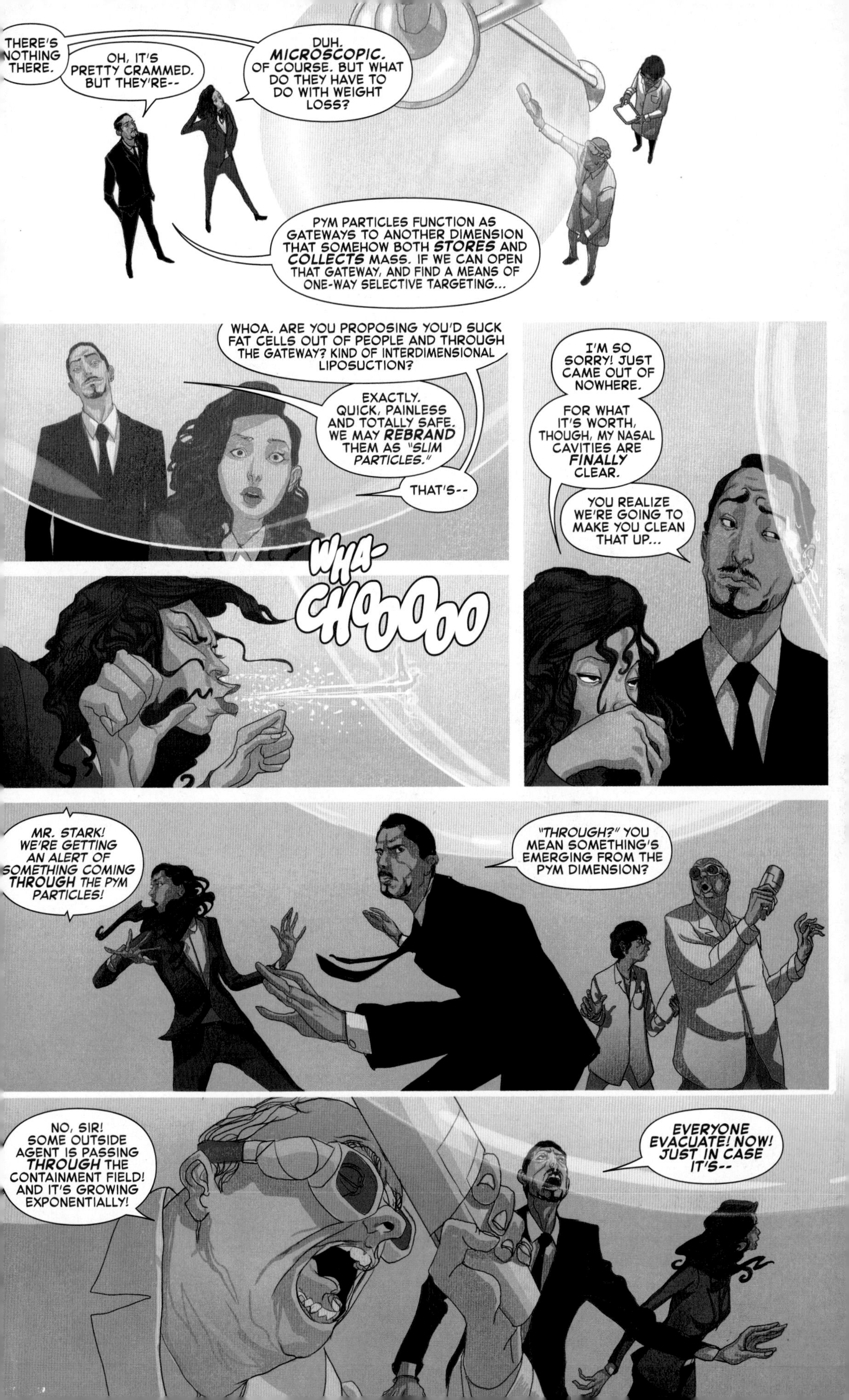
THERE'S NOTHING THERE.
OH, IT'S PRETTY CRAMMED. BUT THEY'RE--
DUH. MICROSCOPIC. OF COURSE. BUT WHAT DO THEY HAVE TO DO WITH WEIGHT LOSS?
PYM PARTICLES FUNCTION AS GATEWAYS TO ANOTHER DIMENSION THAT SOMEHOW BOTH STORES AND COLLECTS MASS. IF WE CAN OPEN THAT GATEWAY, AND FIND A MEANS OF ONE-WAY SELECTIVE TARGETING...
WHOA. ARE YOU PROPOSING YOU'D SUCK FAT CELLS OUT OF PEOPLE AND THROUGH THE GATEWAY? KIND OF INTERDIMENSIONAL LIPOSUCTION?
EXACTLY. QUICK, PAINLESS AND TOTALLY SAFE. WE MAY REBRAND THEM AS "SLIM PARTICLES."
THAT'S--
WHA-CHOOOOO
I'M SO SORRY! JUST CAME OUT OF NOWHERE.
FOR WHAT IT'S WORTH, THOUGH, MY NASAL CAVITIES ARE FINALLY CLEAR.
YOU REALIZE WE'RE GOING TO MAKE YOU CLEAN THAT UP...
MR. STARK! WE'RE GETTING AN ALERT OF SOMETHING COMING THROUGH THE PYM PARTICLES!
"THROUGH?" YOU MEAN SOMETHING'S EMERGING FROM THE PYM DIMENSION?
NO, SIR! SOME OUTSIDE AGENT IS PASSING THROUGH THE CONTAINMENT FIELD! AND IT'S GROWING EXPONENTIALLY!
EVERYONE EVACUATE! NOW! JUST IN CASE IT'S--

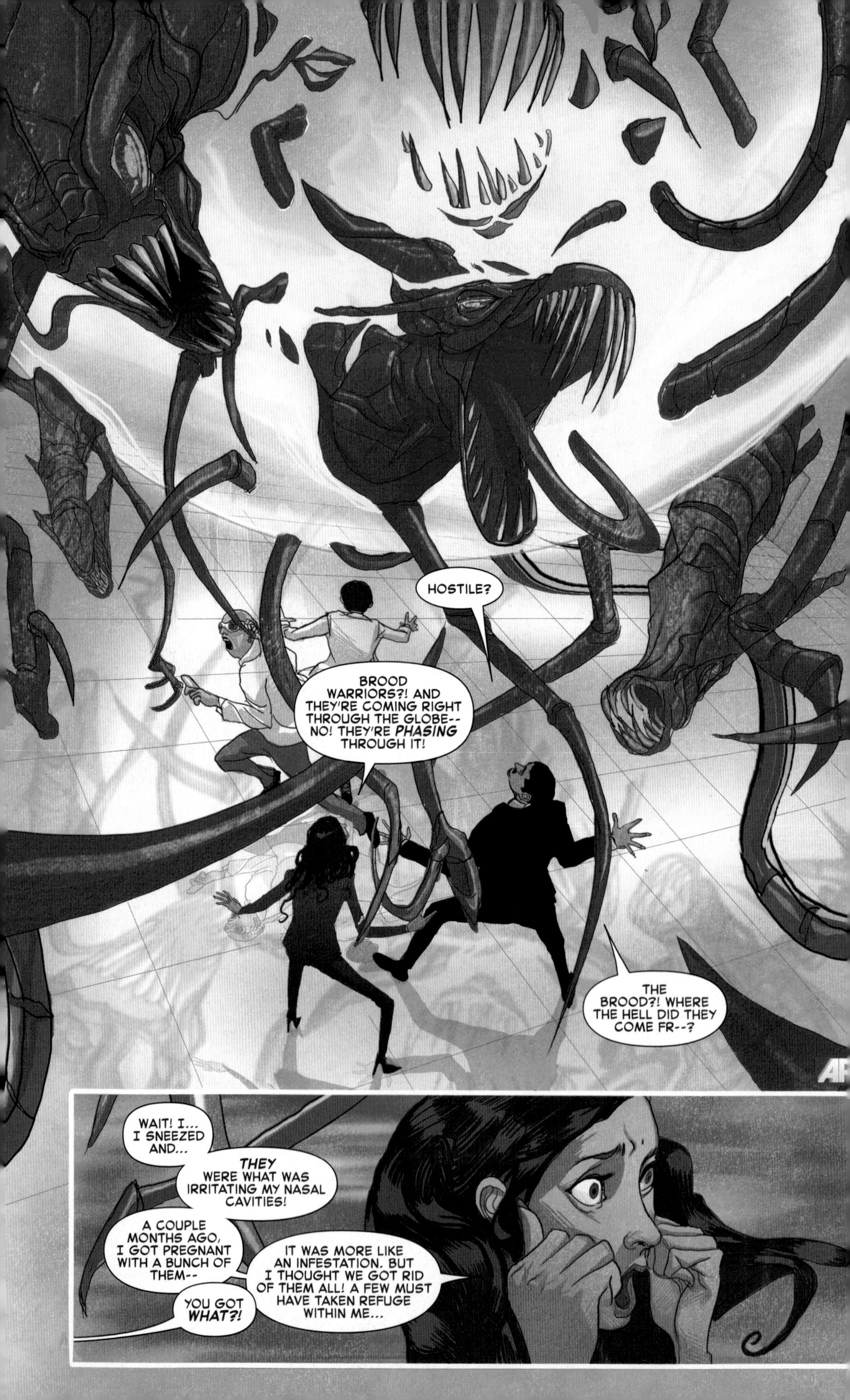

HOSTILE?
BROOD WARRIORS?! AND THEY'RE COMING RIGHT THROUGH THE GLOBE-- NO! THEY'RE *PHASING* THROUGH IT!
THE BROOD?! WHERE THE HELL DID THEY COME FR--?
WAIT! I... I SNEEZED AND...
*THEY* WERE WHAT WAS IRRITATING MY NASAL CAVITIES!
A COUPLE MONTHS AGO, I GOT PREGNANT WITH A BUNCH OF THEM--
YOU GOT *WHAT?!*
IT WAS MORE LIKE AN INFESTATION. BUT I THOUGHT WE GOT RID OF THEM ALL! A FEW MUST HAVE TAKEN REFUGE WITHIN ME...

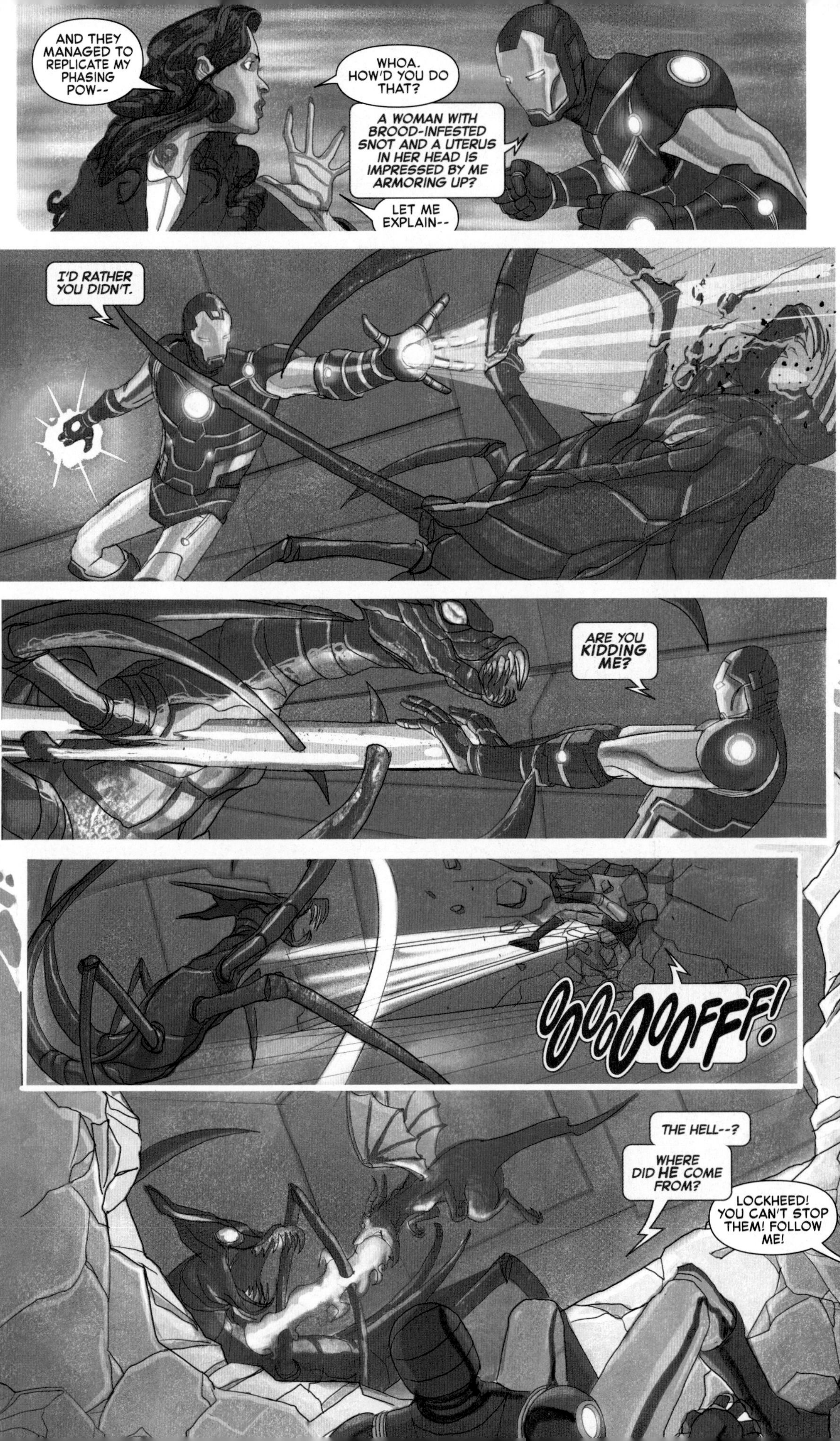
AND THEY MANAGED TO REPLICATE MY PHASING POW--
WHOA. HOW'D YOU DO THAT?
A WOMAN WITH BROOD-INFESTED SNOT AND A UTERUS IN HER HEAD IS IMPRESSED BY ME ARMORING UP?
LET ME EXPLAIN--
I'D RATHER YOU DIDN'T.
ARE YOU KIDDING ME?
OOOOOOOFFF!
THE HELL--?
WHERE DID HE COME FROM?
LOCKHEED! YOU CAN'T STOP THEM! FOLLOW ME!

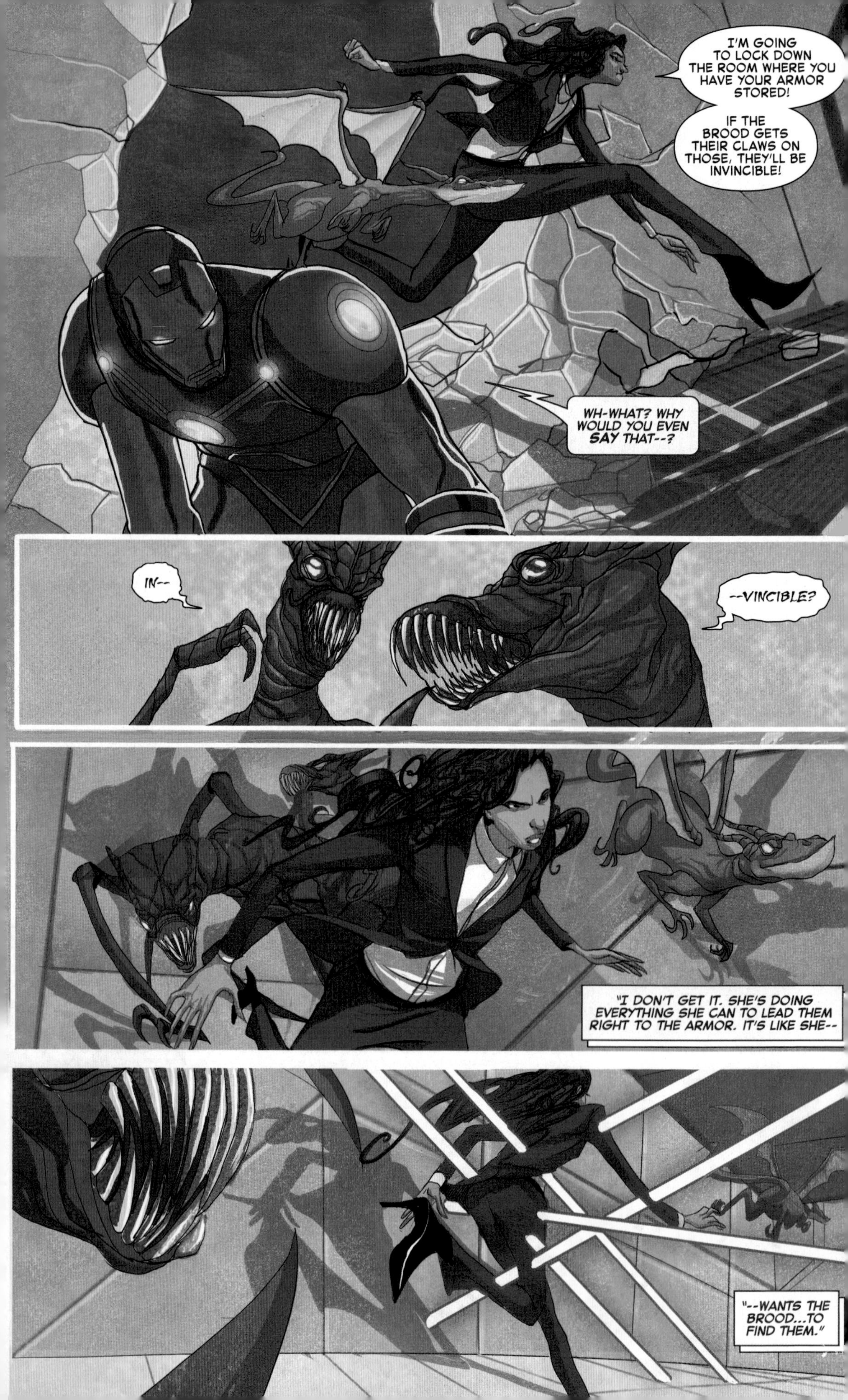
I'M GOING TO LOCK DOWN THE ROOM WHERE YOU HAVE YOUR ARMOR STORED!
IF THE BROOD GETS THEIR CLAWS ON THOSE, THEY'LL BE INVINCIBLE!
WH-WHAT? WHY WOULD YOU EVEN SAY THAT--?
IN--
--VINCIBLE?
"I DON'T GET IT. SHE'S DOING EVERYTHING SHE CAN TO LEAD THEM RIGHT TO THE ARMOR. IT'S LIKE SHE--
"--WANTS THE BROOD...TO FIND THEM."

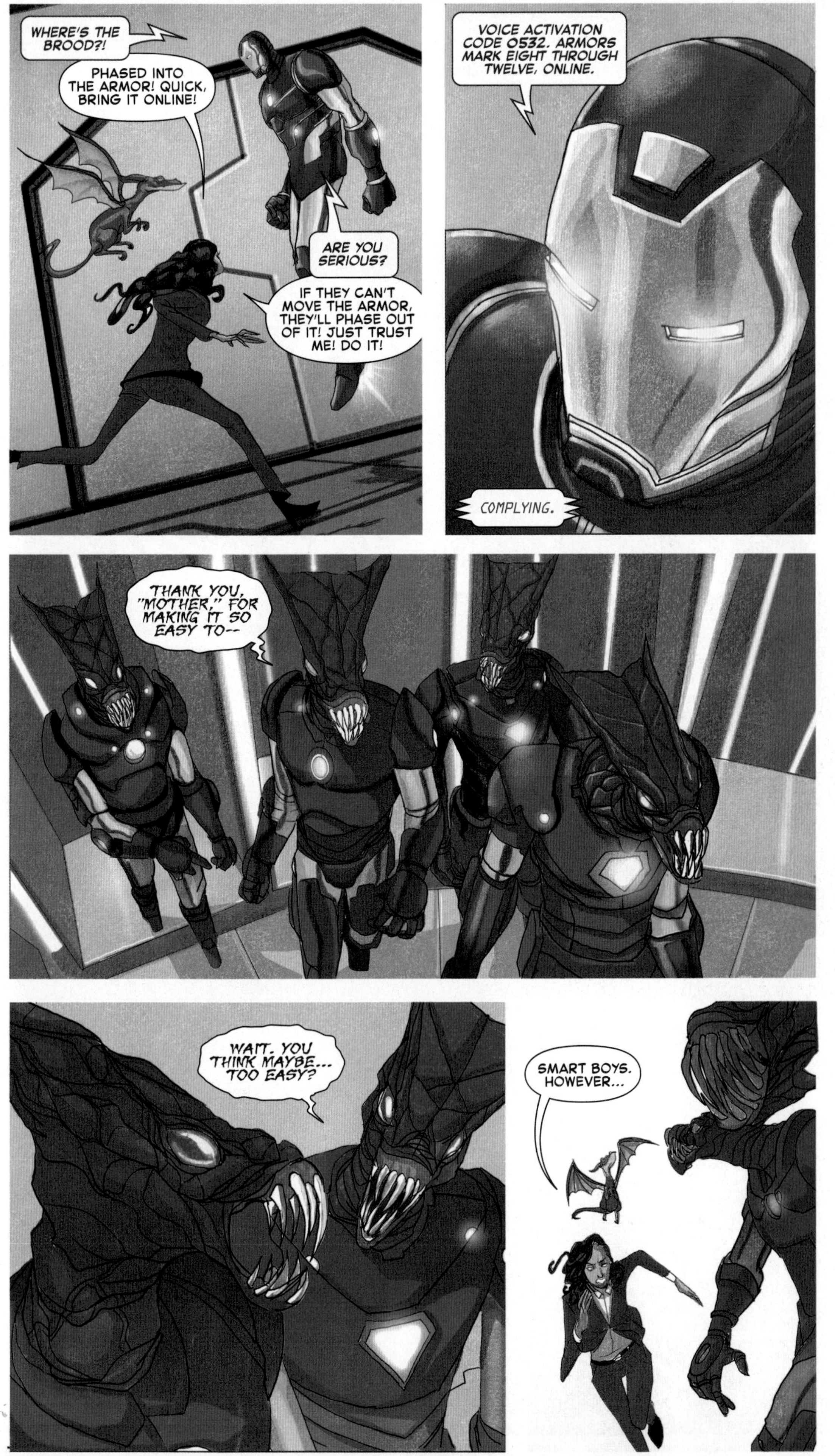
WHERE'S THE BROOD?!
PHASED INTO THE ARMOR! QUICK, BRING IT ONLINE!
ARE YOU SERIOUS?
IF THEY CAN'T MOVE THE ARMOR, THEY'LL PHASE OUT OF IT! JUST TRUST ME! DO IT!
VOICE ACTIVATION CODE 0532. ARMORS MARK EIGHT THROUGH TWELVE, ONLINE.
COMPLYING.
THANK YOU, "MOTHER," FOR MAKING IT SO EASY TO--
WAIT. YOU THINK MAYBE... TOO EASY?
SMART BOYS. HOWEVER...

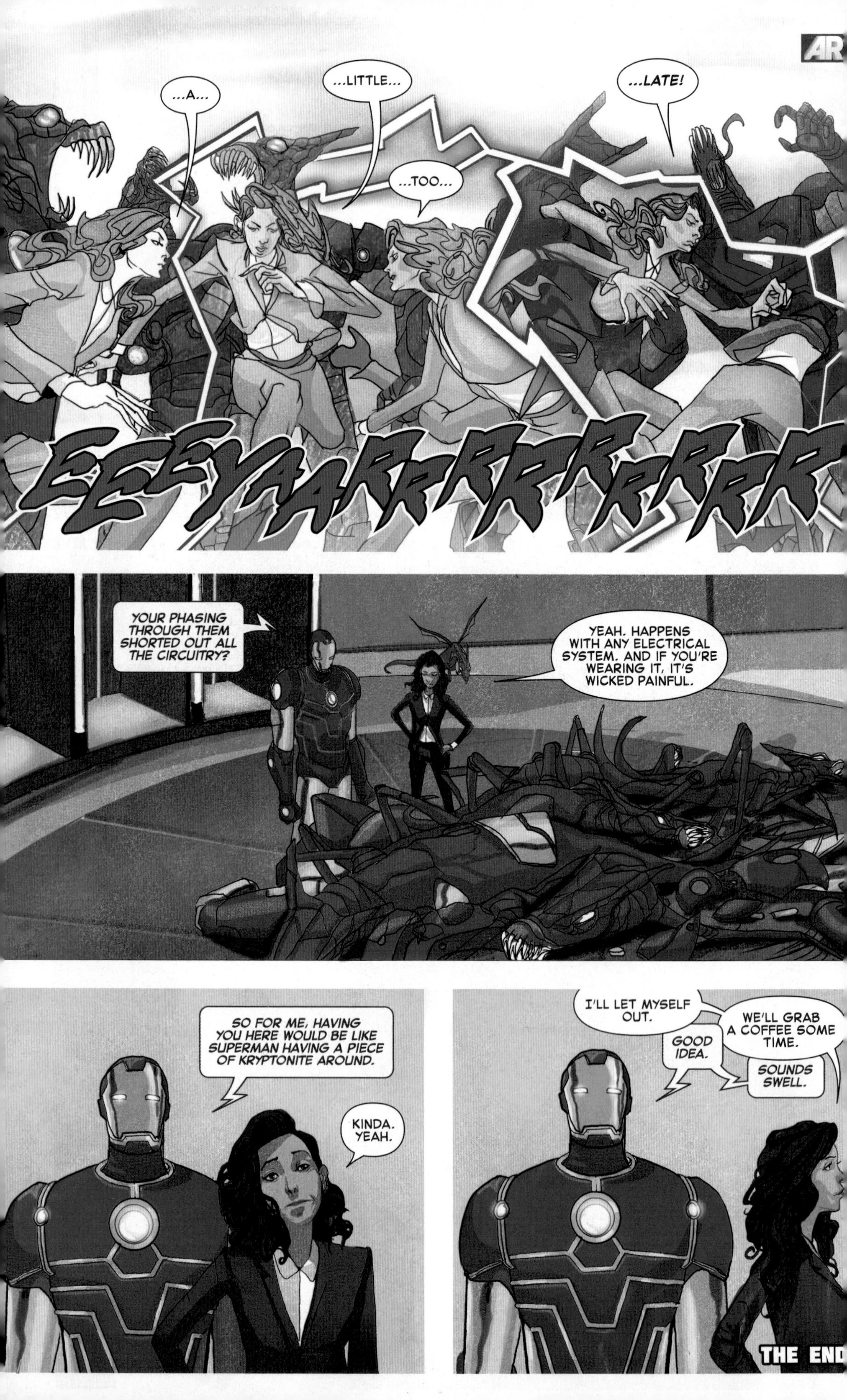
AR
...A...
...LITTLE...
...TOO...
...LATE!
EEEYAARRRRRRRRRRRR
YOUR PHASING THROUGH THEM SHORTED OUT ALL THE CIRCUITRY?
YEAH. HAPPENS WITH ANY ELECTRICAL SYSTEM. AND IF YOU'RE WEARING IT, IT'S WICKED PAINFUL.
SO FOR ME, HAVING YOU HERE WOULD BE LIKE SUPERMAN HAVING A PIECE OF KRYPTONITE AROUND.
KINDA. YEAH.
I'LL LET MYSELF OUT.
GOOD IDEA.
WE'LL GRAB A COFFEE SOME TIME.
SOUNDS SWELL.
THE END

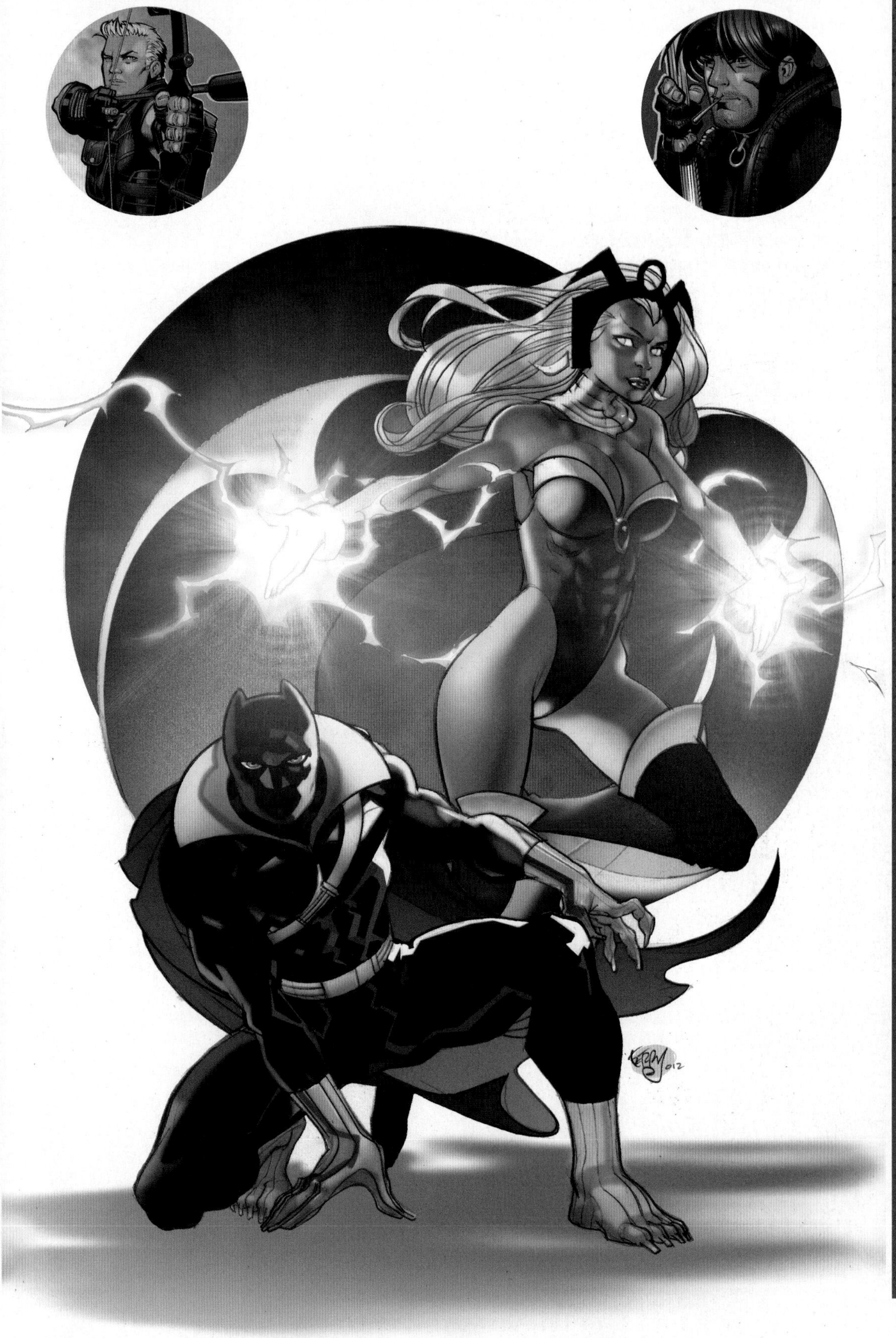

# A + X = 3

Q: My, my, my—what have we here? A comic book?
A: Not A comic book—THE comic book! It's A+X #3, where we add one Avenger and one X-Man together to get EPIC ACTION TEAM-UPS the likes of which have NEVER BEFORE BEEN SEEN!

Q: That's a bold claim. What makes them so epic?
A: ARE YOU KIDDING ME? Before now, Avengers and X-Men wouldn't be caught DEAD hanging out together! Now, they're BEST BUDS and partners in WALING ON CRIMINALS!

Q: OK, I'm on board so far. Who's in this issue?
A: We got TWO WHOLE STORIES for you. First up, there's BLACK PANTHER, super-smart African royalty empowered by his panther god, and STORM, mutant-powered weather controller and Black Panther's FORMER WIFE! THAT'S gonna be awkward!

Q: Sounds good so far. How about the second story?
A: That one's got the sharp-shooting Avenger HAWKEYE crossing paths with charming, roguish X-Man GAMBIT! I am VAGUELY UNCOMFORTABLE with the amount ladies seem to LOVE these two men!

Q: That...is too much personal information from you, I think.
A: Then TURN THE PAGE and we can FORGET THIS EVER HAPPENED!

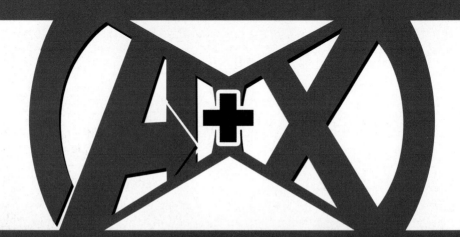

 **+**

**BLACK PANTHER + STORM**

JASON **AARON** WRITER

PASQUAL **FERRY** ARTIST

BRIAN **REBER** COLOR ARTIST

VC'S CLAYTON **COWLES** LETTERER

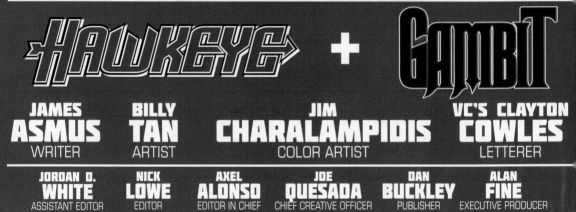 **+**

**HAWKEYE + GAMBIT**

JAMES **ASMUS** WRITER

BILLY **TAN** ARTIST

JIM **CHARALAMPIDIS** COLOR ARTIST

VC'S CLAYTON **COWLES** LETTERER

JORDAN D. **WHITE** ASSISTANT EDITOR

NICK **LOWE** EDITOR

AXEL **ALONSO** EDITOR IN CHIEF

JOE **QUESADA** CHIEF CREATIVE OFFICER

DAN **BUCKLEY** PUBLISHER

ALAN **FINE** EXECUTIVE PRODUCER

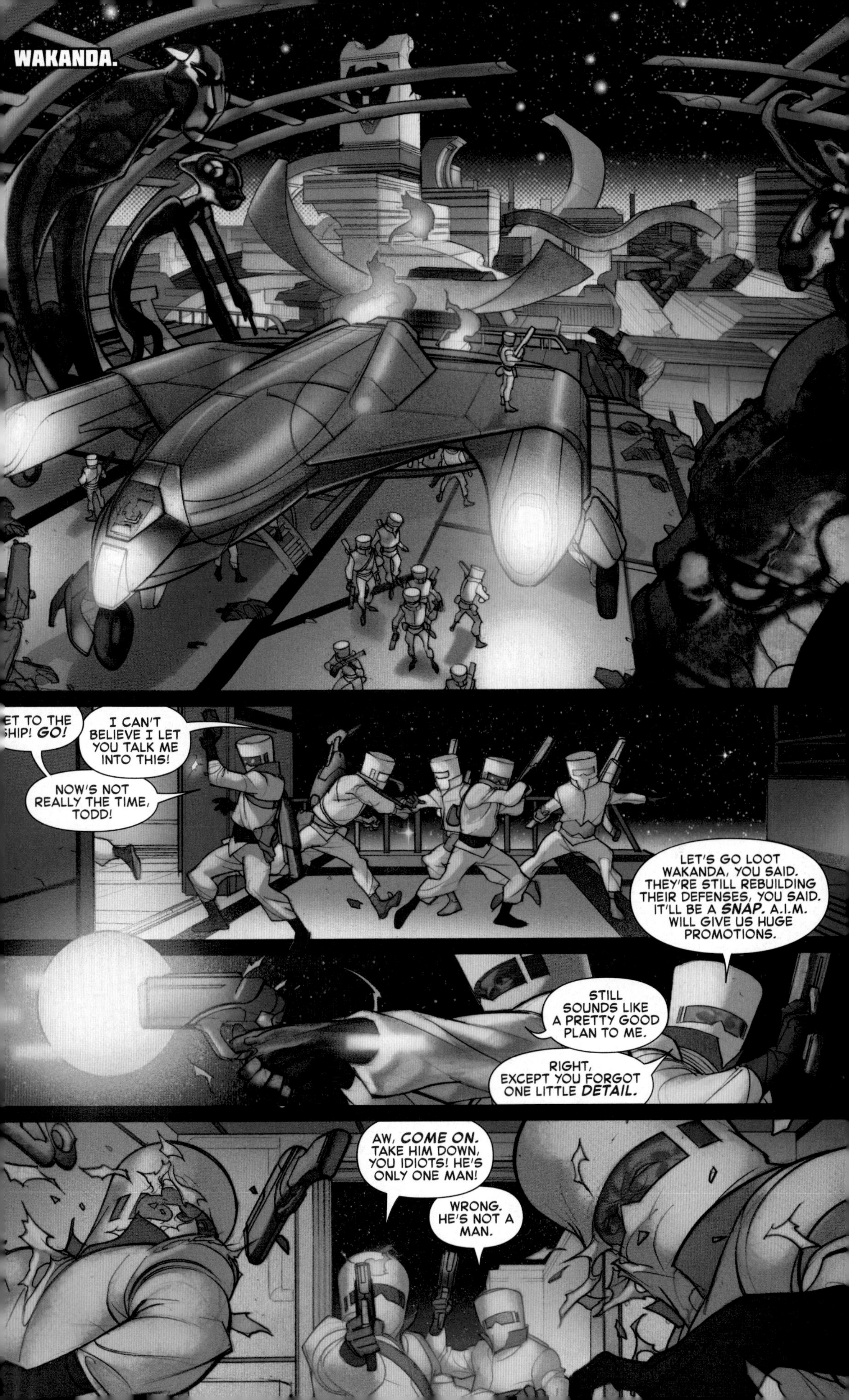
WAKANDA.
ET TO THE
SHIP! GO!
I CAN'T BELIEVE I LET YOU TALK ME INTO THIS!
NOW'S NOT REALLY THE TIME, TODD!
LET'S GO LOOT WAKANDA, YOU SAID. THEY'RE STILL REBUILDING THEIR DEFENSES, YOU SAID. IT'LL BE A SNAP. A.I.M. WILL GIVE US HUGE PROMOTIONS.
STILL SOUNDS LIKE A PRETTY GOOD PLAN TO ME.
RIGHT, EXCEPT YOU FORGOT ONE LITTLE DETAIL.
AW, COME ON. TAKE HIM DOWN, YOU IDIOTS! HE'S ONLY ONE MAN!
WRONG. HE'S NOT A MAN.

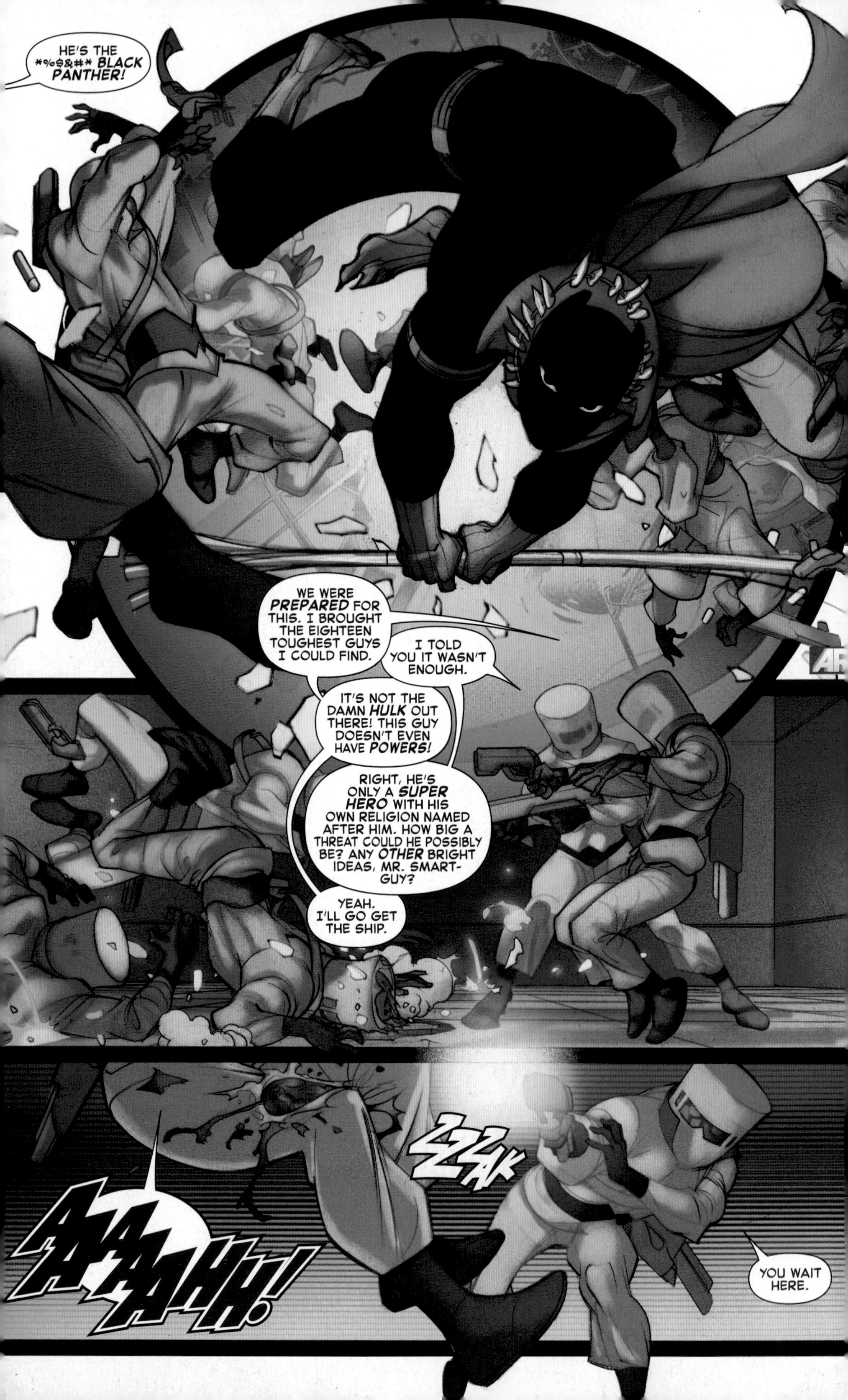
HE'S THE *%$&#* BLACK PANTHER!
WE WERE PREPARED FOR THIS. I BROUGHT THE EIGHTEEN TOUGHEST GUYS I COULD FIND.
I TOLD YOU IT WASN'T ENOUGH.
IT'S NOT THE DAMN HULK OUT THERE! THIS GUY DOESN'T EVEN HAVE POWERS!
RIGHT, HE'S ONLY A SUPER HERO WITH HIS OWN RELIGION NAMED AFTER HIM. HOW BIG A THREAT COULD HE POSSIBLY BE? ANY OTHER BRIGHT IDEAS, MR. SMART-GUY?
YEAH. I'LL GO GET THE SHIP.
AAAAHH!
ZZZAK
YOU WAIT HERE.

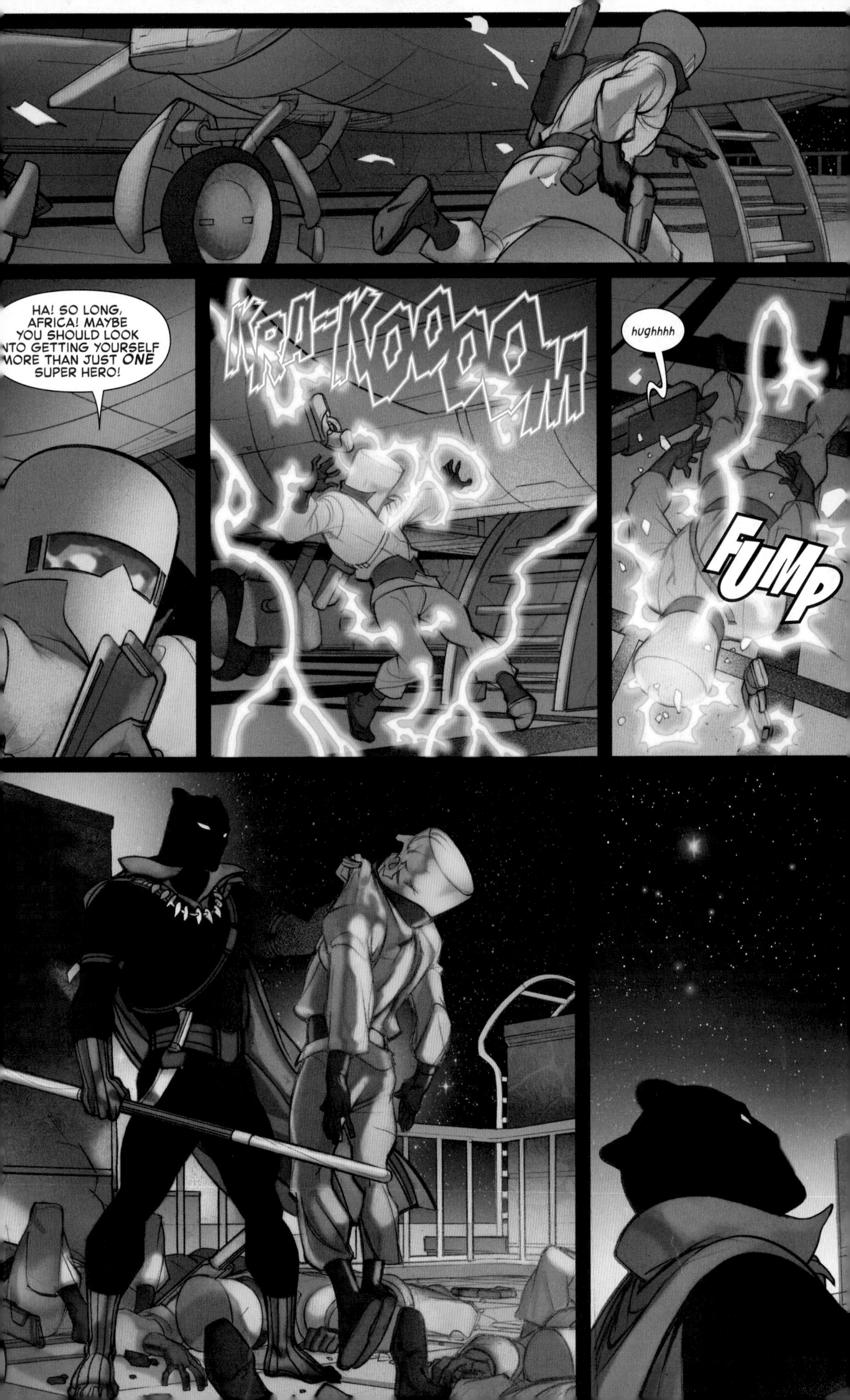
HA! SO LONG, AFRICA! MAYBE YOU SHOULD LOOK INTO GETTING YOURSELF MORE THAN JUST ONE SUPER HERO!
KRA-KOOOOM
hughhhh
FUMP

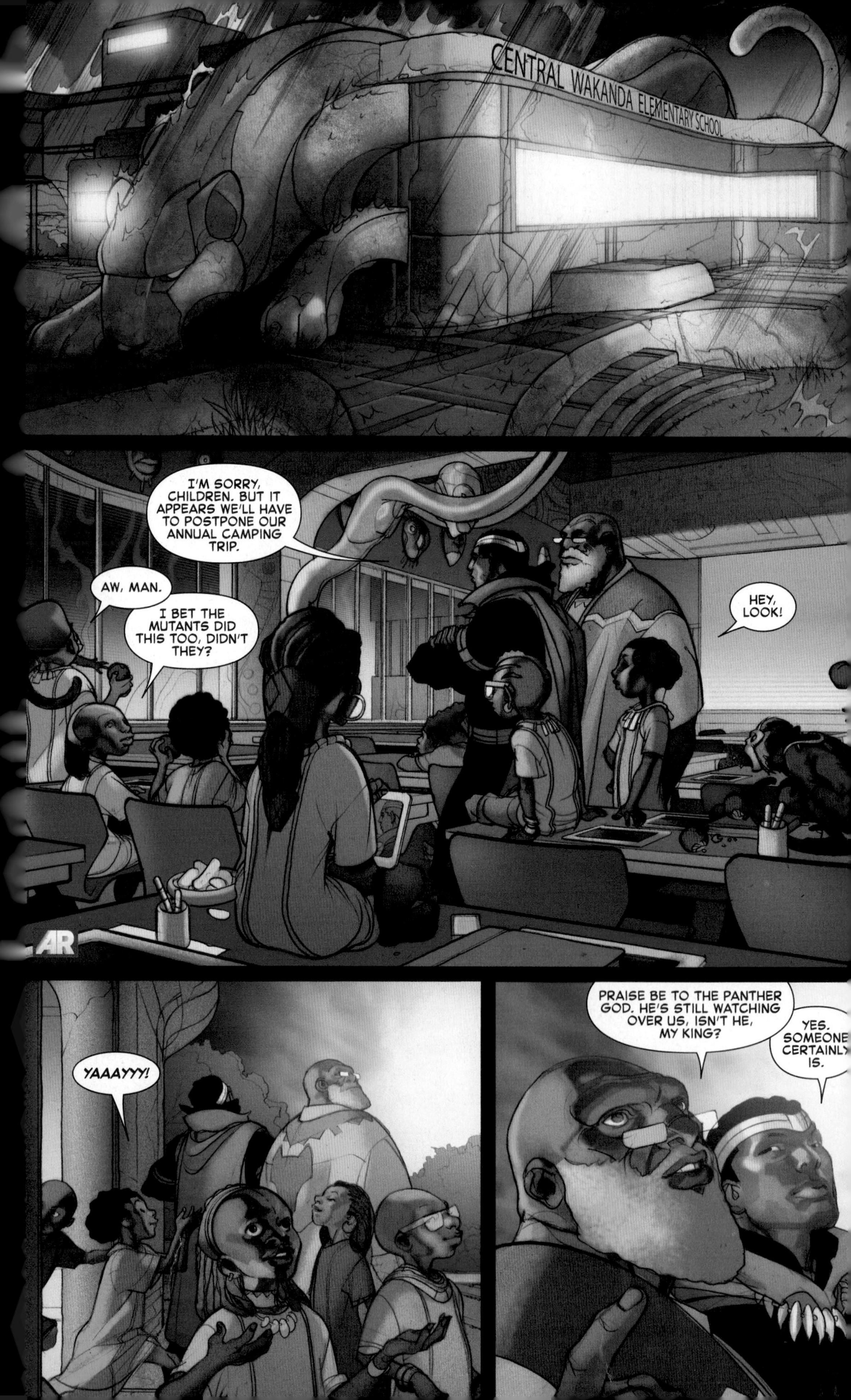
CENTRAL WAKANDA ELEMENTARY SCHOOL
I'M SORRY, CHILDREN. BUT IT APPEARS WE'LL HAVE TO POSTPONE OUR ANNUAL CAMPING TRIP.
AW, MAN.
I BET THE MUTANTS DID THIS TOO, DIDN'T THEY?
HEY, LOOK!
YAAAYYY!
PRAISE BE TO THE PANTHER GOD. HE'S STILL WATCHING OVER US, ISN'T HE, MY KING?
YES. SOMEONE CERTAINLY IS.

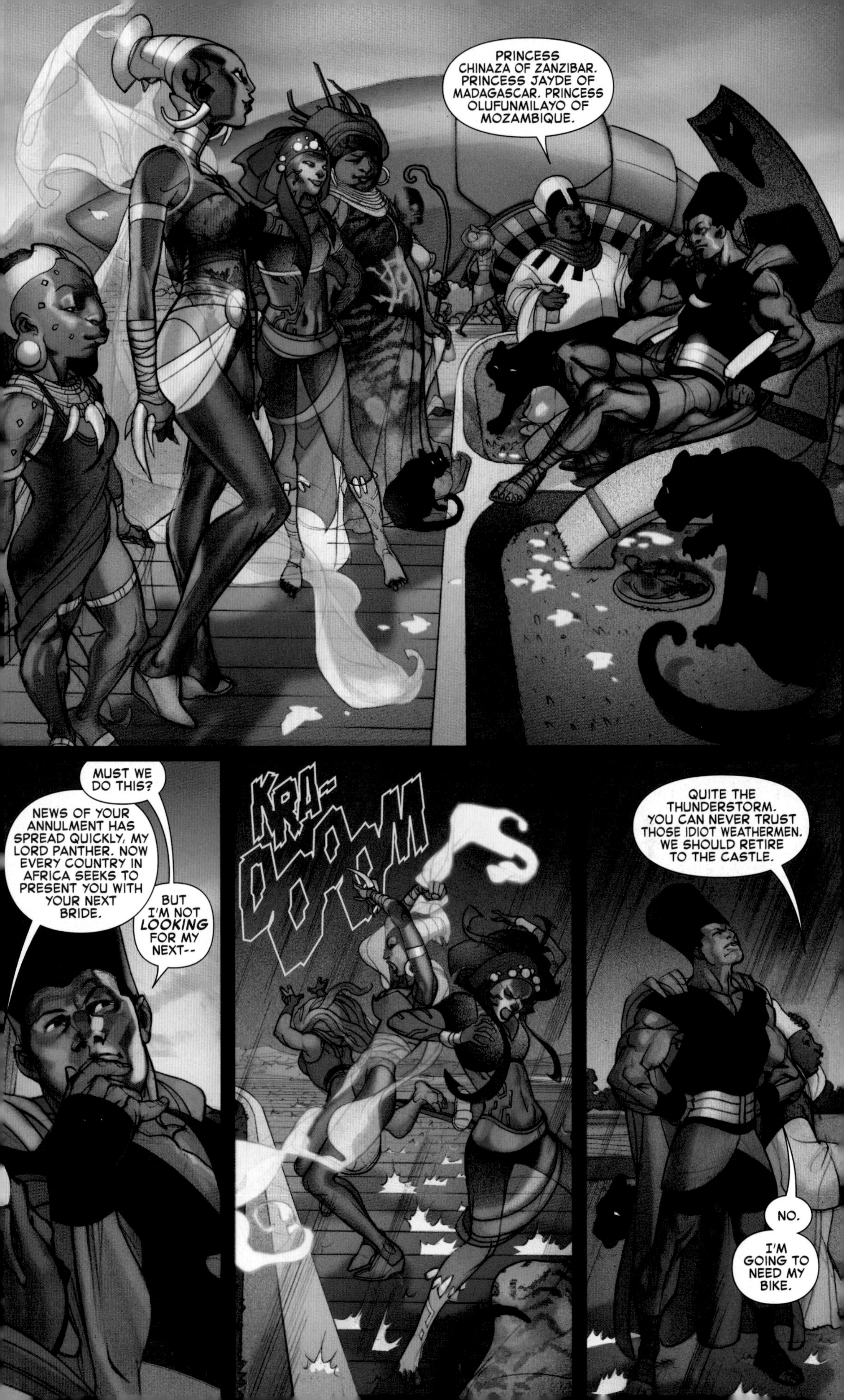
PRINCESS CHINAZA OF ZANZIBAR. PRINCESS JAYDE OF MADAGASCAR. PRINCESS OLUFUNMILAYO OF MOZAMBIQUE.
MUST WE DO THIS?
NEWS OF YOUR ANNULMENT HAS SPREAD QUICKLY, MY LORD PANTHER. NOW EVERY COUNTRY IN AFRICA SEEKS TO PRESENT YOU WITH YOUR NEXT BRIDE.
BUT I'M NOT *LOOKING* FOR MY NEXT--
KRA-DOOOM
QUITE THE THUNDERSTORM. YOU CAN NEVER TRUST THOSE IDIOT WEATHERMEN. WE SHOULD RETIRE TO THE CASTLE.
NO.
I'M GOING TO NEED MY BIKE.

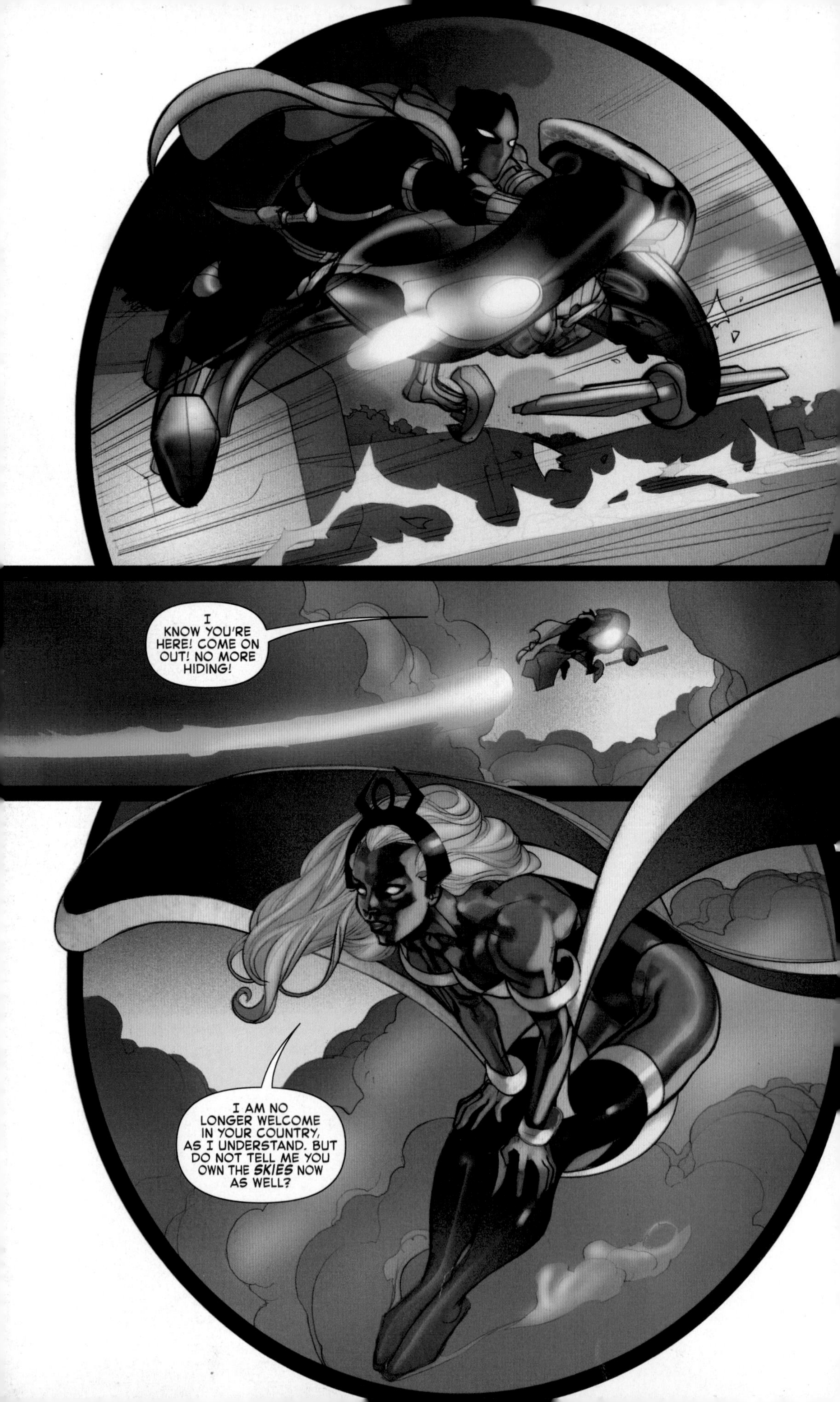
I KNOW YOU'RE HERE! COME ON OUT! NO MORE HIDING!
I AM NO LONGER WELCOME IN YOUR COUNTRY, AS I UNDERSTAND. BUT DO NOT TELL ME YOU OWN THE SKIES NOW AS WELL?

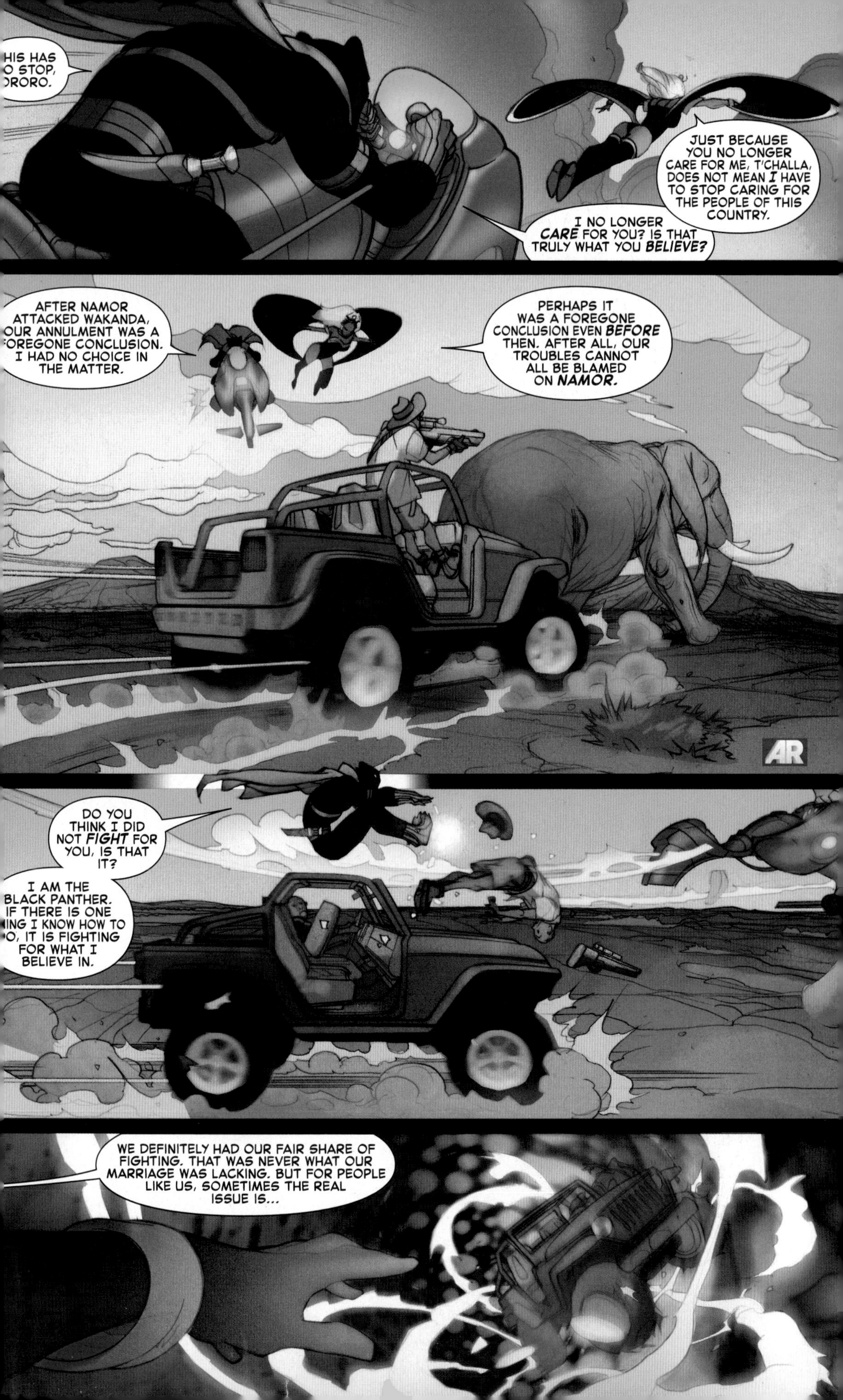

HIS HAS
O STOP,
ORORO.
JUST BECAUSE YOU NO LONGER CARE FOR ME, T'CHALLA, DOES NOT MEAN I HAVE TO STOP CARING FOR THE PEOPLE OF THIS COUNTRY.
I NO LONGER CARE FOR YOU? IS THAT TRULY WHAT YOU BELIEVE?
AFTER NAMOR ATTACKED WAKANDA, OUR ANNULMENT WAS A FOREGONE CONCLUSION. I HAD NO CHOICE IN THE MATTER.
PERHAPS IT WAS A FOREGONE CONCLUSION EVEN BEFORE THEN. AFTER ALL, OUR TROUBLES CANNOT ALL BE BLAMED ON NAMOR.
AR
DO YOU THINK I DID NOT FIGHT FOR YOU, IS THAT IT?
I AM THE BLACK PANTHER. IF THERE IS ONE ING I KNOW HOW TO O, IT IS FIGHTING FOR WHAT I BELIEVE IN.
WE DEFINITELY HAD OUR FAIR SHARE OF FIGHTING. THAT WAS NEVER WHAT OUR MARRIAGE WAS LACKING. BUT FOR PEOPLE LIKE US, SOMETIMES THE REAL ISSUE IS...

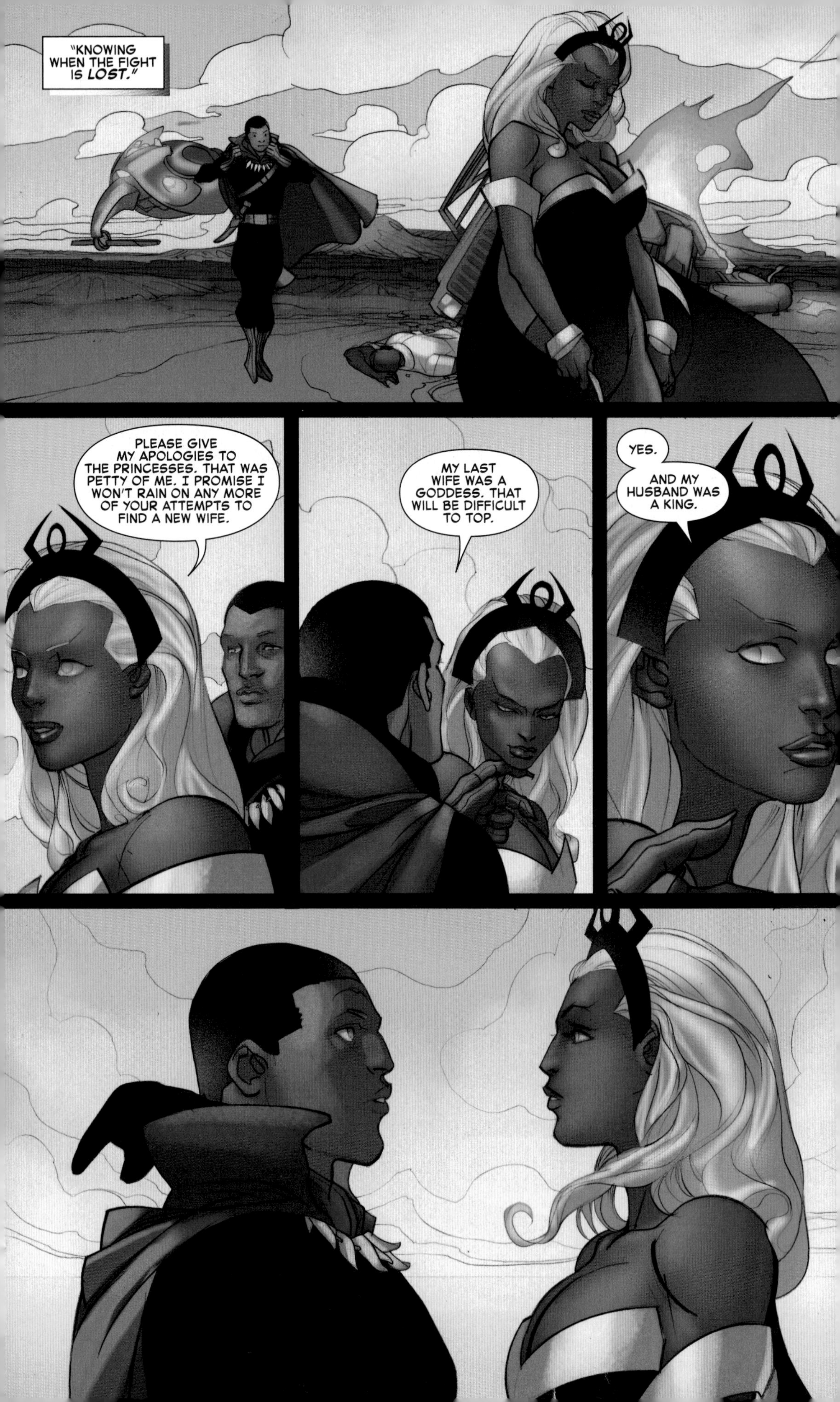
"KNOWING WHEN THE FIGHT IS LOST."
PLEASE GIVE MY APOLOGIES TO THE PRINCESSES. THAT WAS PETTY OF ME. I PROMISE I WON'T RAIN ON ANY MORE OF YOUR ATTEMPTS TO FIND A NEW WIFE.
MY LAST WIFE WAS A GODDESS. THAT WILL BE DIFFICULT TO TOP.
YES.
AND MY HUSBAND WAS A KING.

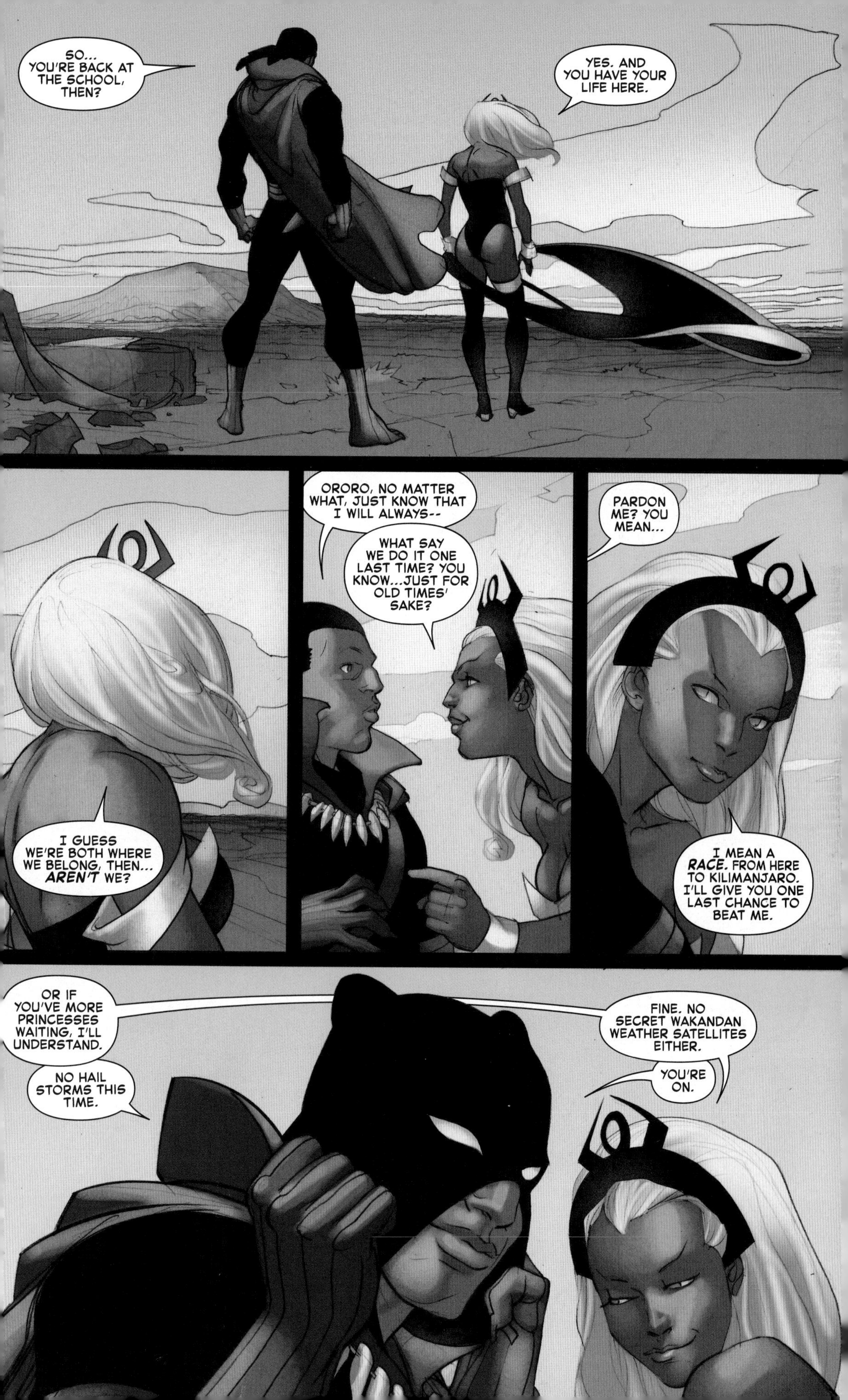
SO... YOU'RE BACK AT THE SCHOOL, THEN?
YES. AND YOU HAVE YOUR LIFE HERE.
I GUESS WE'RE BOTH WHERE WE BELONG, THEN... *AREN'T* WE?
ORORO, NO MATTER WHAT, JUST KNOW THAT I WILL ALWAYS--
WHAT SAY WE DO IT ONE LAST TIME? YOU KNOW...JUST FOR OLD TIMES' SAKE?
PARDON ME? YOU MEAN...
I MEAN A *RACE*. FROM HERE TO KILIMANJARO. I'LL GIVE YOU ONE LAST CHANCE TO BEAT ME.
OR IF YOU'VE MORE PRINCESSES WAITING, I'LL UNDERSTAND.
NO HAIL STORMS THIS TIME.
FINE. NO SECRET WAKANDAN WEATHER SATELLITES EITHER.
YOU'RE ON.

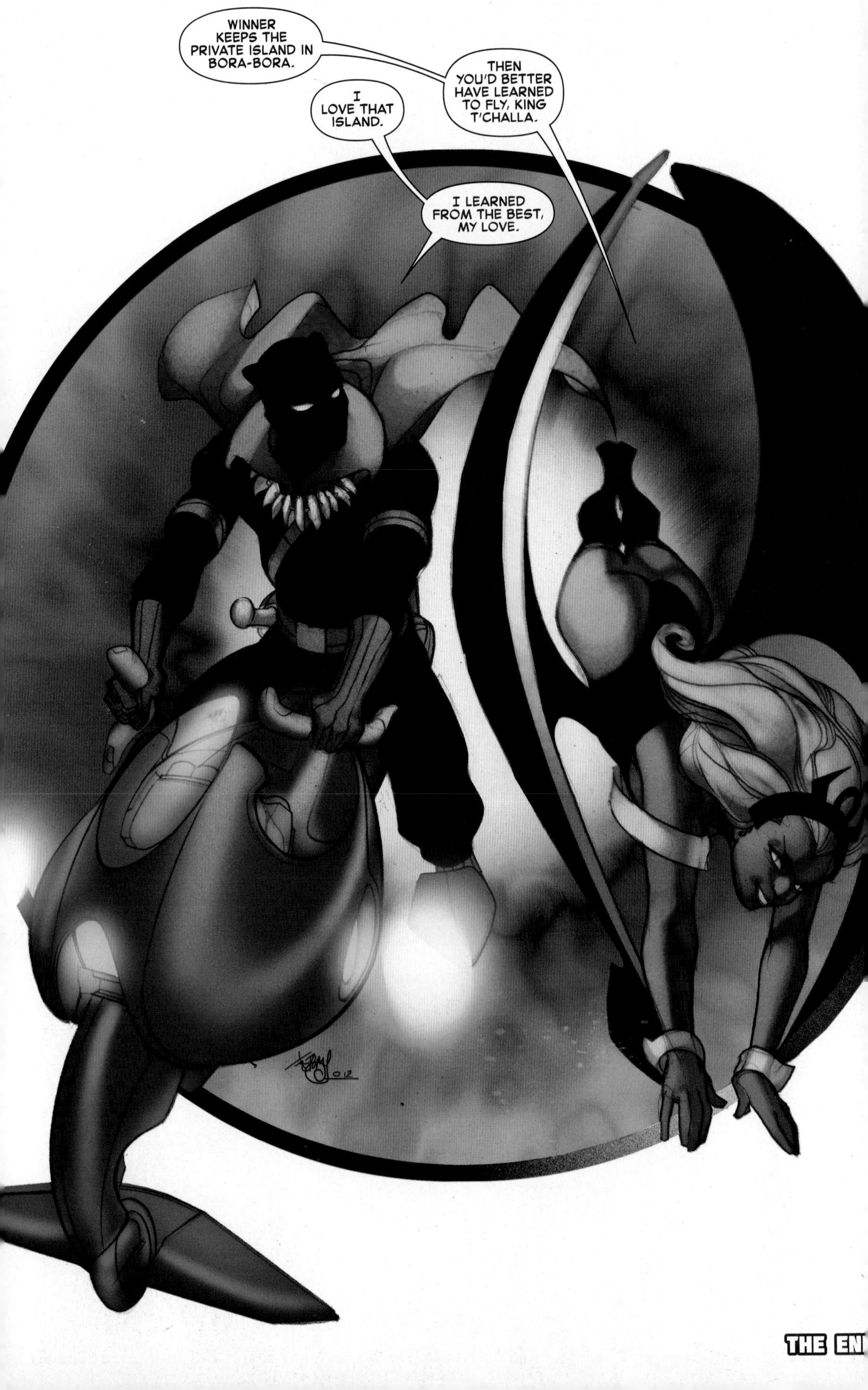
WINNER KEEPS THE PRIVATE ISLAND IN BORA-BORA.
I LOVE THAT ISLAND.
THEN YOU'D BETTER HAVE LEARNED TO FLY, KING T'CHALLA.
I LEARNED FROM THE BEST, MY LOVE.
THE EN

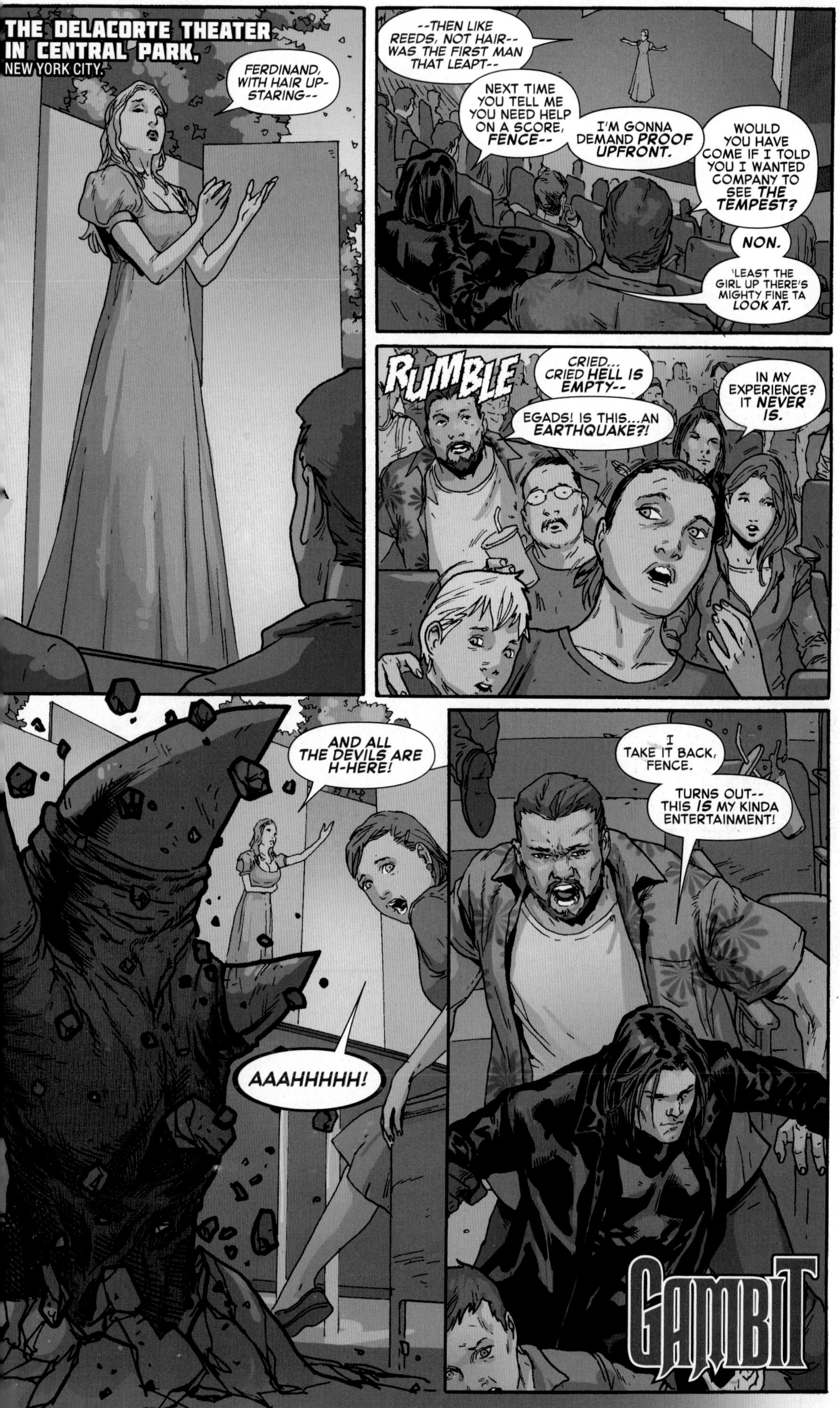
THE DELACORTE THEATER IN CENTRAL PARK,
NEW YORK CITY.
FERDINAND, WITH HAIR UP-STARING--
--THEN LIKE REEDS, NOT HAIR--WAS THE FIRST MAN THAT LEAPT--
NEXT TIME YOU TELL ME YOU NEED HELP ON A SCORE, FENCE--
I'M GONNA DEMAND PROOF UPFRONT.
WOULD YOU HAVE COME IF I TOLD YOU I WANTED COMPANY TO SEE THE TEMPEST?
NON.
'LEAST THE GIRL UP THERE'S MIGHTY FINE TA LOOK AT.
RUMBLE
CRIED... CRIED HELL IS EMPTY--
EGADS! IS THIS...AN EARTHQUAKE?!
IN MY EXPERIENCE? IT NEVER IS.
AND ALL THE DEVILS ARE H-HERE!
AAAHHHHH!
I TAKE IT BACK, FENCE.
TURNS OUT--THIS IS MY KINDA ENTERTAINMENT!
GAMBIT

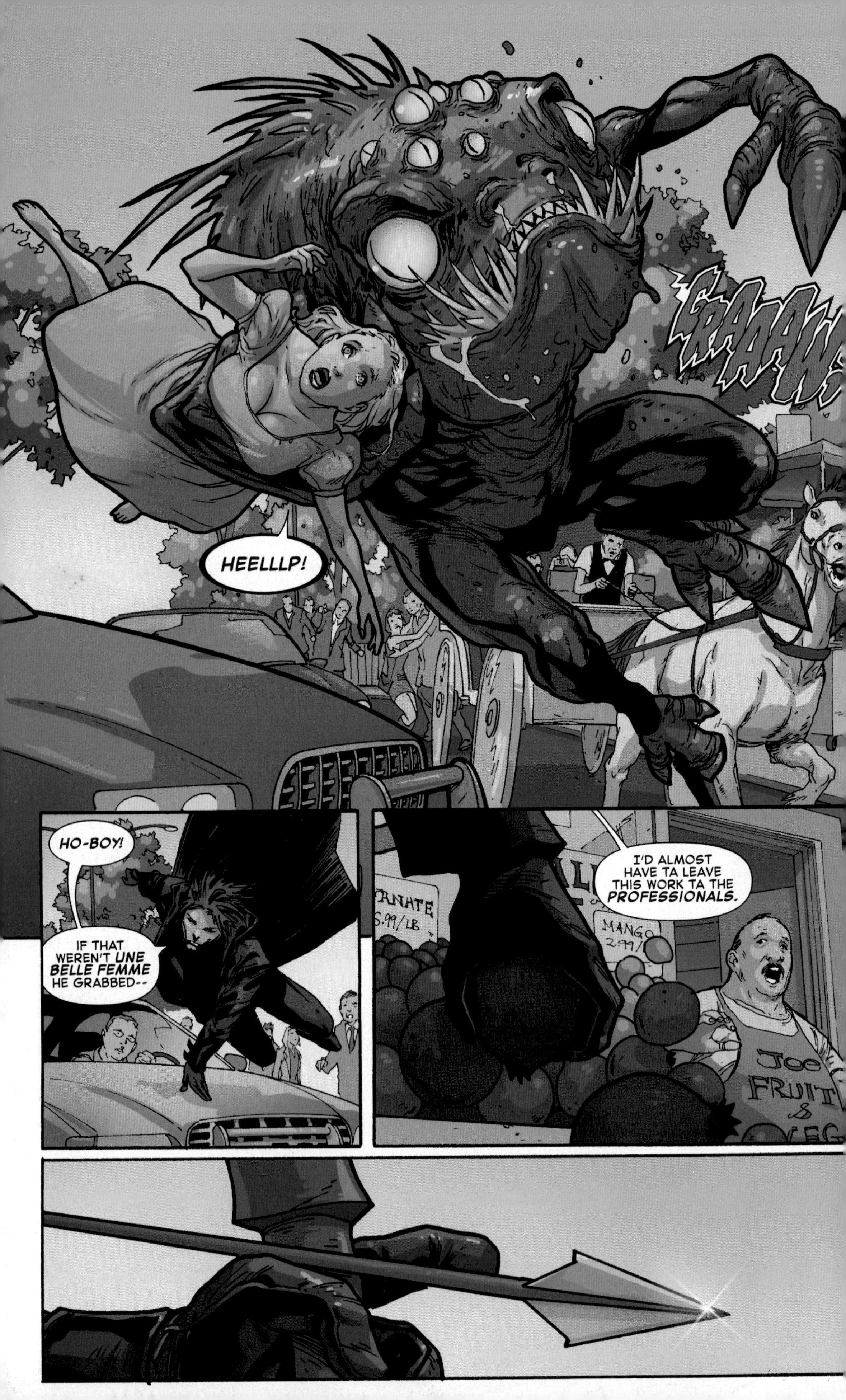
GRAAAWW
HEELLLP!
HO-BOY!
IF THAT WEREN'T UNE BELLE FEMME HE GRABBED--
I'D ALMOST HAVE TA LEAVE THIS WORK TA THE PROFESSIONALS.
MANGO
JOE FRUIT

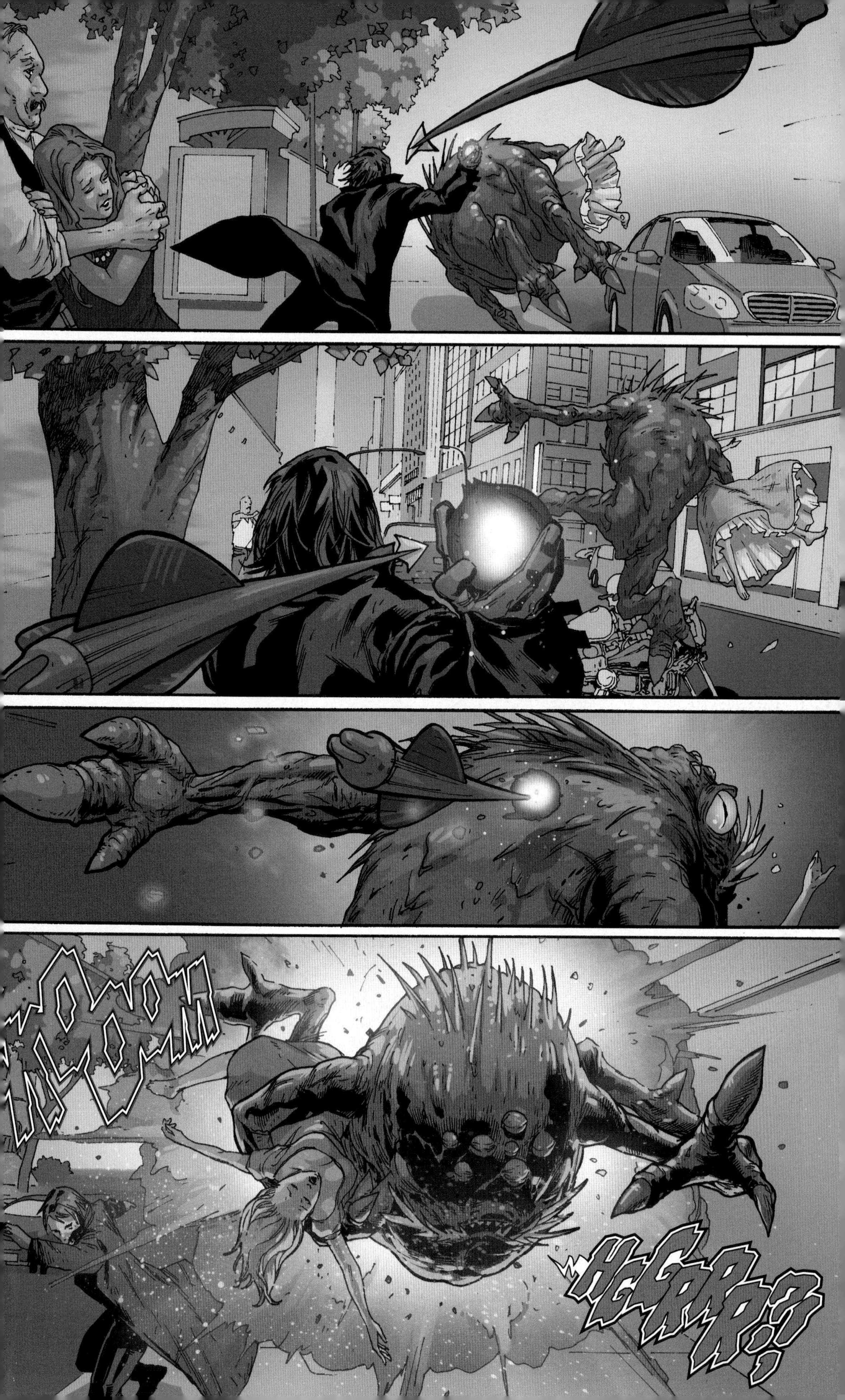
WHOOOM
HGRR?!

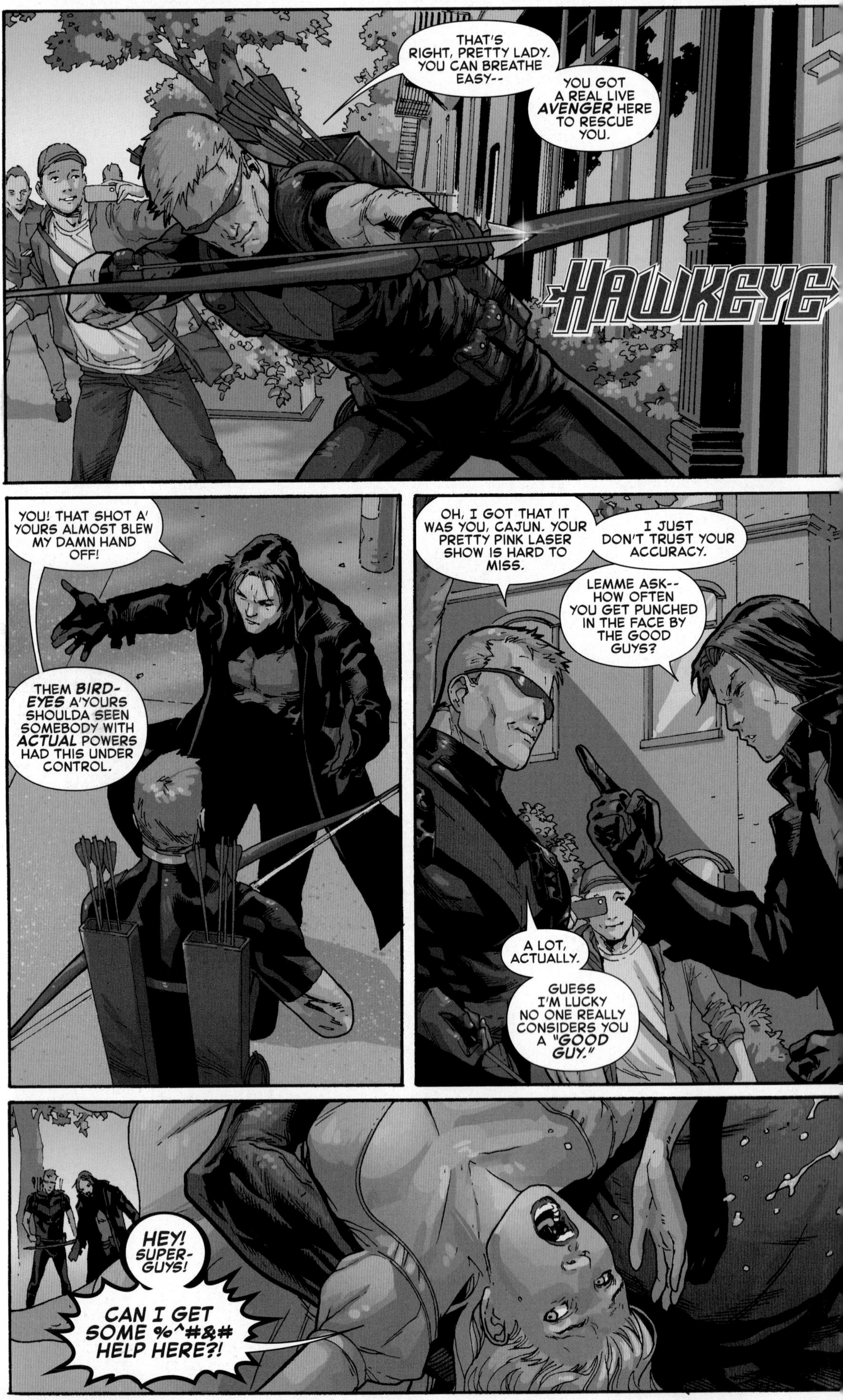
THAT'S RIGHT, PRETTY LADY. YOU CAN BREATHE EASY--
YOU GOT A REAL LIVE AVENGER HERE TO RESCUE YOU.
HAWKEYE
YOU! THAT SHOT A' YOURS ALMOST BLEW MY DAMN HAND OFF!
THEM BIRD-EYES A'YOURS SHOULDA SEEN SOMEBODY WITH ACTUAL POWERS HAD THIS UNDER CONTROL.
OH, I GOT THAT IT WAS YOU, CAJUN. YOUR PRETTY PINK LASER SHOW IS HARD TO MISS.
I JUST DON'T TRUST YOUR ACCURACY.
LEMME ASK-- HOW OFTEN YOU GET PUNCHED IN THE FACE BY THE GOOD GUYS?
A LOT, ACTUALLY.
GUESS I'M LUCKY NO ONE REALLY CONSIDERS YOU A "GOOD GUY."
HEY! SUPER-GUYS!
CAN I GET SOME %^#&# HELP HERE?!

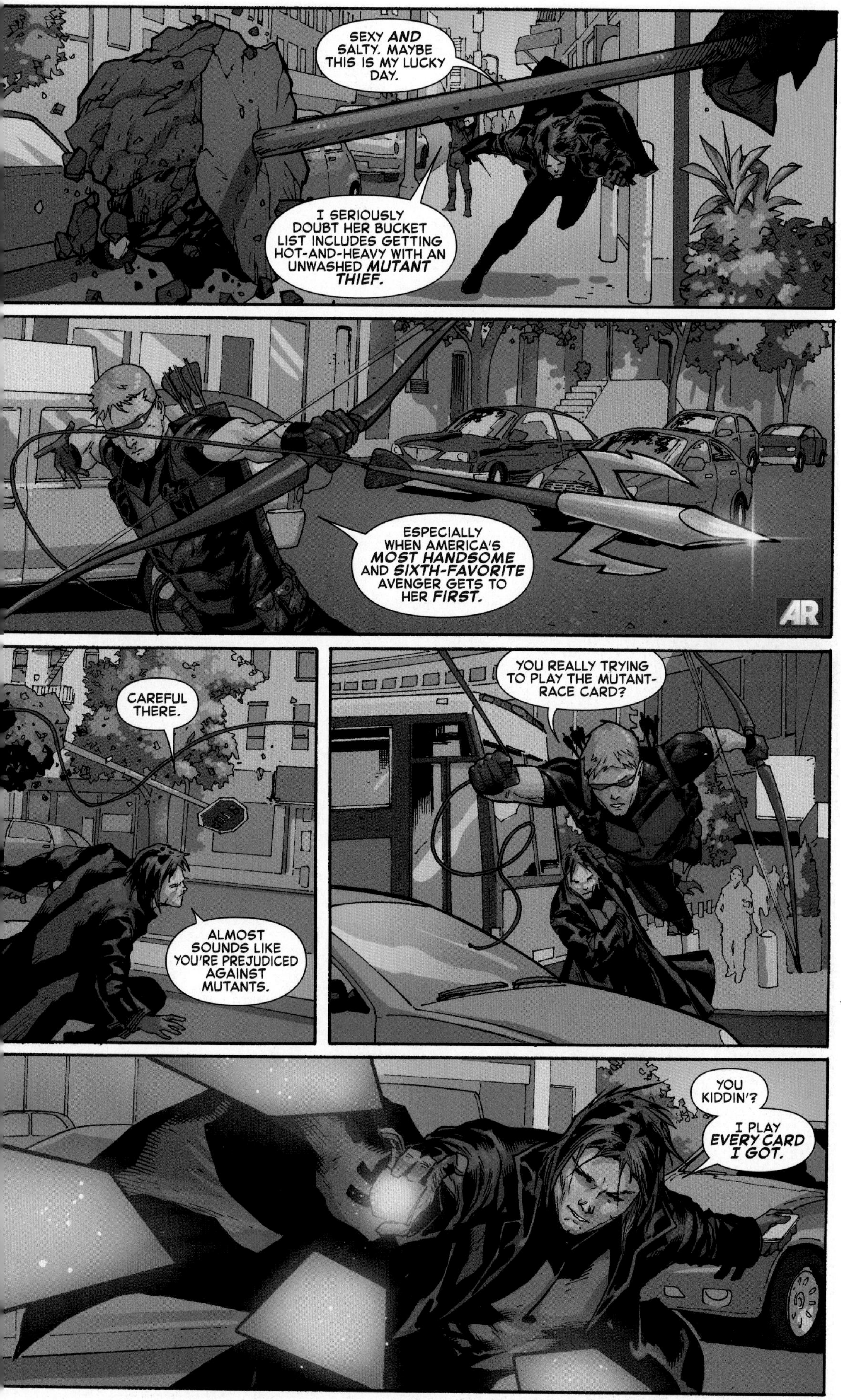
SEXY AND SALTY. MAYBE THIS IS MY LUCKY DAY.
I SERIOUSLY DOUBT HER BUCKET LIST INCLUDES GETTING HOT-AND-HEAVY WITH AN UNWASHED MUTANT THIEF.
ESPECIALLY WHEN AMERICA'S MOST HANDSOME AND SIXTH-FAVORITE AVENGER GETS TO HER FIRST.
AR
CAREFUL THERE.
ALMOST SOUNDS LIKE YOU'RE PREJUDICED AGAINST MUTANTS.
YOU REALLY TRYING TO PLAY THE MUTANT-RACE CARD?
YOU KIDDIN'?
I PLAY EVERY CARD I GOT.

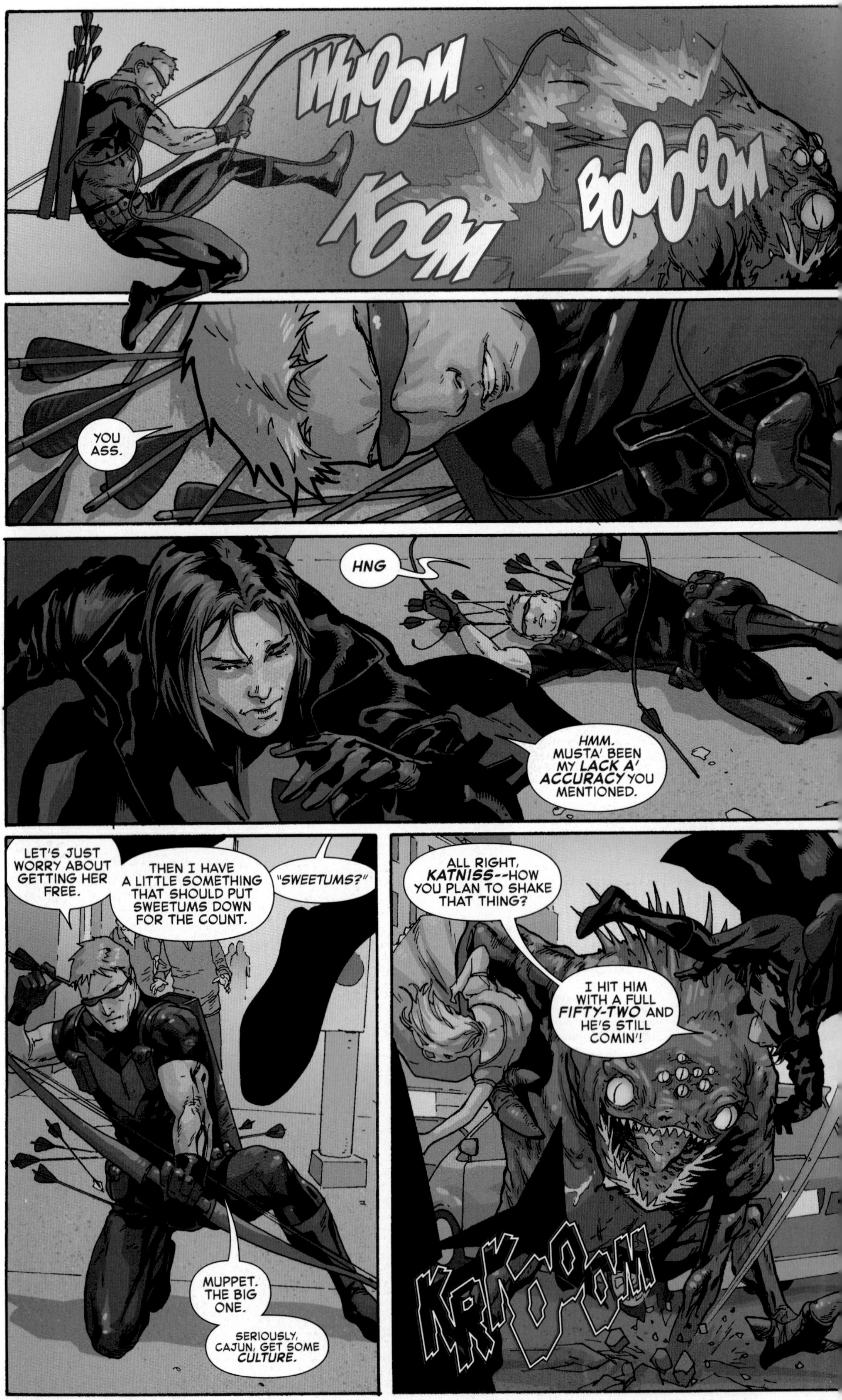
WHOOM
KOOM
BOOOOOM
YOU ASS.
HNG
HMM. MUSTA' BEEN MY LACK A' ACCURACY YOU MENTIONED.
LET'S JUST WORRY ABOUT GETTING HER FREE.
THEN I HAVE A LITTLE SOMETHING THAT SHOULD PUT SWEETUMS DOWN FOR THE COUNT.
"SWEETUMS?"
MUPPET. THE BIG ONE.
SERIOUSLY, CAJUN, GET SOME CULTURE.
ALL RIGHT, KATNISS--HOW YOU PLAN TO SHAKE THAT THING?
I HIT HIM WITH A FULL FIFTY-TWO AND HE'S STILL COMIN'!
KRKOOOOM

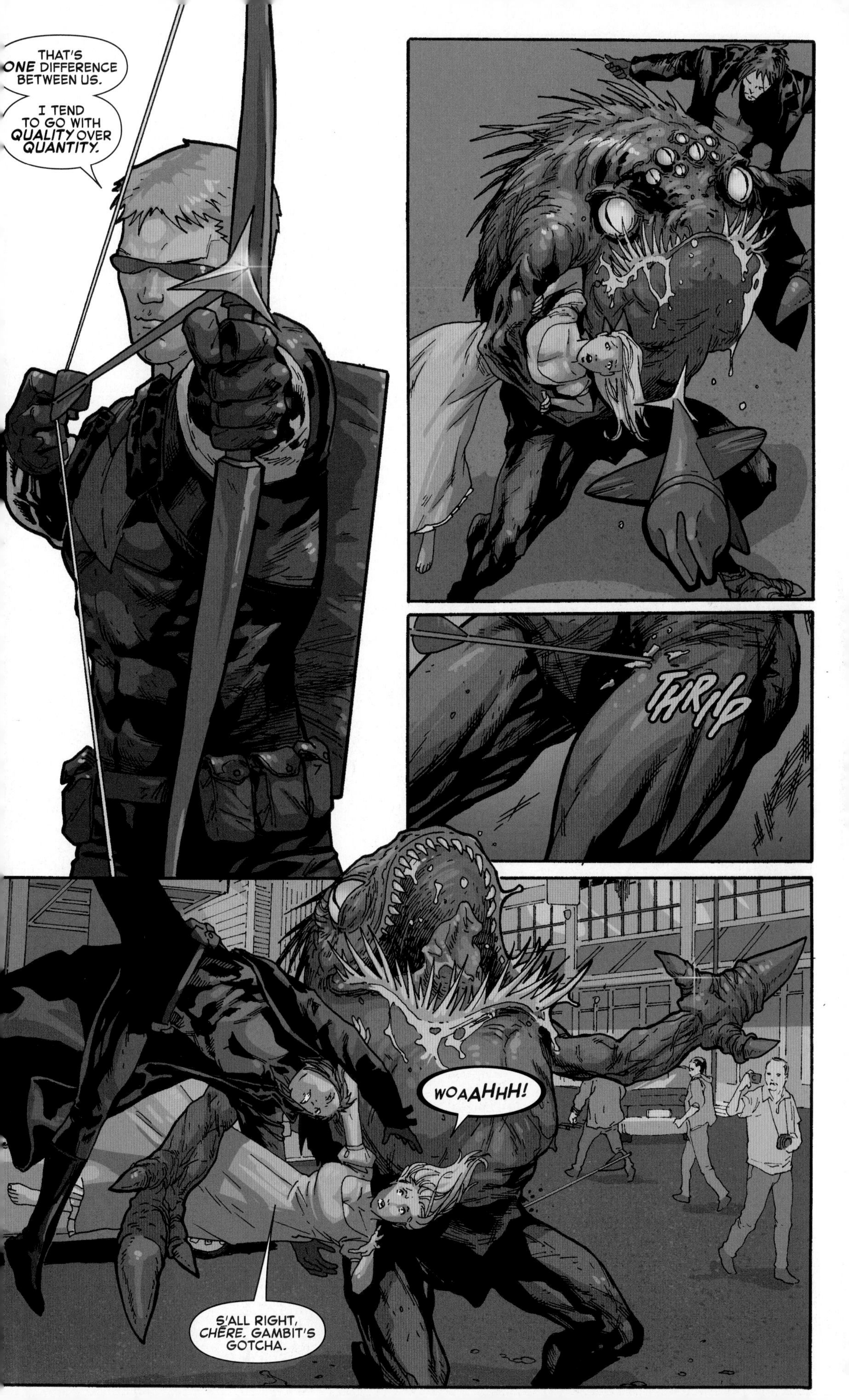
THAT'S ONE DIFFERENCE BETWEEN US.
I TEND TO GO WITH QUALITY OVER QUANTITY.
THRIP
WOAAHHH!
S'ALL RIGHT, CHÈRE. GAMBIT'S GOTCHA.

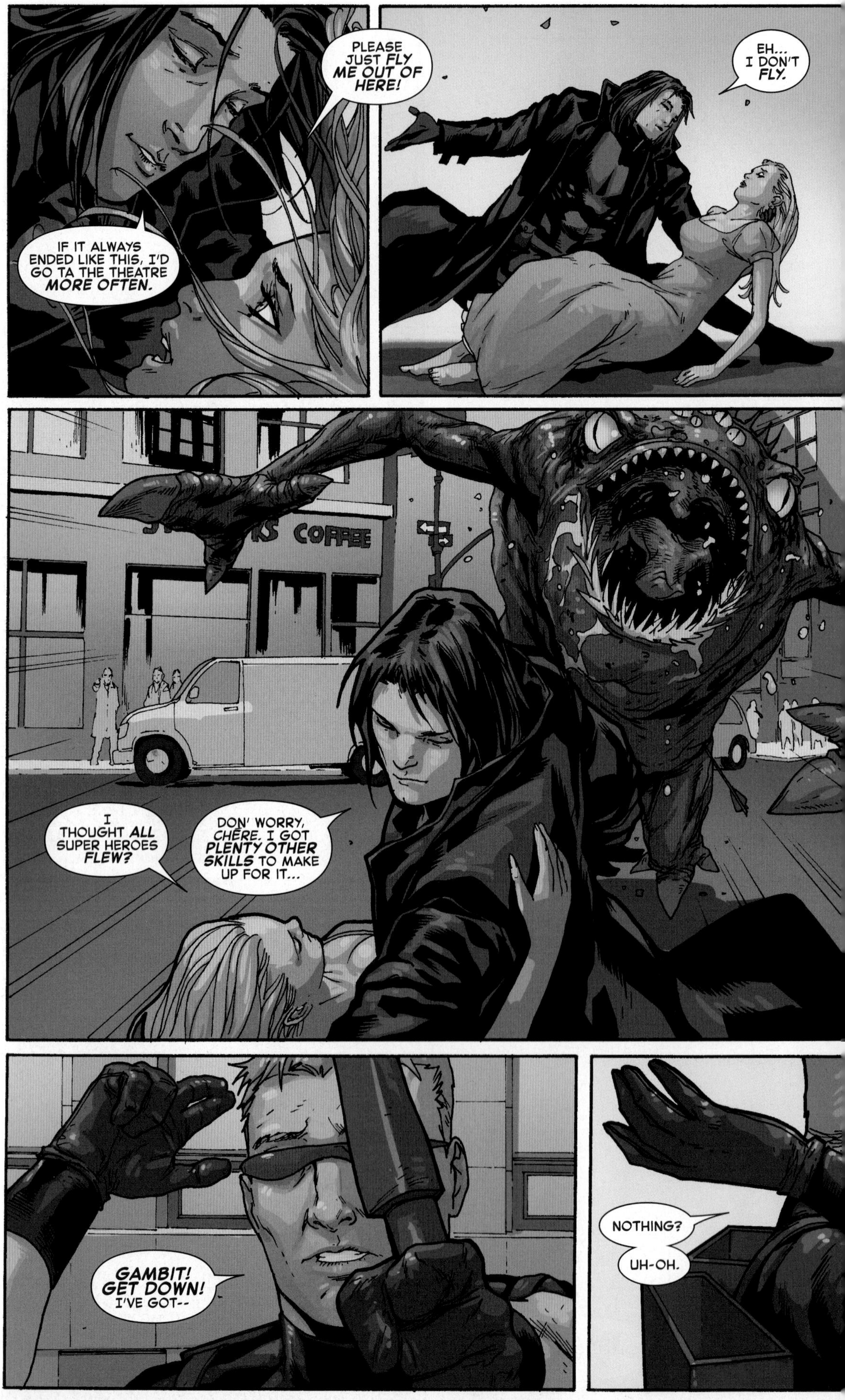
PLEASE JUST FLY ME OUT OF HERE!
IF IT ALWAYS ENDED LIKE THIS, I'D GO TA THE THEATRE MORE OFTEN.
EH... I DON'T FLY.
COFFEE
I THOUGHT ALL SUPER HEROES FLEW?
DON' WORRY, CHÈRE. I GOT PLENTY OTHER SKILLS TO MAKE UP FOR IT...
GAMBIT! GET DOWN! I'VE GOT--
NOTHING?
UH-OH.

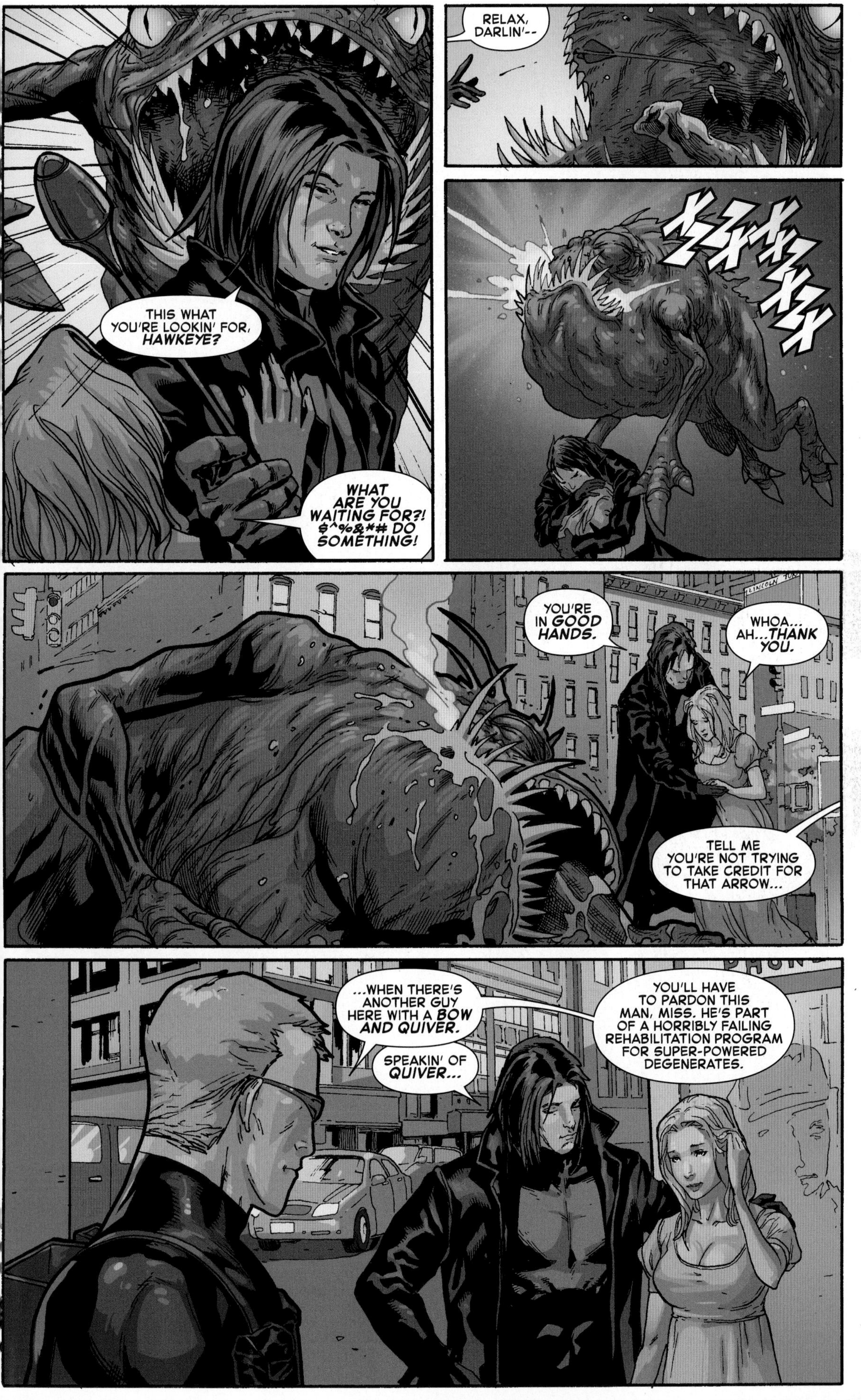

THIS WHAT YOU'RE LOOKIN' FOR, HAWKEYE?
WHAT ARE YOU WAITING FOR?! $^%&*# DO SOMETHING!
RELAX, DARLIN'--
YOU'RE IN GOOD HANDS.
WHOA... AH...THANK YOU.
LINCOLN
TELL ME YOU'RE NOT TRYING TO TAKE CREDIT FOR THAT ARROW...
...WHEN THERE'S ANOTHER GUY HERE WITH A BOW AND QUIVER.
SPEAKIN' OF QUIVER...
YOU'LL HAVE TO PARDON THIS MAN, MISS. HE'S PART OF A HORRIBLY FAILING REHABILITATION PROGRAM FOR SUPER-POWERED DEGENERATES.

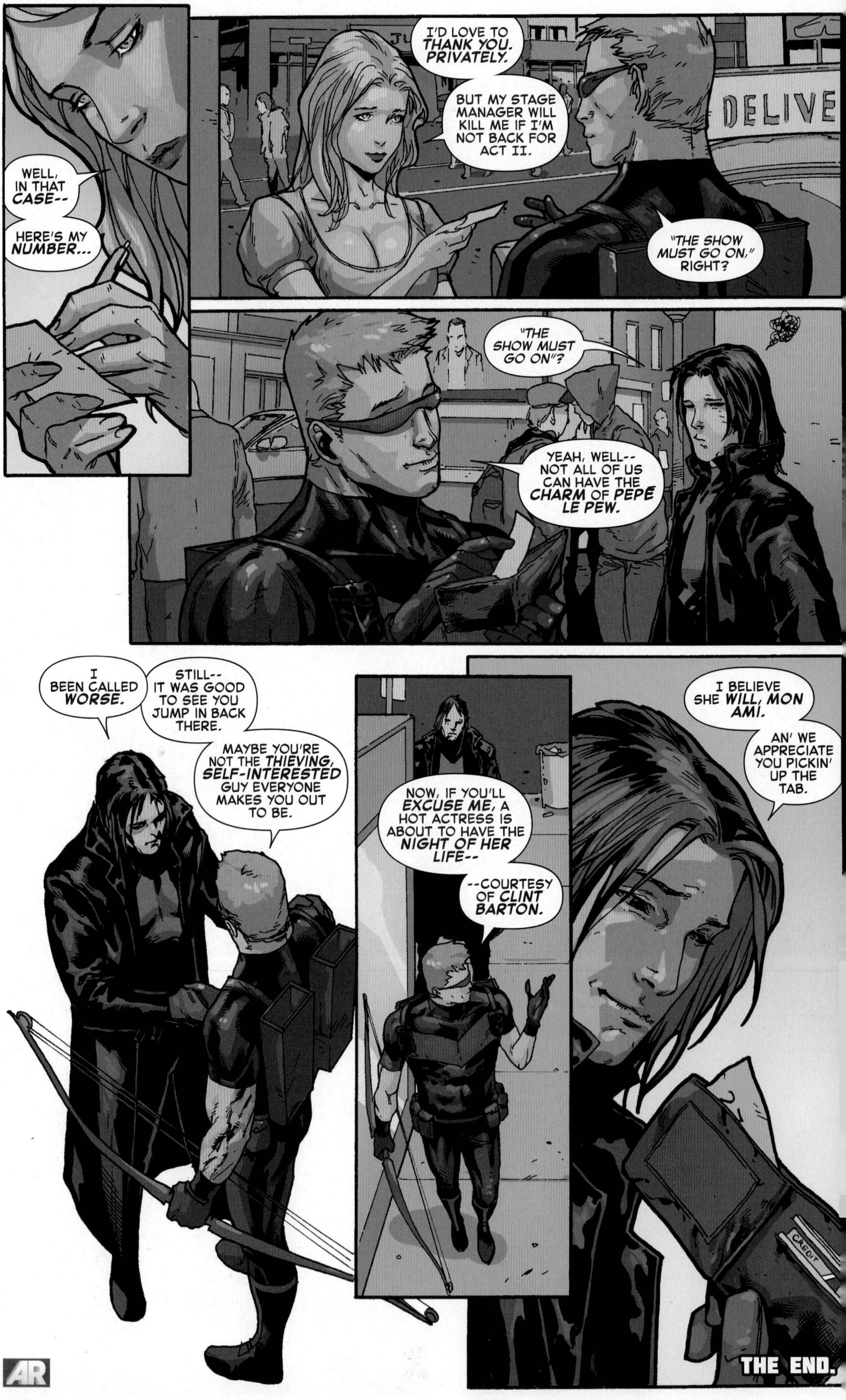

WELL, IN THAT CASE--
HERE'S MY NUMBER...
I'D LOVE TO THANK YOU. PRIVATELY.
BUT MY STAGE MANAGER WILL KILL ME IF I'M NOT BACK FOR ACT II.
"THE SHOW MUST GO ON," RIGHT?
DELIVE
"THE SHOW MUST GO ON"?
YEAH, WELL-- NOT ALL OF US CAN HAVE THE CHARM OF PEPE LE PEW.
I BEEN CALLED WORSE.
STILL-- IT WAS GOOD TO SEE YOU JUMP IN BACK THERE.
MAYBE YOU'RE NOT THE THIEVING, SELF-INTERESTED GUY EVERYONE MAKES YOU OUT TO BE.
NOW, IF YOU'LL EXCUSE ME, A HOT ACTRESS IS ABOUT TO HAVE THE NIGHT OF HER LIFE--
--COURTESY OF CLINT BARTON.
I BELIEVE SHE WILL, MON AMI.
AN' WE APPRECIATE YOU PICKIN' UP THE TAB.
CREDIT
THE END.

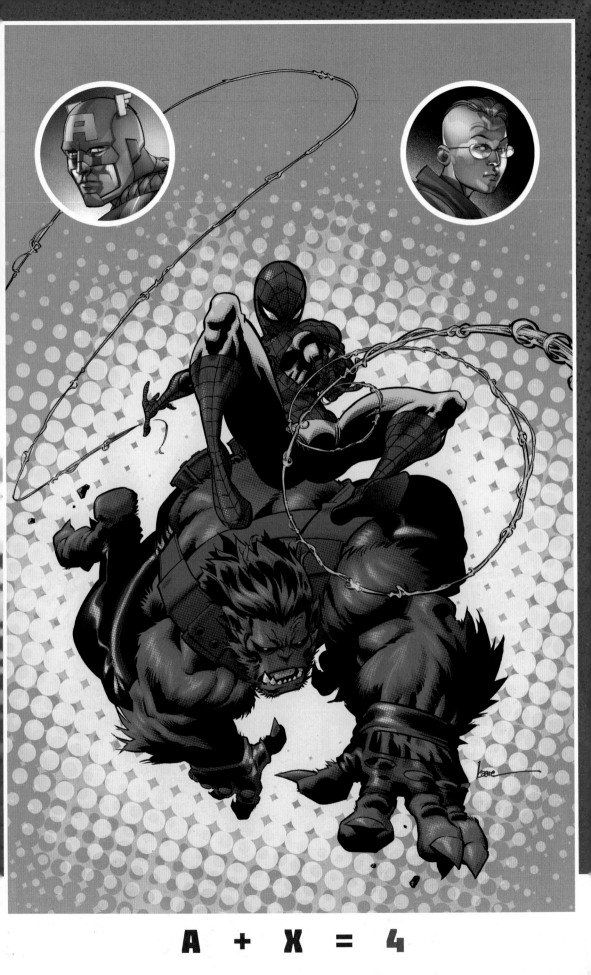

A + X = 4

Q: Oh, my...what is this thing I'm reading?
A: It's the new issue of A+X, the BEST COMIC where one AVENGER and one X-MAN team up together EVER MADE!

Q: Wow, really?
A: I WOULD STAKE YOUR LIFE ON IT! And not only that, it has TWO STORIES of A's being added to X's for DOUBLE THE AWESOME! BELIEVE IT!

Q: All right, I will! So what are the stories about?
A: The first one takes the X-Men's blue, furry, cat-faced genius, BEAST, and teams him up with the fun-loving friendly neighborhood wall-crawler, SPIDER-MAN!

Q: Wait—didn't Beast get turned ape-like instead of cat-like? And...didn't Spider-Man's brain get replaced with—
A: WHATEVER! You think I read other comic books? THIS IS THE ONLY COMIC BOOK YOU NEED! And, uh...it takes place before those comics.

Q: Oh, okay. And what's the second story?
A: Only the story fans have been waiting for since 1941—the sentinel of liberty himself, CAPTAIN AMERICA, finally teams up with the rabble-rousing self-proclaimed best X-Man ever, KID OMEGA, a.k.a. QUENTIN QUIRE!

Q: Okay, so where in Wolverine & the X-Men continuity does this story—
A: SHUT UP! READ THE COMIC!

THE BEAST + the AMAZING SPIDER-MAN

KAARE **ANDREWS**
WRITER/ARTIST

LEE **LOUGHRIDGE**
COLOR ARTIST

VC'S CLAYTON **COWLES**
LETTERER

CAPTAIN AMERICA + QUENTIN QUIRE

JASON **LATOUR**
WRITER

DAVID **LÓPEZ**
PENCILER

ALVARO **LÓPEZ**
INKER

JIM **CHARALAMPIDIS**
COLORIST

VC'S CLAYTON **COWLES**
LETTERER

JORDAN D. **WHITE**
ASSOCIATE EDITOR

NICK **LOWE**
EDITOR

AXEL **ALONSO**
EDITOR IN CHIEF

JOE **QUESADA**
CHIEF CREATIVE OFFICER

DAN **BUCKLEY**
PUBLISHER

ALAN **FINE**
EXECUTIVE PRODUCER

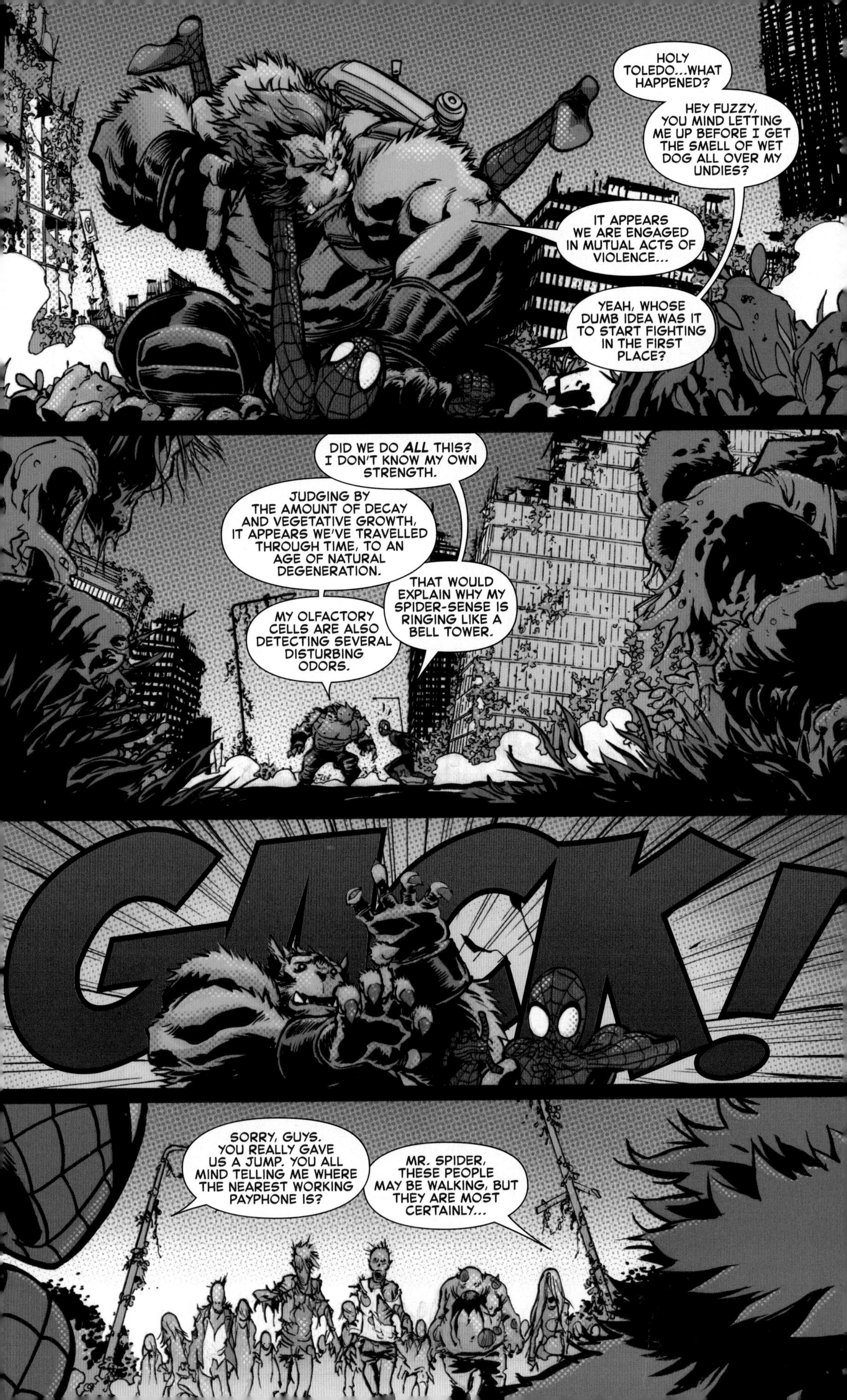
HOLY TOLEDO...WHAT HAPPENED?
HEY FUZZY, YOU MIND LETTING ME UP BEFORE I GET THE SMELL OF WET DOG ALL OVER MY UNDIES?
IT APPEARS WE ARE ENGAGED IN MUTUAL ACTS OF VIOLENCE...
YEAH, WHOSE DUMB IDEA WAS IT TO START FIGHTING IN THE FIRST PLACE?
DID WE DO *ALL* THIS? I DON'T KNOW MY OWN STRENGTH.
JUDGING BY THE AMOUNT OF DECAY AND VEGETATIVE GROWTH, IT APPEARS WE'VE TRAVELLED THROUGH TIME, TO AN AGE OF NATURAL DEGENERATION.
MY OLFACTORY CELLS ARE ALSO DETECTING SEVERAL DISTURBING ODORS.
THAT WOULD EXPLAIN WHY MY SPIDER-SENSE IS RINGING LIKE A BELL TOWER.
GACK!
SORRY, GUYS. YOU REALLY GAVE US A JUMP. YOU ALL MIND TELLING ME WHERE THE NEAREST WORKING PAYPHONE IS?
MR. SPIDER, THESE PEOPLE MAY BE WALKING, BUT THEY ARE MOST CERTAINLY...

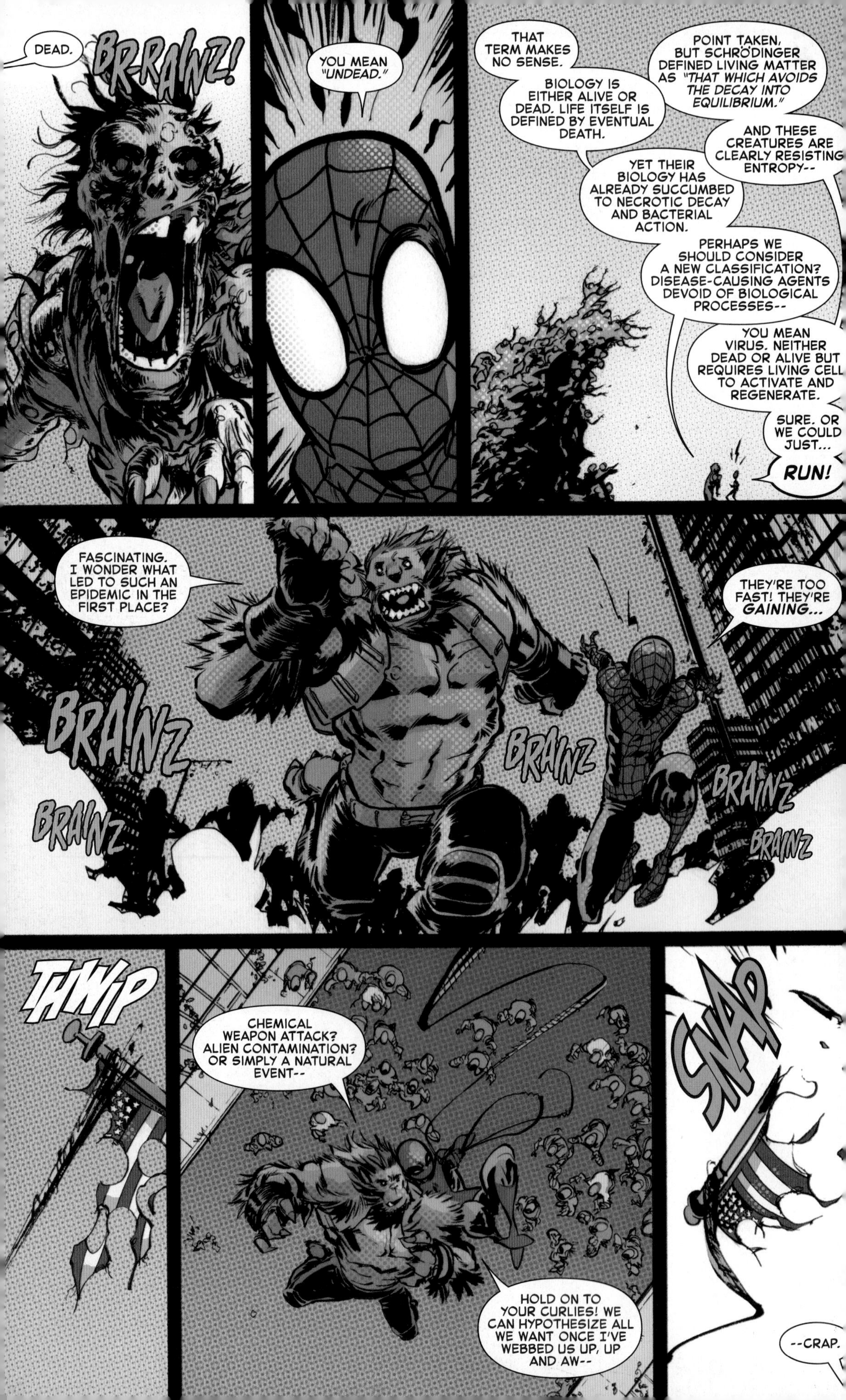
DEAD.
BR-RAINZ!
YOU MEAN "UNDEAD."
THAT TERM MAKES NO SENSE.
BIOLOGY IS EITHER ALIVE OR DEAD. LIFE ITSELF IS DEFINED BY EVENTUAL DEATH.
POINT TAKEN, BUT SCHRÖDINGER DEFINED LIVING MATTER AS "THAT WHICH AVOIDS THE DECAY INTO EQUILIBRIUM."
AND THESE CREATURES ARE CLEARLY RESISTING ENTROPY--
YET THEIR BIOLOGY HAS ALREADY SUCCUMBED TO NECROTIC DECAY AND BACTERIAL ACTION.
PERHAPS WE SHOULD CONSIDER A NEW CLASSIFICATION? DISEASE-CAUSING AGENTS DEVOID OF BIOLOGICAL PROCESSES--
YOU MEAN VIRUS. NEITHER DEAD OR ALIVE BUT REQUIRES LIVING CELL TO ACTIVATE AND REGENERATE.
SURE. OR WE COULD JUST...
RUN!
FASCINATING. I WONDER WHAT LED TO SUCH AN EPIDEMIC IN THE FIRST PLACE?
THEY'RE TOO FAST! THEY'RE GAINING...
BRAINZ
BRAINZ
BRAINZ
BRAINZ
BRAINZ
THWIP
CHEMICAL WEAPON ATTACK? ALIEN CONTAMINATION? OR SIMPLY A NATURAL EVENT--
HOLD ON TO YOUR CURLIES! WE CAN HYPOTHESIZE ALL WE WANT ONCE I'VE WEBBED US UP, UP AND AW--
SNAP
--CRAP.

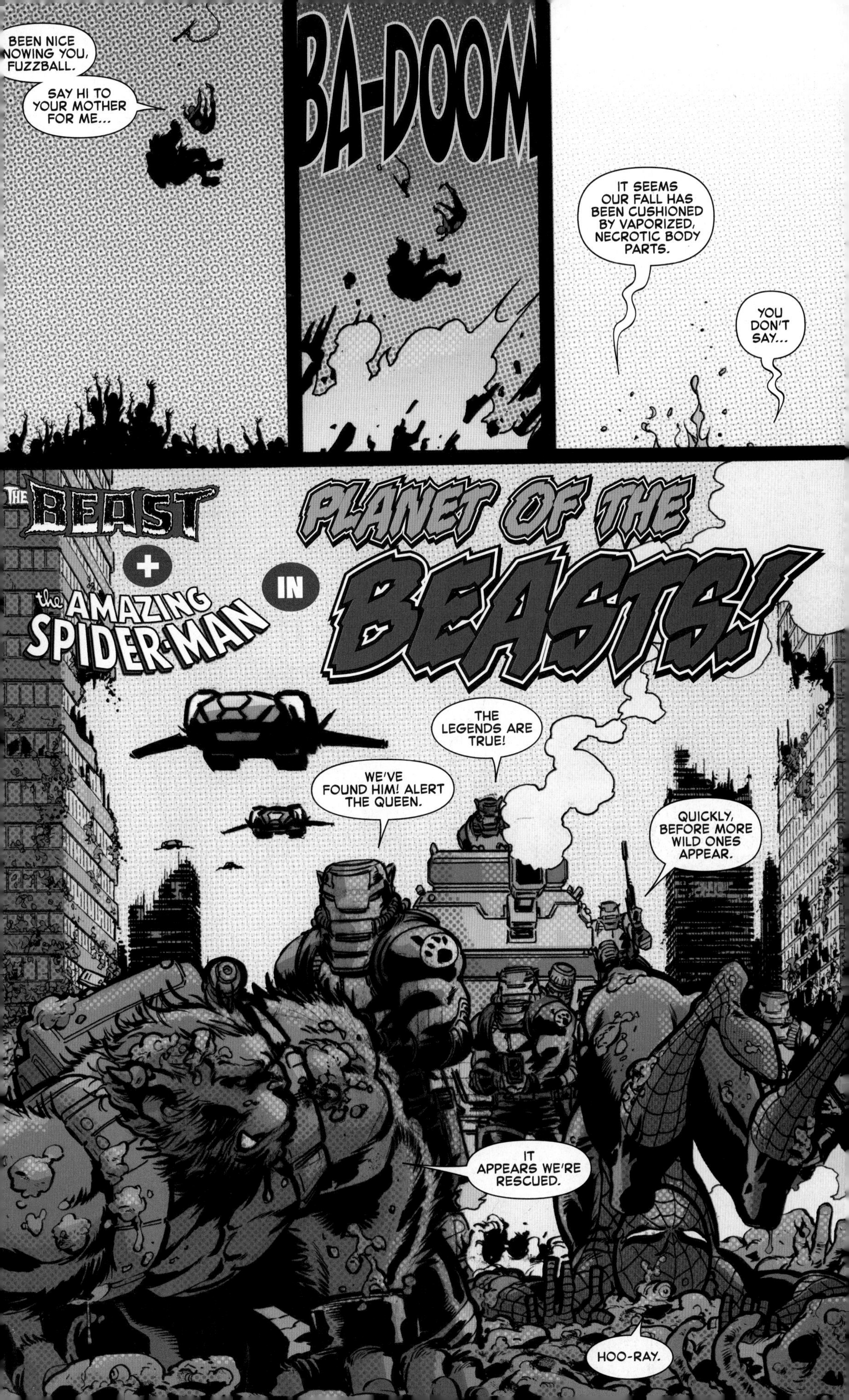
BEEN NICE NOWING YOU, FUZZBALL.
SAY HI TO YOUR MOTHER FOR ME...
BA-DOOM
IT SEEMS OUR FALL HAS BEEN CUSHIONED BY VAPORIZED, NECROTIC BODY PARTS.
YOU DON'T SAY...
THE BEAST + THE AMAZING SPIDER-MAN IN PLANET OF THE BEASTS!
THE LEGENDS ARE TRUE!
WE'VE FOUND HIM! ALERT THE QUEEN.
QUICKLY, BEFORE MORE WILD ONES APPEAR.
IT APPEARS WE'RE RESCUED.
HOO-RAY.

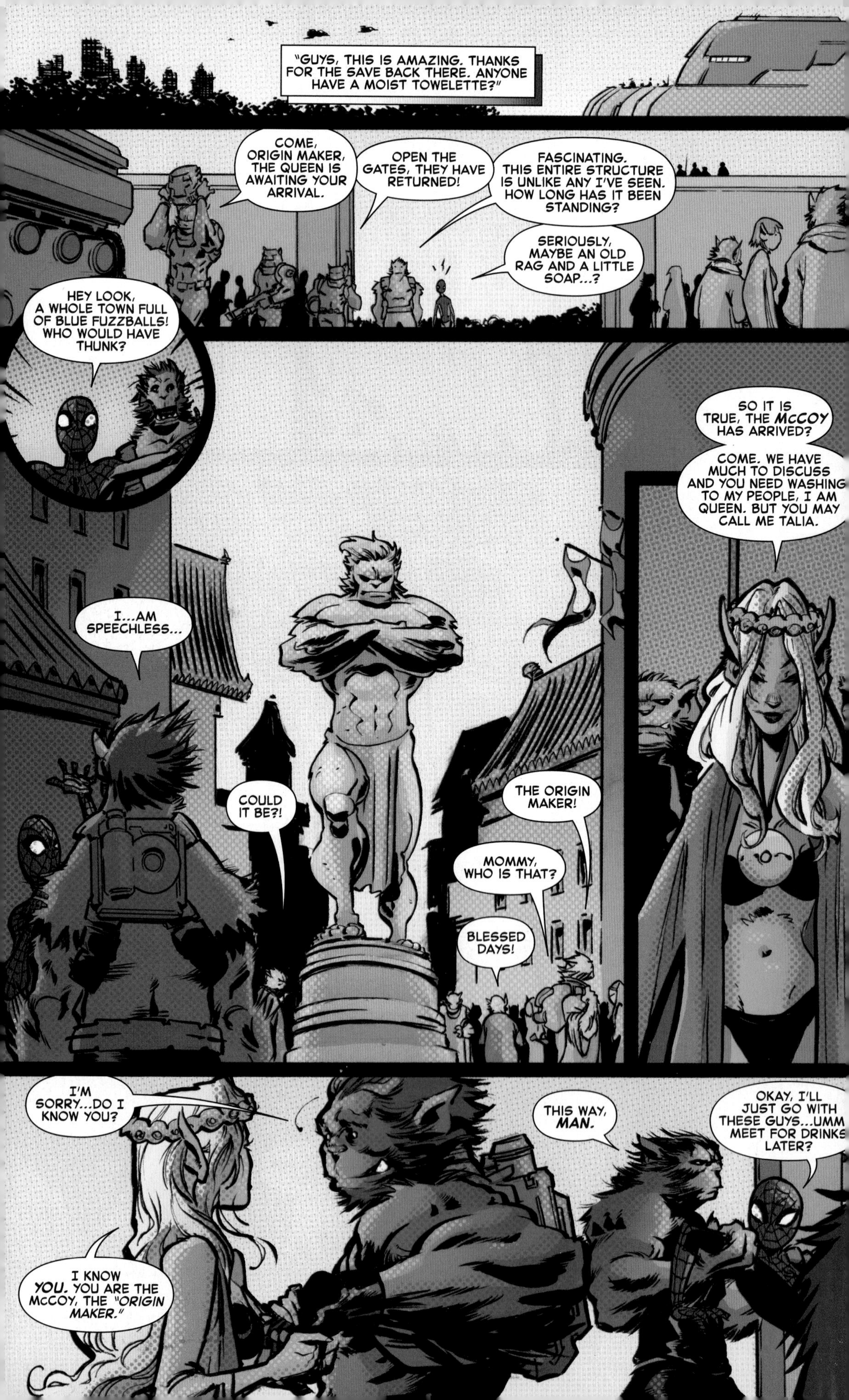
"GUYS, THIS IS AMAZING. THANKS FOR THE SAVE BACK THERE. ANYONE HAVE A MOIST TOWELETTE?"
COME, ORIGIN MAKER, THE QUEEN IS AWAITING YOUR ARRIVAL.
OPEN THE GATES, THEY HAVE RETURNED!
FASCINATING. THIS ENTIRE STRUCTURE IS UNLIKE ANY I'VE SEEN. HOW LONG HAS IT BEEN STANDING?
SERIOUSLY, MAYBE AN OLD RAG AND A LITTLE SOAP...?
HEY LOOK, A WHOLE TOWN FULL OF BLUE FUZZBALLS! WHO WOULD HAVE THUNK?
SO IT IS TRUE, THE McCOY HAS ARRIVED?
COME. WE HAVE MUCH TO DISCUSS AND YOU NEED WASHING. TO MY PEOPLE, I AM QUEEN. BUT YOU MAY CALL ME TALIA.
I...AM SPEECHLESS...
COULD IT BE?!
THE ORIGIN MAKER!
MOMMY, WHO IS THAT?
BLESSED DAYS!
I'M SORRY...DO I KNOW YOU?
I KNOW YOU. YOU ARE THE McCOY, THE "ORIGIN MAKER."
THIS WAY, MAN.
OKAY, I'LL JUST GO WITH THESE GUYS...UMM MEET FOR DRINKS LATER?

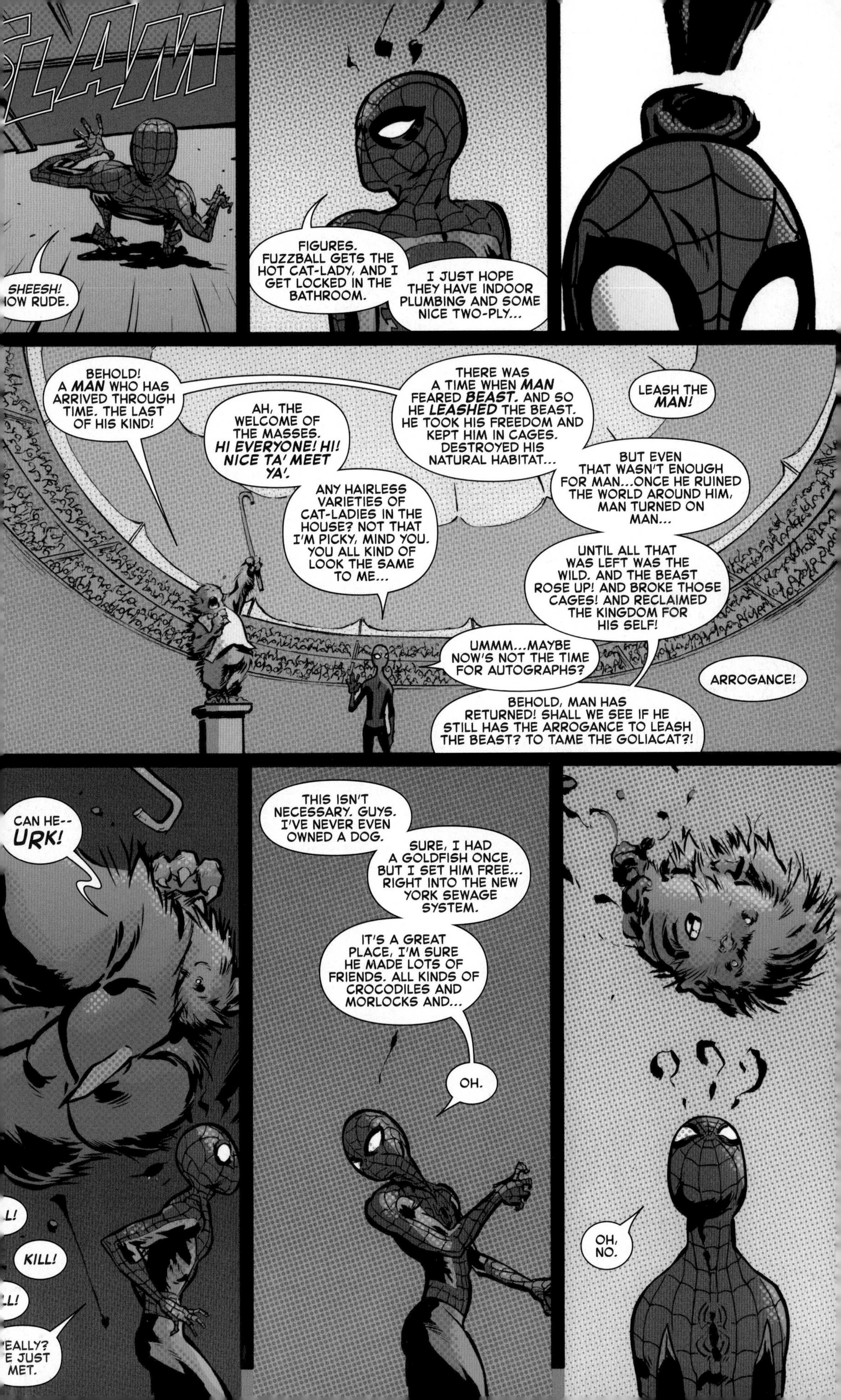

LAM
SHEESH! IOW RUDE.
FIGURES. FUZZBALL GETS THE HOT CAT-LADY, AND I GET LOCKED IN THE BATHROOM.
I JUST HOPE THEY HAVE INDOOR PLUMBING AND SOME NICE TWO-PLY...
BEHOLD! A **MAN** WHO HAS ARRIVED THROUGH TIME. THE LAST OF HIS KIND!
AH, THE WELCOME OF THE MASSES. ***HI EVERYONE! HI! NICE TA' MEET YA'.***
ANY HAIRLESS VARIETIES OF CAT-LADIES IN THE HOUSE? NOT THAT I'M PICKY, MIND YOU. YOU ALL KIND OF LOOK THE SAME TO ME...
THERE WAS A TIME WHEN **MAN** FEARED ***BEAST.*** AND SO HE ***LEASHED*** THE BEAST. HE TOOK HIS FREEDOM AND KEPT HIM IN CAGES. DESTROYED HIS NATURAL HABITAT...
LEASH THE ***MAN!***
BUT EVEN THAT WASN'T ENOUGH FOR MAN...ONCE HE RUINED THE WORLD AROUND HIM, MAN TURNED ON MAN...
UNTIL ALL THAT WAS LEFT WAS THE WILD. AND THE BEAST ROSE UP! AND BROKE THOSE CAGES! AND RECLAIMED THE KINGDOM FOR HIS SELF!
UMMM...MAYBE NOW'S NOT THE TIME FOR AUTOGRAPHS?
ARROGANCE!
BEHOLD, MAN HAS RETURNED! SHALL WE SEE IF HE STILL HAS THE ARROGANCE TO LEASH THE BEAST? TO TAME THE GOLIACAT?!
CAN HE-- **URK!**
LL!
KILL!
LL!
EALLY? E JUST MET.
THIS ISN'T NECESSARY. GUYS. I'VE NEVER EVEN OWNED A DOG.
SURE, I HAD A GOLDFISH ONCE, BUT I SET HIM FREE... RIGHT INTO THE NEW YORK SEWAGE SYSTEM.
IT'S A GREAT PLACE, I'M SURE HE MADE LOTS OF FRIENDS. ALL KINDS OF CROCODILES AND MORLOCKS AND...
OH.
OH, NO.

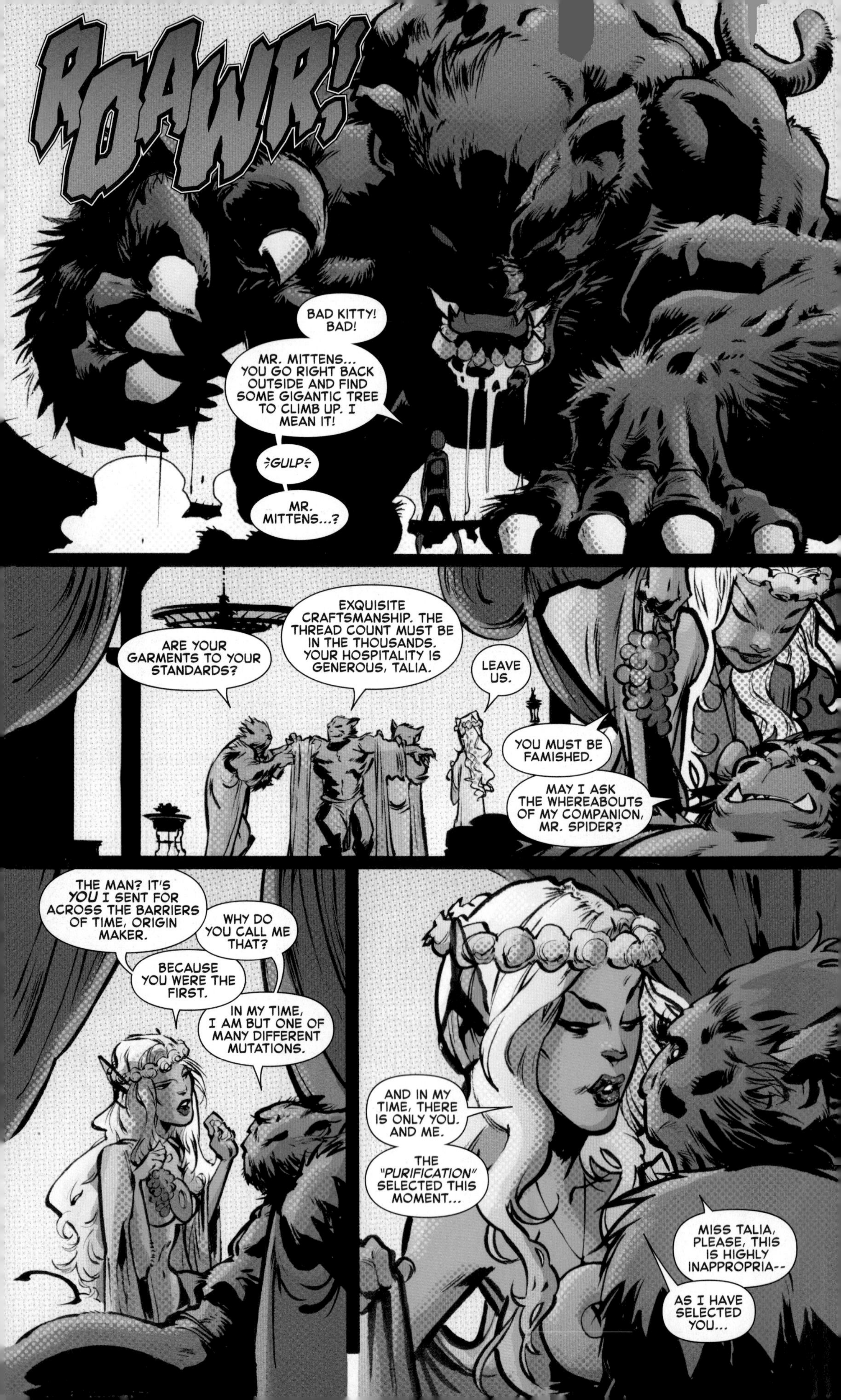
ROAWR!
BAD KITTY! BAD!
MR. MITTENS... YOU GO RIGHT BACK OUTSIDE AND FIND SOME GIGANTIC TREE TO CLIMB UP. I MEAN IT!
GULP
MR. MITTENS...?
ARE YOUR GARMENTS TO YOUR STANDARDS?
EXQUISITE CRAFTSMANSHIP. THE THREAD COUNT MUST BE IN THE THOUSANDS. YOUR HOSPITALITY IS GENEROUS, TALIA.
LEAVE US.
YOU MUST BE FAMISHED.
MAY I ASK THE WHEREABOUTS OF MY COMPANION, MR. SPIDER?
THE MAN? IT'S *YOU* I SENT FOR ACROSS THE BARRIERS OF TIME, ORIGIN MAKER.
WHY DO YOU CALL ME THAT?
BECAUSE YOU WERE THE FIRST.
IN MY TIME, I AM BUT ONE OF MANY DIFFERENT MUTATIONS.
AND IN MY TIME, THERE IS ONLY YOU. AND ME.
THE *"PURIFICATION"* SELECTED THIS MOMENT...
MISS TALIA, PLEASE, THIS IS HIGHLY INAPPROPRIA--
AS I HAVE SELECTED YOU...

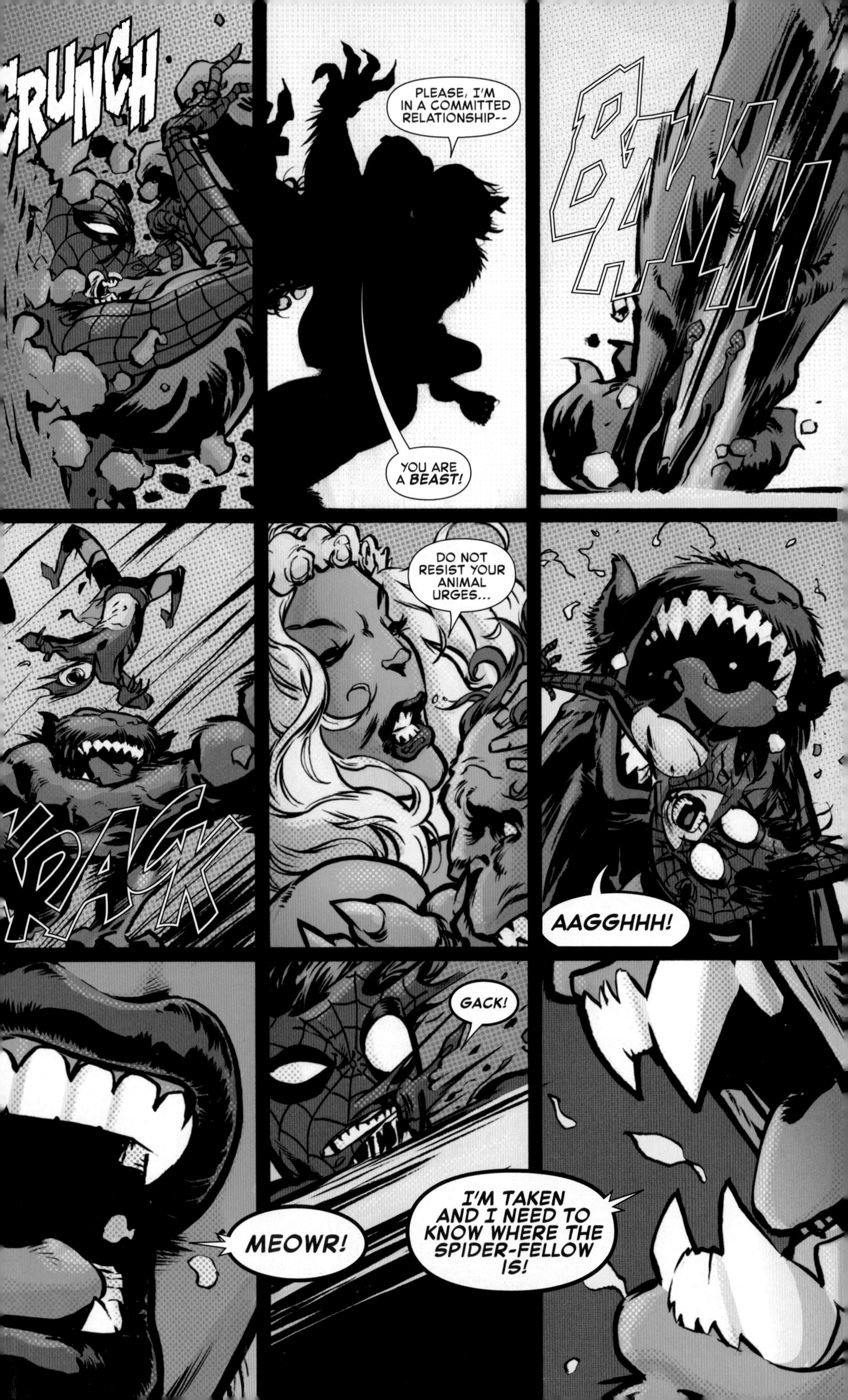
CRUNCH
PLEASE, I'M IN A COMMITTED RELATIONSHIP--
YOU ARE A BEAST!
BAMM
DO NOT RESIST YOUR ANIMAL URGES...
KRAAK
AAGGHHH!
GACK!
MEOWR!
I'M TAKEN AND I NEED TO KNOW WHERE THE SPIDER-FELLOW IS!

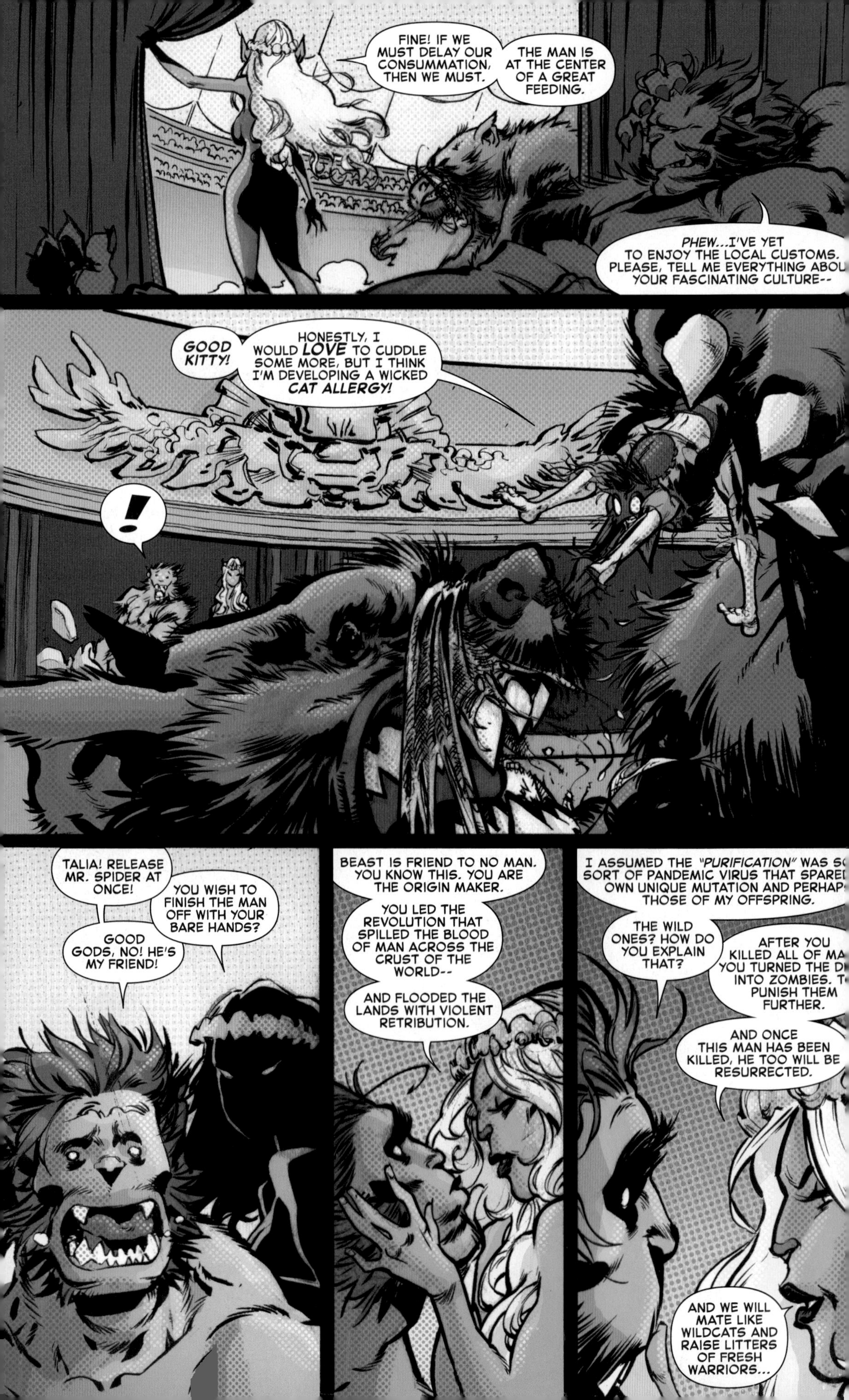
FINE! IF WE MUST DELAY OUR CONSUMMATION, THEN WE MUST.
THE MAN IS AT THE CENTER OF A GREAT FEEDING.
PHEW...I'VE YET TO ENJOY THE LOCAL CUSTOMS. PLEASE, TELL ME EVERYTHING ABOU YOUR FASCINATING CULTURE--
GOOD KITTY!
HONESTLY, I WOULD LOVE TO CUDDLE SOME MORE, BUT I THINK I'M DEVELOPING A WICKED CAT ALLERGY!
!
TALIA! RELEASE MR. SPIDER AT ONCE!
YOU WISH TO FINISH THE MAN OFF WITH YOUR BARE HANDS?
GOOD GODS, NO! HE'S MY FRIEND!
BEAST IS FRIEND TO NO MAN. YOU KNOW THIS. YOU ARE THE ORIGIN MAKER.
YOU LED THE REVOLUTION THAT SPILLED THE BLOOD OF MAN ACROSS THE CRUST OF THE WORLD--
AND FLOODED THE LANDS WITH VIOLENT RETRIBUTION.
I ASSUMED THE "PURIFICATION" WAS S SORT OF PANDEMIC VIRUS THAT SPARE OWN UNIQUE MUTATION AND PERHAP THOSE OF MY OFFSPRING.
THE WILD ONES? HOW DO YOU EXPLAIN THAT?
AFTER YOU KILLED ALL OF MA YOU TURNED THE D INTO ZOMBIES. T PUNISH THEM FURTHER.
AND ONCE THIS MAN HAS BEEN KILLED, HE TOO WILL BE RESURRECTED.
AND WE WILL MATE LIKE WILDCATS AND RAISE LITTERS OF FRESH WARRIORS...

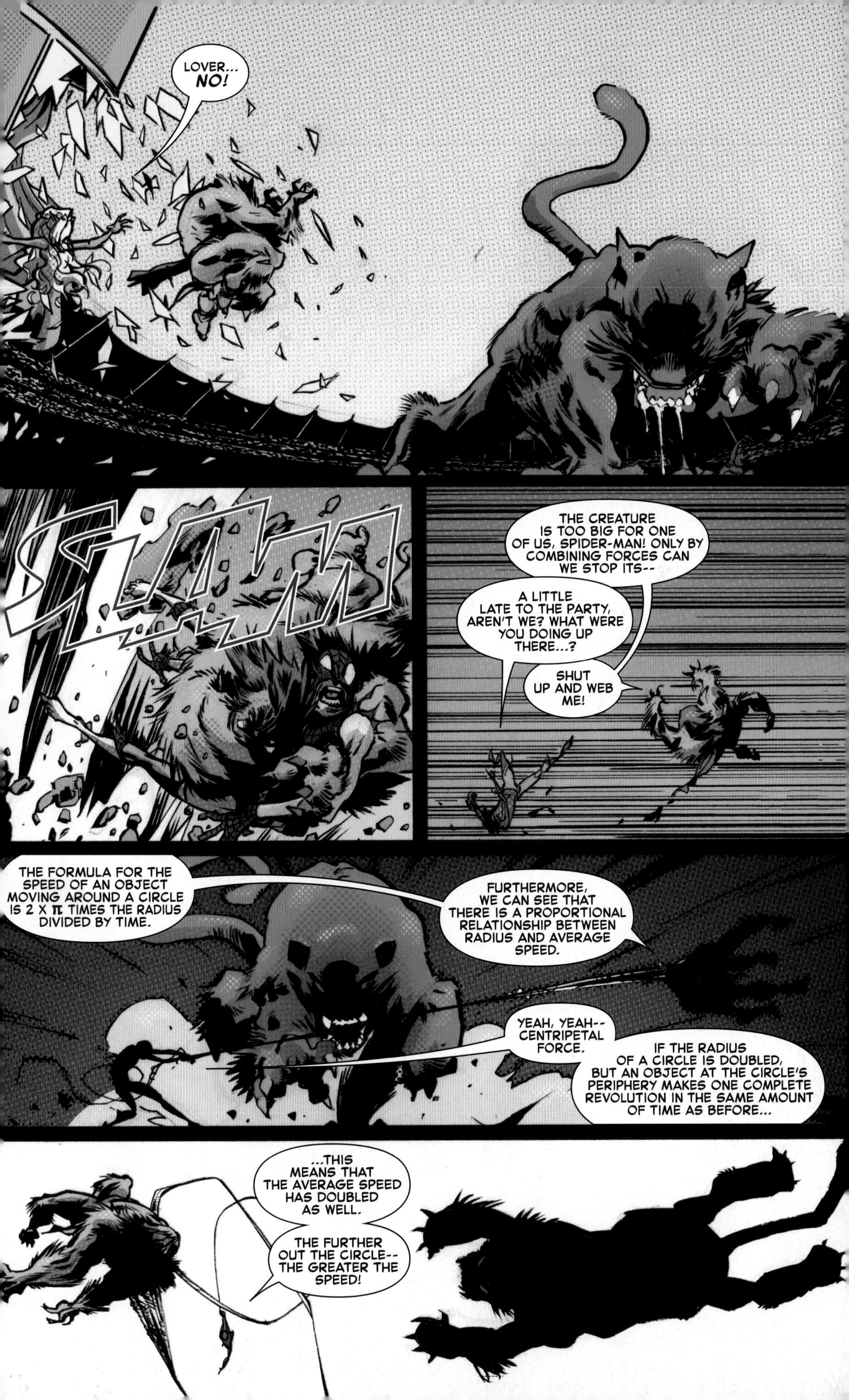
LOVER... NO!
SLAM
THE CREATURE IS TOO BIG FOR ONE OF US, SPIDER-MAN! ONLY BY COMBINING FORCES CAN WE STOP ITS--
A LITTLE LATE TO THE PARTY, AREN'T WE? WHAT WERE YOU DOING UP THERE...?
SHUT UP AND WEB ME!
THE FORMULA FOR THE SPEED OF AN OBJECT MOVING AROUND A CIRCLE IS 2 X π TIMES THE RADIUS DIVIDED BY TIME.
FURTHERMORE, WE CAN SEE THAT THERE IS A PROPORTIONAL RELATIONSHIP BETWEEN RADIUS AND AVERAGE SPEED.
YEAH, YEAH-- CENTRIPETAL FORCE.
IF THE RADIUS OF A CIRCLE IS DOUBLED, BUT AN OBJECT AT THE CIRCLE'S PERIPHERY MAKES ONE COMPLETE REVOLUTION IN THE SAME AMOUNT OF TIME AS BEFORE...
...THIS MEANS THAT THE AVERAGE SPEED HAS DOUBLED AS WELL.
THE FURTHER OUT THE CIRCLE-- THE GREATER THE SPEED!

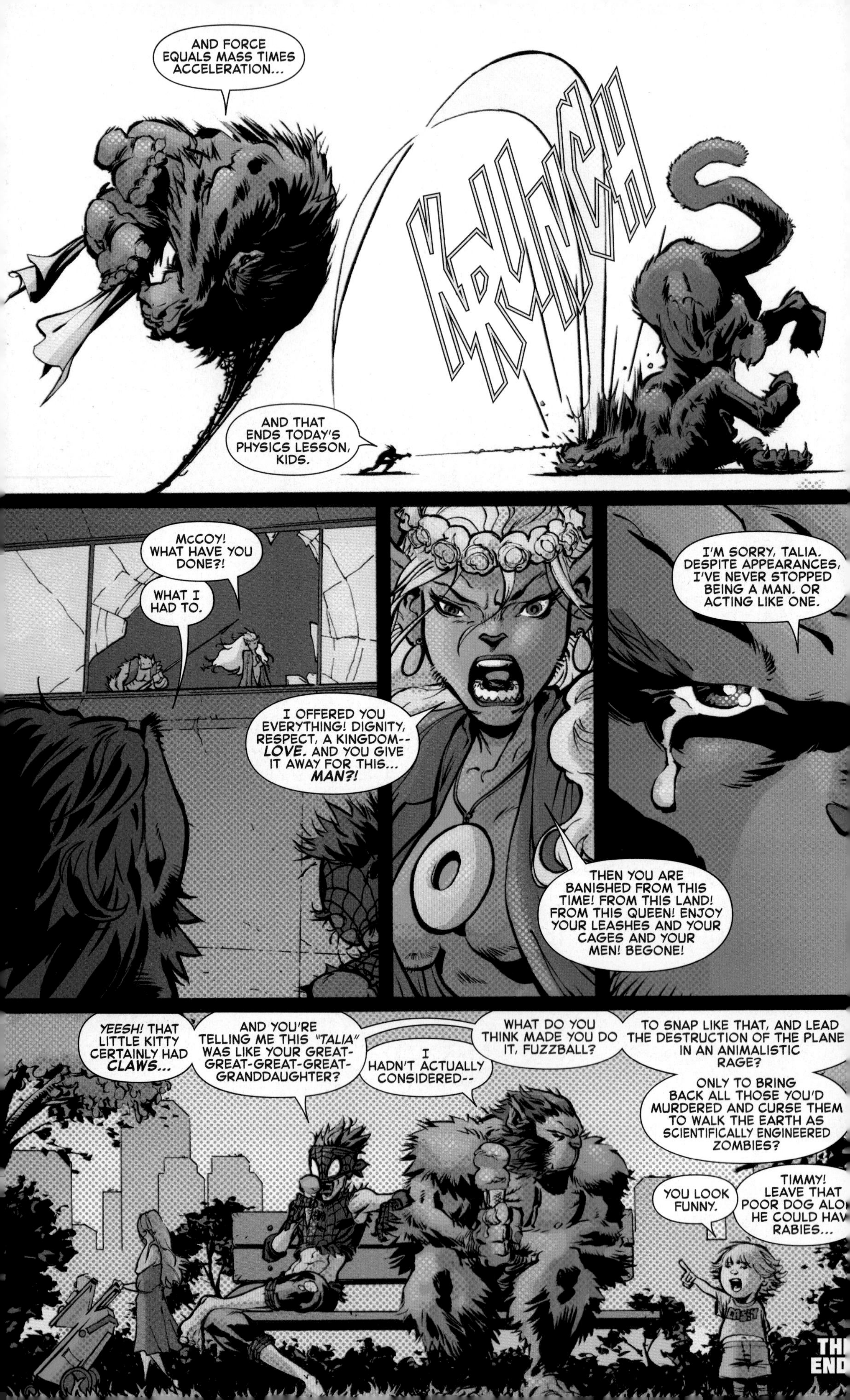
AND FORCE EQUALS MASS TIMES ACCELERATION...
KRUNCH
AND THAT ENDS TODAY'S PHYSICS LESSON, KIDS.
McCOY! WHAT HAVE YOU DONE?!
WHAT I HAD TO.
I OFFERED YOU EVERYTHING! DIGNITY, RESPECT, A KINGDOM-- LOVE. AND YOU GIVE IT AWAY FOR THIS... MAN?!
I'M SORRY, TALIA. DESPITE APPEARANCES, I'VE NEVER STOPPED BEING A MAN. OR ACTING LIKE ONE.
THEN YOU ARE BANISHED FROM THIS TIME! FROM THIS LAND! FROM THIS QUEEN! ENJOY YOUR LEASHES AND YOUR CAGES AND YOUR MEN! BEGONE!
YEESH! THAT LITTLE KITTY CERTAINLY HAD CLAWS...
AND YOU'RE TELLING ME THIS "TALIA" WAS LIKE YOUR GREAT-GREAT-GREAT-GREAT-GRANDDAUGHTER?
I HADN'T ACTUALLY CONSIDERED--
WHAT DO YOU THINK MADE YOU DO IT, FUZZBALL?
TO SNAP LIKE THAT, AND LEAD THE DESTRUCTION OF THE PLANE IN AN ANIMALISTIC RAGE?
ONLY TO BRING BACK ALL THOSE YOU'D MURDERED AND CURSE THEM TO WALK THE EARTH AS SCIENTIFICALLY ENGINEERED ZOMBIES?
YOU LOOK FUNNY.
TIMMY! LEAVE THAT POOR DOG ALO HE COULD HAV RABIES...
THE END

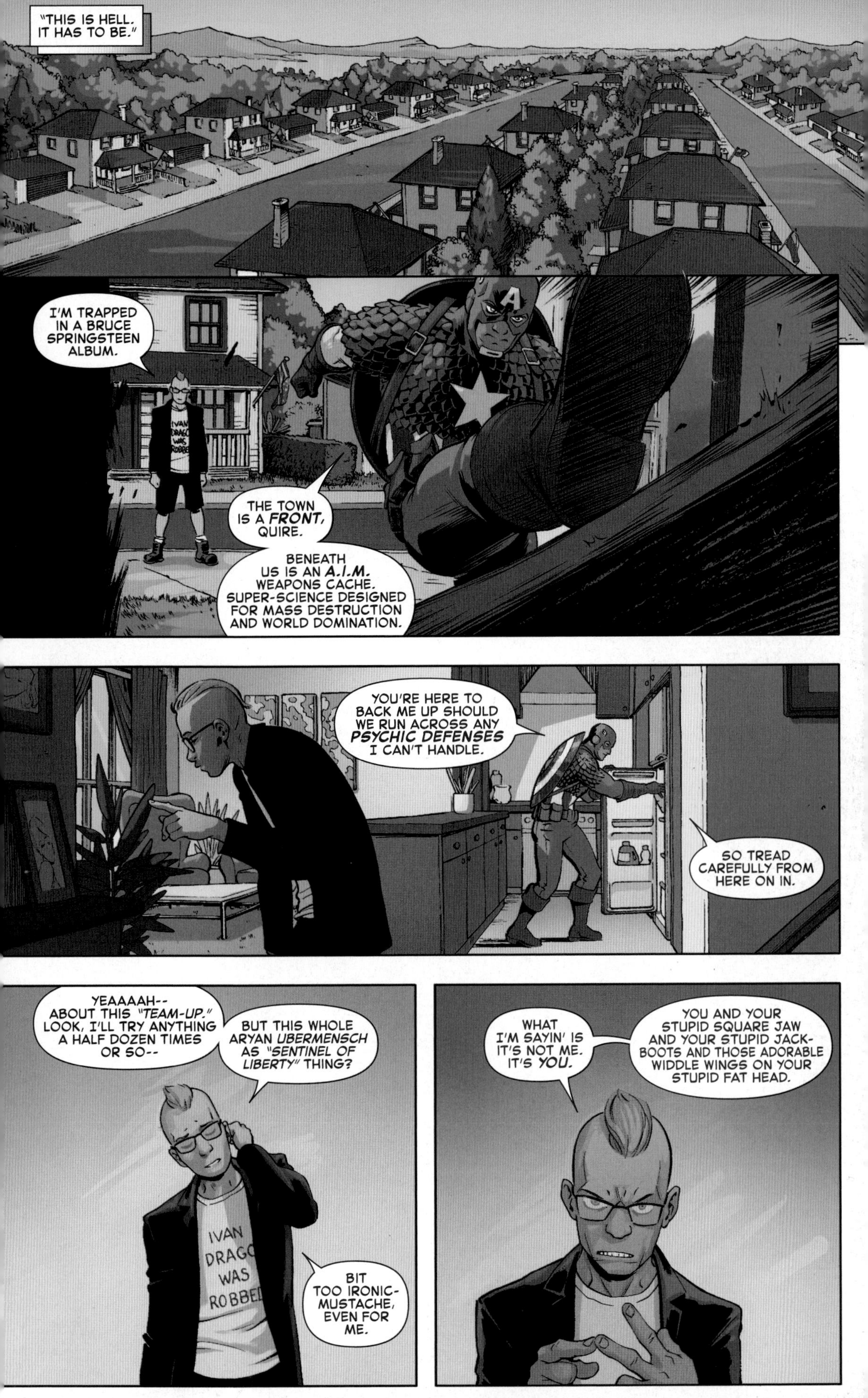
"THIS IS HELL. IT HAS TO BE."
I'M TRAPPED IN A BRUCE SPRINGSTEEN ALBUM.
IVAN DRAGO WAS ROBBED
THE TOWN IS A *FRONT,* QUIRE.
BENEATH US IS AN *A.I.M.* WEAPONS CACHE. SUPER-SCIENCE DESIGNED FOR MASS DESTRUCTION AND WORLD DOMINATION.
YOU'RE HERE TO BACK ME UP SHOULD WE RUN ACROSS ANY *PSYCHIC DEFENSES* I CAN'T HANDLE.
SO TREAD CAREFULLY FROM HERE ON IN.
YEAAAAH-- ABOUT THIS *"TEAM-UP."* LOOK, I'LL TRY ANYTHING A HALF DOZEN TIMES OR SO--
BUT THIS WHOLE ARYAN *UBERMENSCH* AS *"SENTINEL OF LIBERTY"* THING?
IVAN DRAGO WAS ROBBED
BIT TOO IRONIC-MUSTACHE, EVEN FOR ME.
WHAT I'M SAYIN' IS IT'S NOT ME. IT'S *YOU.*
YOU AND YOUR STUPID SQUARE JAW AND YOUR STUPID JACK-BOOTS AND THOSE ADORABLE WIDDLE WINGS ON YOUR STUPID FAT HEAD.

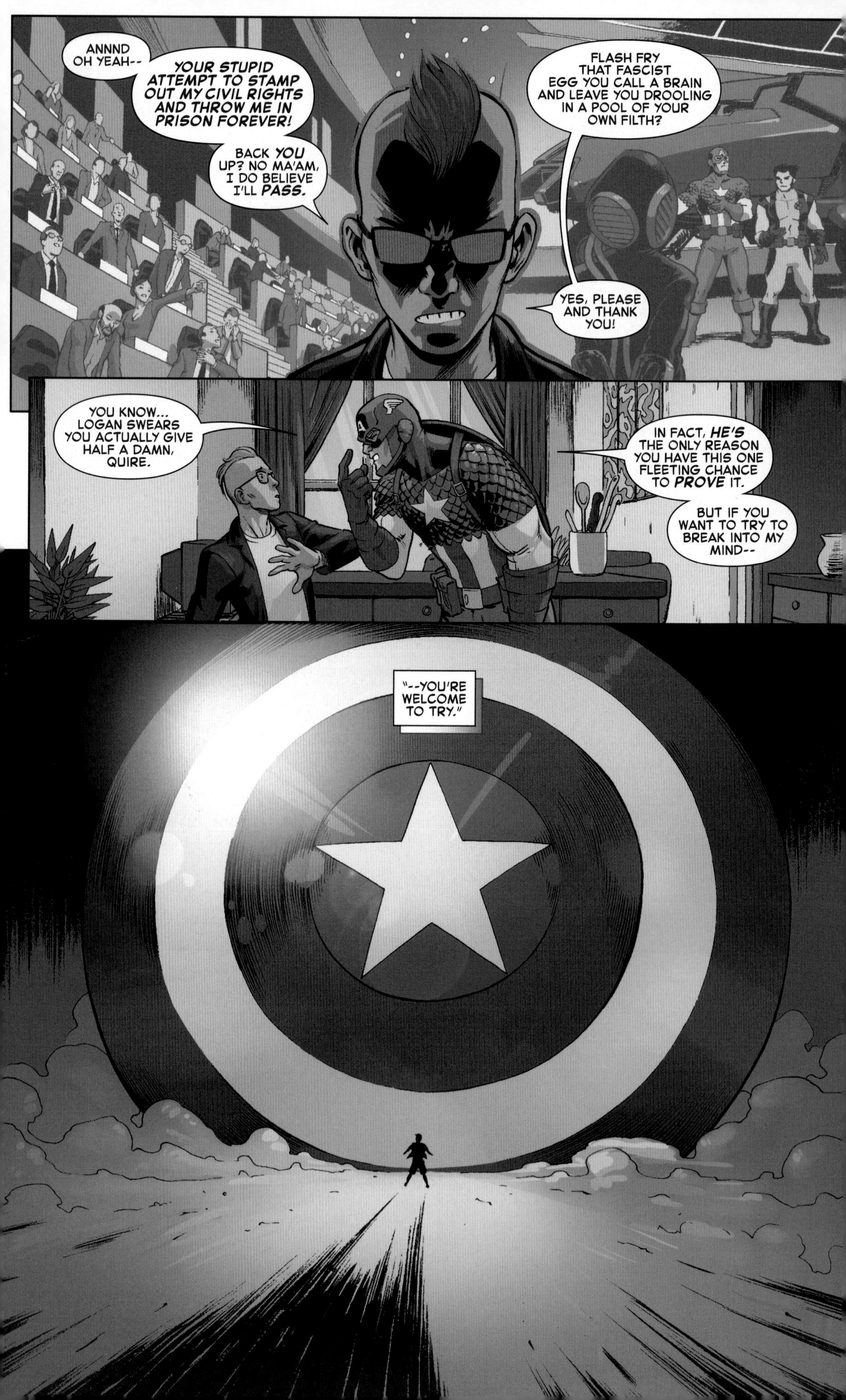
ANNND OH YEAH--
YOUR STUPID ATTEMPT TO STAMP OUT MY CIVIL RIGHTS AND THROW ME IN PRISON FOREVER!
BACK YOU UP? NO MA'AM, I DO BELIEVE I'LL PASS.
FLASH FRY THAT FASCIST EGG YOU CALL A BRAIN AND LEAVE YOU DROOLING IN A POOL OF YOUR OWN FILTH?
YES, PLEASE AND THANK YOU!
YOU KNOW... LOGAN SWEARS YOU ACTUALLY GIVE HALF A DAMN, QUIRE.
IN FACT, HE'S THE ONLY REASON YOU HAVE THIS ONE FLEETING CHANCE TO PROVE IT.
BUT IF YOU WANT TO TRY TO BREAK INTO MY MIND--
"--YOU'RE WELCOME TO TRY."

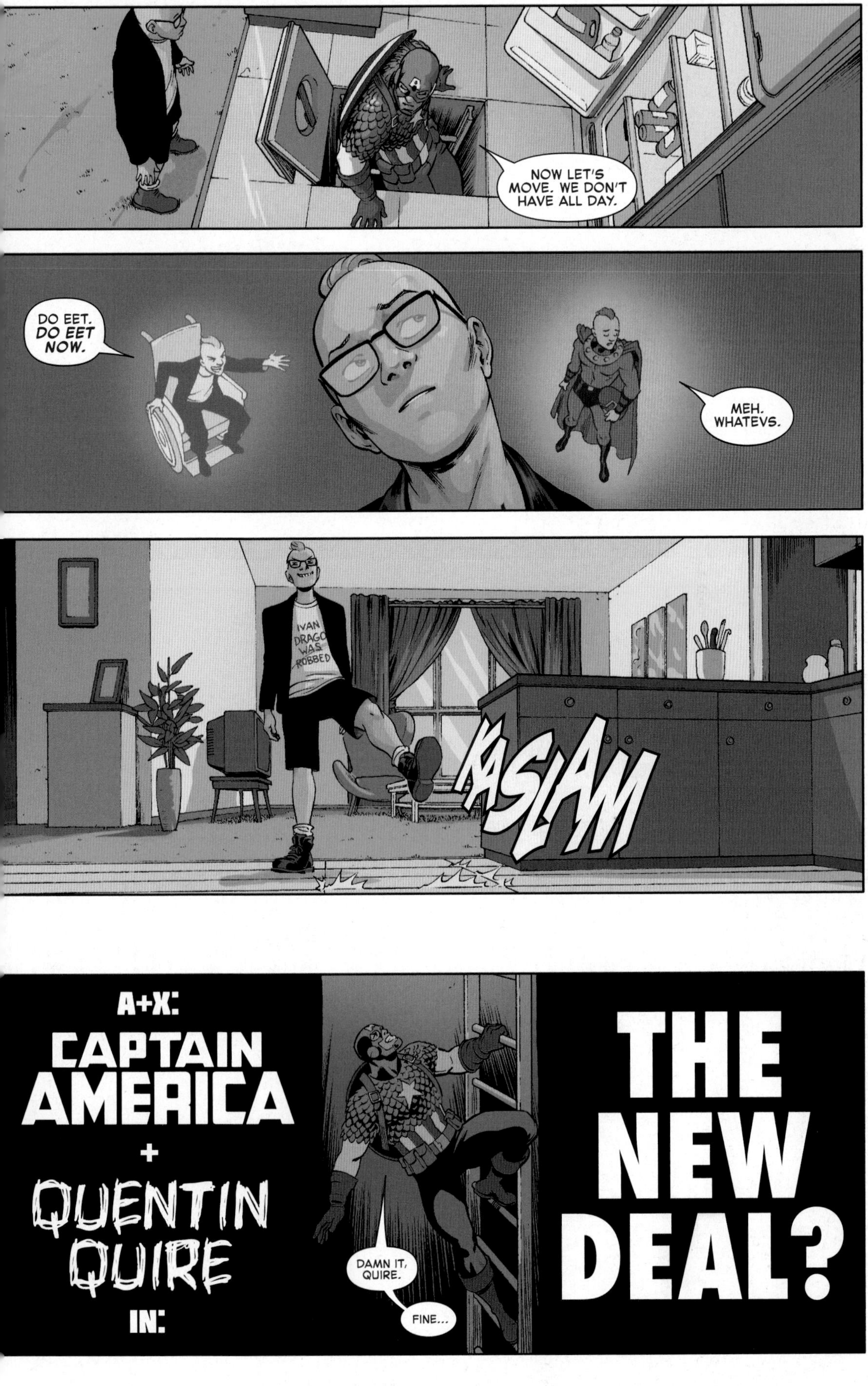
NOW LET'S MOVE. WE DON'T HAVE ALL DAY.
DO EET. DO EET NOW.
MEH. WHATEVS.
IVAN DRAGO WAS ROBBED
KASLAM
A+X: CAPTAIN AMERICA + QUENTIN QUIRE IN:
DAMN IT, QUIRE.
FINE...
THE NEW DEAL?

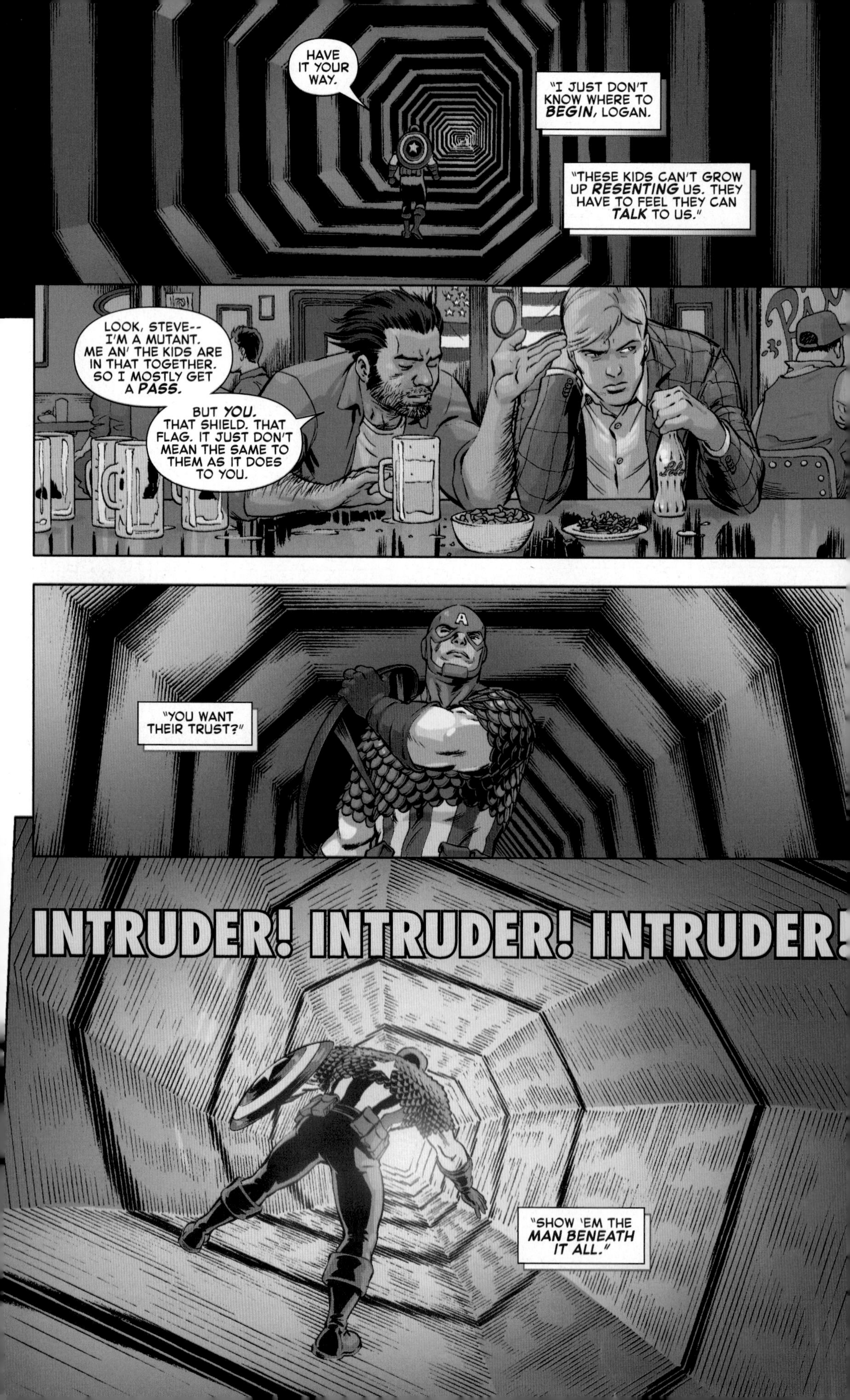
HAVE IT YOUR WAY.
"I JUST DON'T KNOW WHERE TO BEGIN, LOGAN.
"THESE KIDS CAN'T GROW UP RESENTING US. THEY HAVE TO FEEL THEY CAN TALK TO US."
LOOK, STEVE-- I'M A MUTANT. ME AN' THE KIDS ARE IN THAT TOGETHER. SO I MOSTLY GET A PASS.
BUT YOU. THAT SHIELD. THAT FLAG. IT JUST DON'T MEAN THE SAME TO THEM AS IT DOES TO YOU.
"YOU WANT THEIR TRUST?"
INTRUDER! INTRUDER! INTRUDER!
"SHOW 'EM THE MAN BENEATH IT ALL."

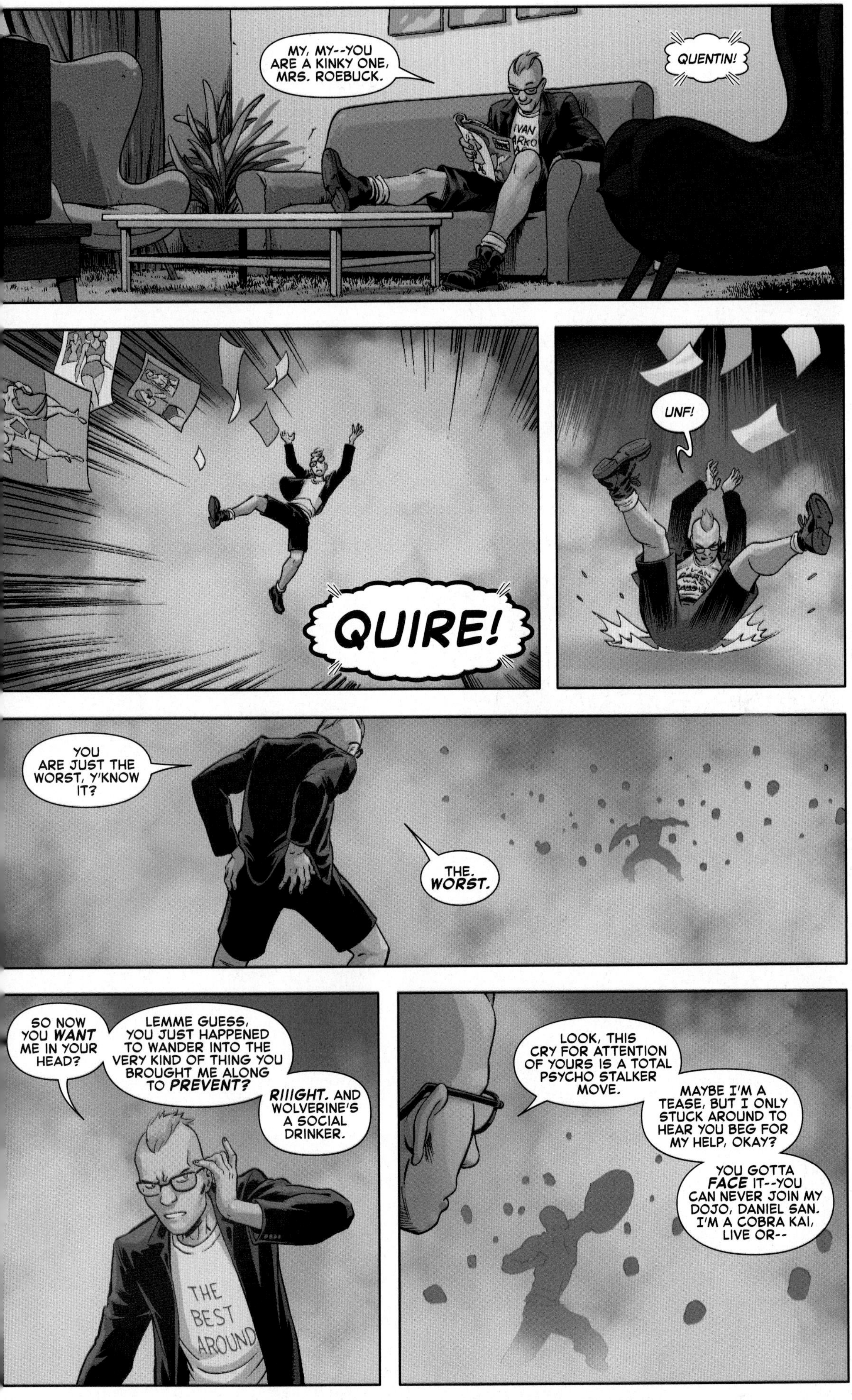
MY, MY--YOU ARE A KINKY ONE, MRS. ROEBUCK.
QUENTIN!
IVAN ARKO
QUIRE!
UNF!
YOU ARE JUST THE WORST, Y'KNOW IT?
THE. WORST.
SO NOW YOU WANT ME IN YOUR HEAD?
LEMME GUESS, YOU JUST HAPPENED TO WANDER INTO THE VERY KIND OF THING YOU BROUGHT ME ALONG TO PREVENT?
RIIIGHT. AND WOLVERINE'S A SOCIAL DRINKER.
THE BEST AROUND
LOOK, THIS CRY FOR ATTENTION OF YOURS IS A TOTAL PSYCHO STALKER MOVE.
MAYBE I'M A TEASE, BUT I ONLY STUCK AROUND TO HEAR YOU BEG FOR MY HELP, OKAY?
YOU GOTTA FACE IT--YOU CAN NEVER JOIN MY DOJO, DANIEL SAN. I'M A COBRA KAI, LIVE OR--

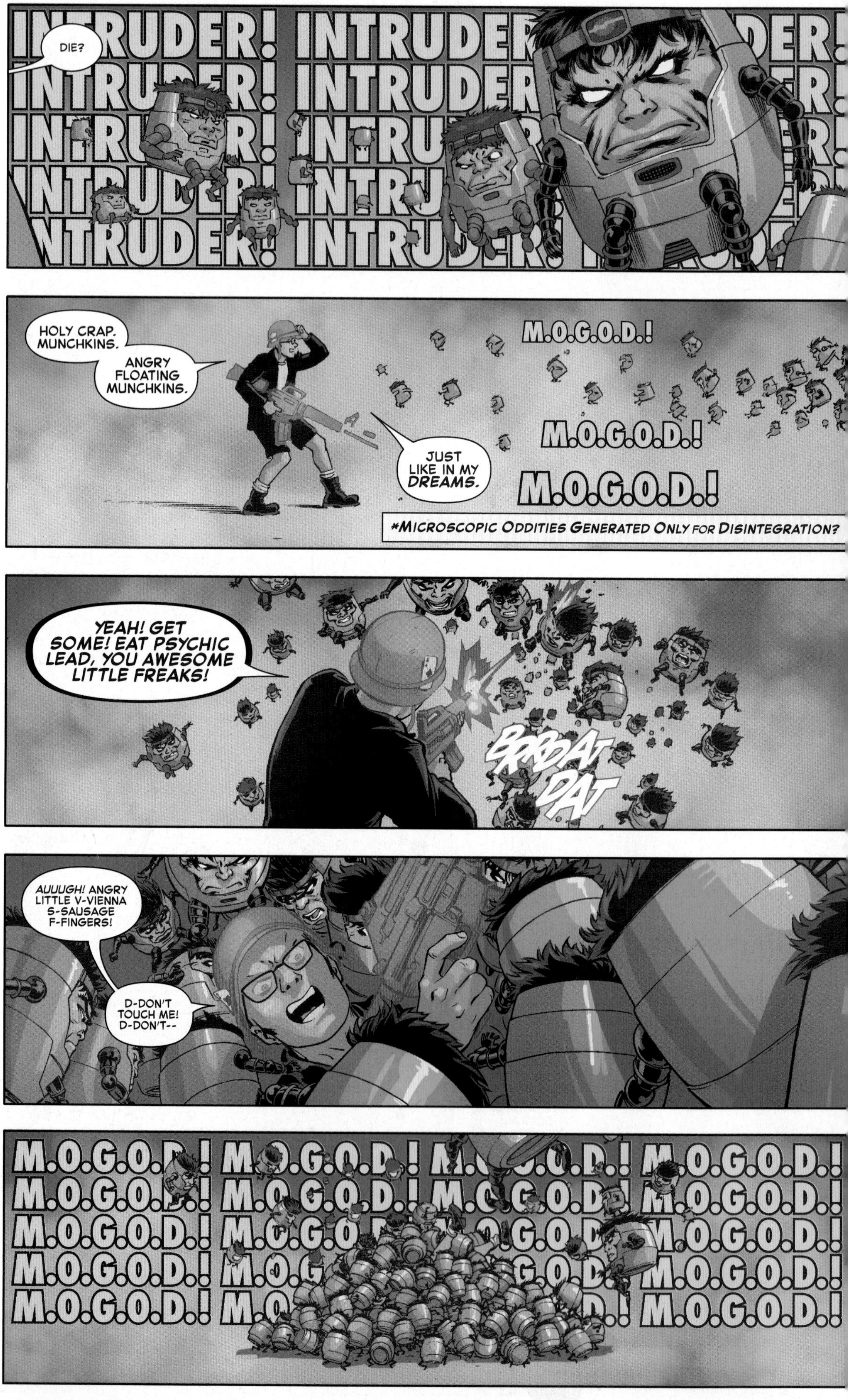

DIE?
INTRUDER! INTRUDER!
INTRUDER! INTRUDER!
INTRUDER! INTRUDER!
INTRUDER! INTRUDER!
INTRUDER! INTRUDER!
HOLY CRAP. MUNCHKINS.
ANGRY FLOATING MUNCHKINS.
M.O.G.O.D.!
M.O.G.O.D.!
JUST LIKE IN MY DREAMS.
M.O.G.O.D.!
*MICROSCOPIC ODDITIES GENERATED ONLY FOR DISINTEGRATION?
YEAH! GET SOME! EAT PSYCHIC LEAD, YOU AWESOME LITTLE FREAKS!
BRRDAT DAT
AUUUGH! ANGRY LITTLE V-VIENNA S-SAUSAGE F-FINGERS!
D-DON'T TOUCH ME! D-DON'T--
M.O.G.O.D.! M.O.G.O.D.! M.O.G.O.D.! M.O.G.O.D.!
M.O.G.O.D.! M.O.G.O.D.! M.O.G.O.D.! M.O.G.O.D.!
M.O.G.O.D.! M.O.G.O.D.! M.O.G.O.D.! M.O.G.O.D.!
M.O.G.O.D.! M.O.G.O.D.! M.O.G.O.D.! M.O.G.O.D.!
M.O.G.O.D.! M.O.G.O.D.! M.O.G.O.D.! M.O.G.O.D.!

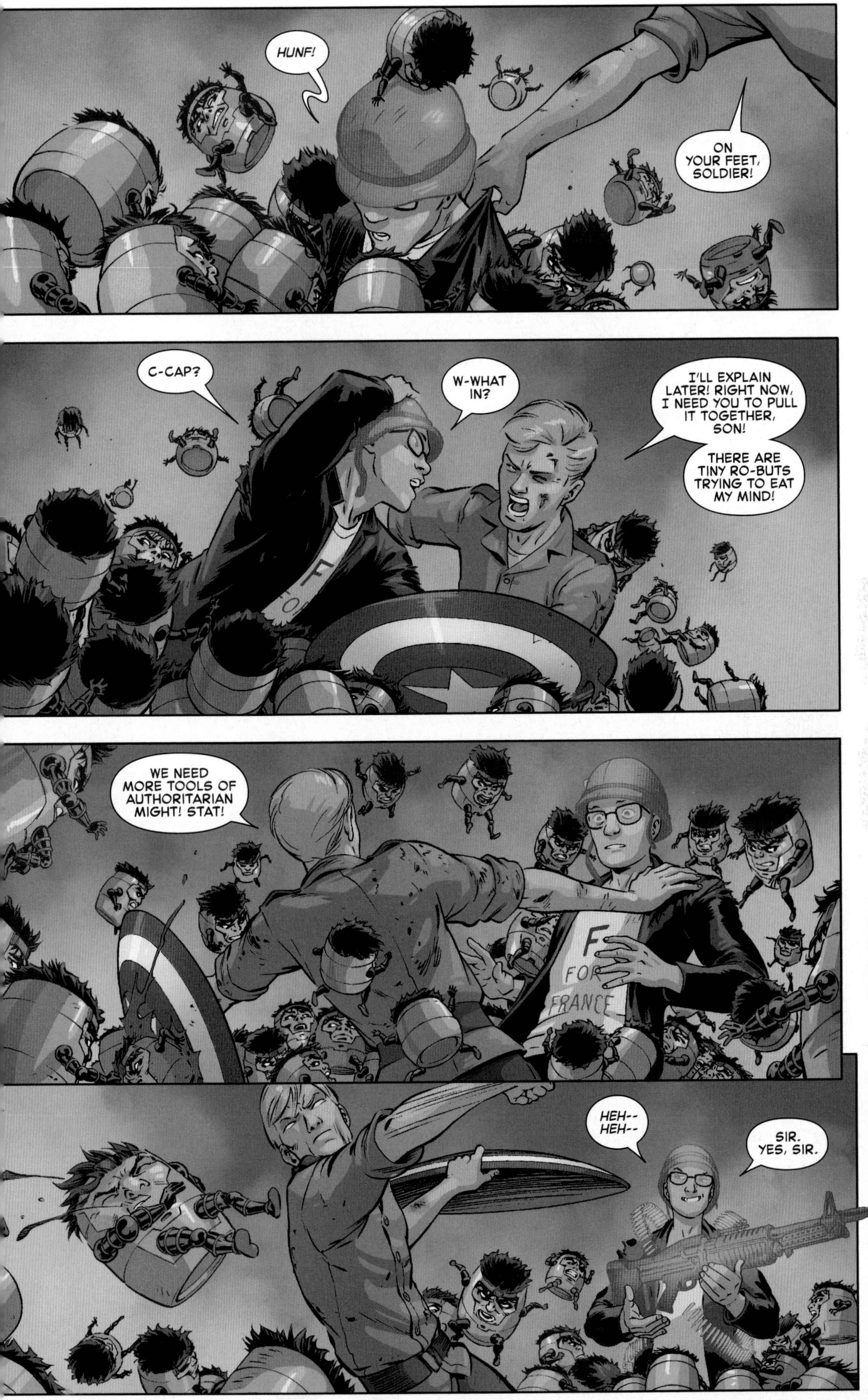
HUNF!
ON YOUR FEET, SOLDIER!
C-CAP?
W-WHAT IN?
I'LL EXPLAIN LATER! RIGHT NOW, I NEED YOU TO PULL IT TOGETHER, SON!
THERE ARE TINY RO-BUTS TRYING TO EAT MY MIND!
WE NEED MORE TOOLS OF AUTHORITARIAN MIGHT! STAT!
F FOR FRANCE
HEH-- HEH--
SIR. YES, SIR.

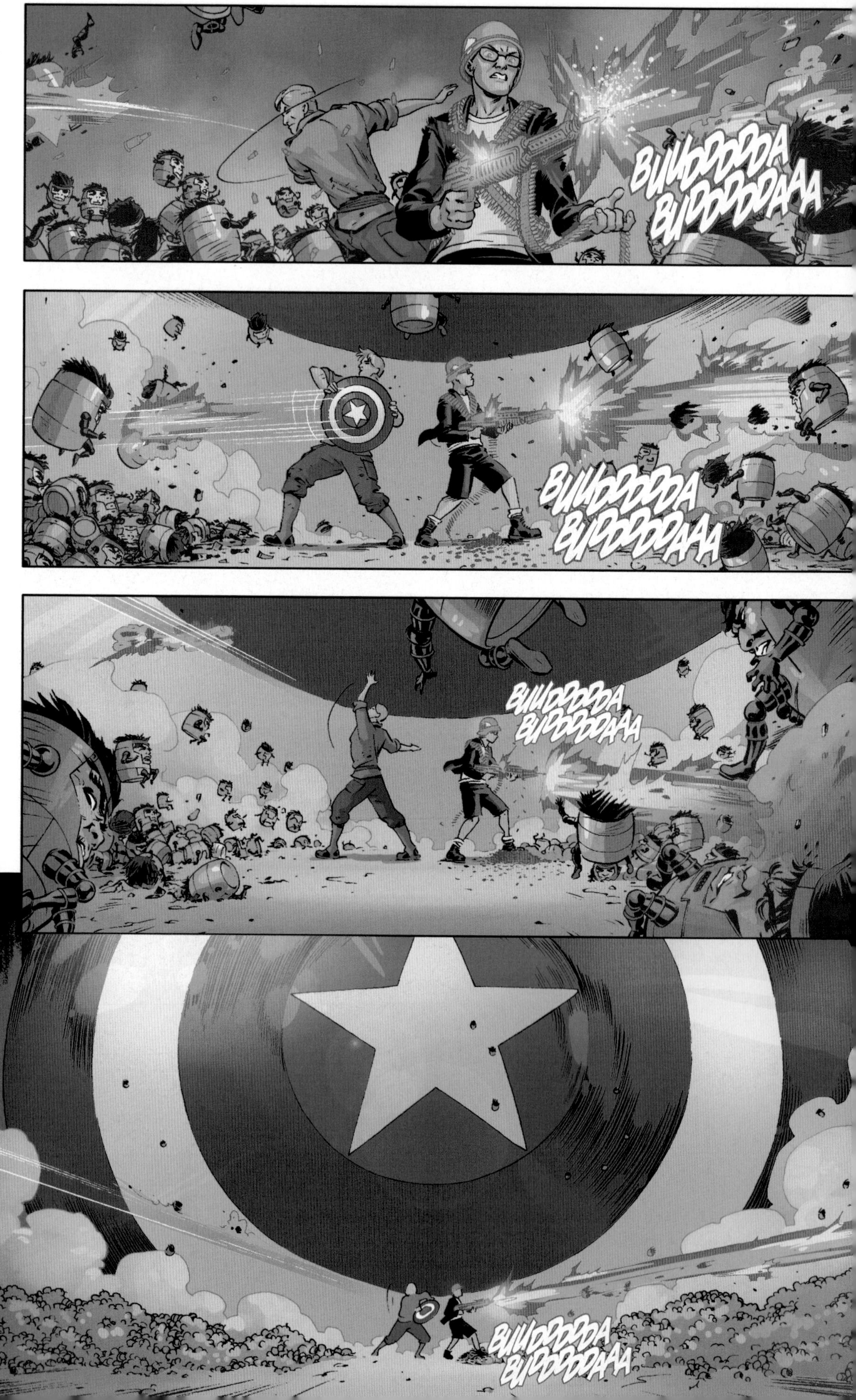
BUUDDDDA
BUDDDDAAA
BUUDDDDA
BUDDDDAAA
BUUDDDDA
BUDDDDAAA
BUUDDDDA
BUDDDDAAA

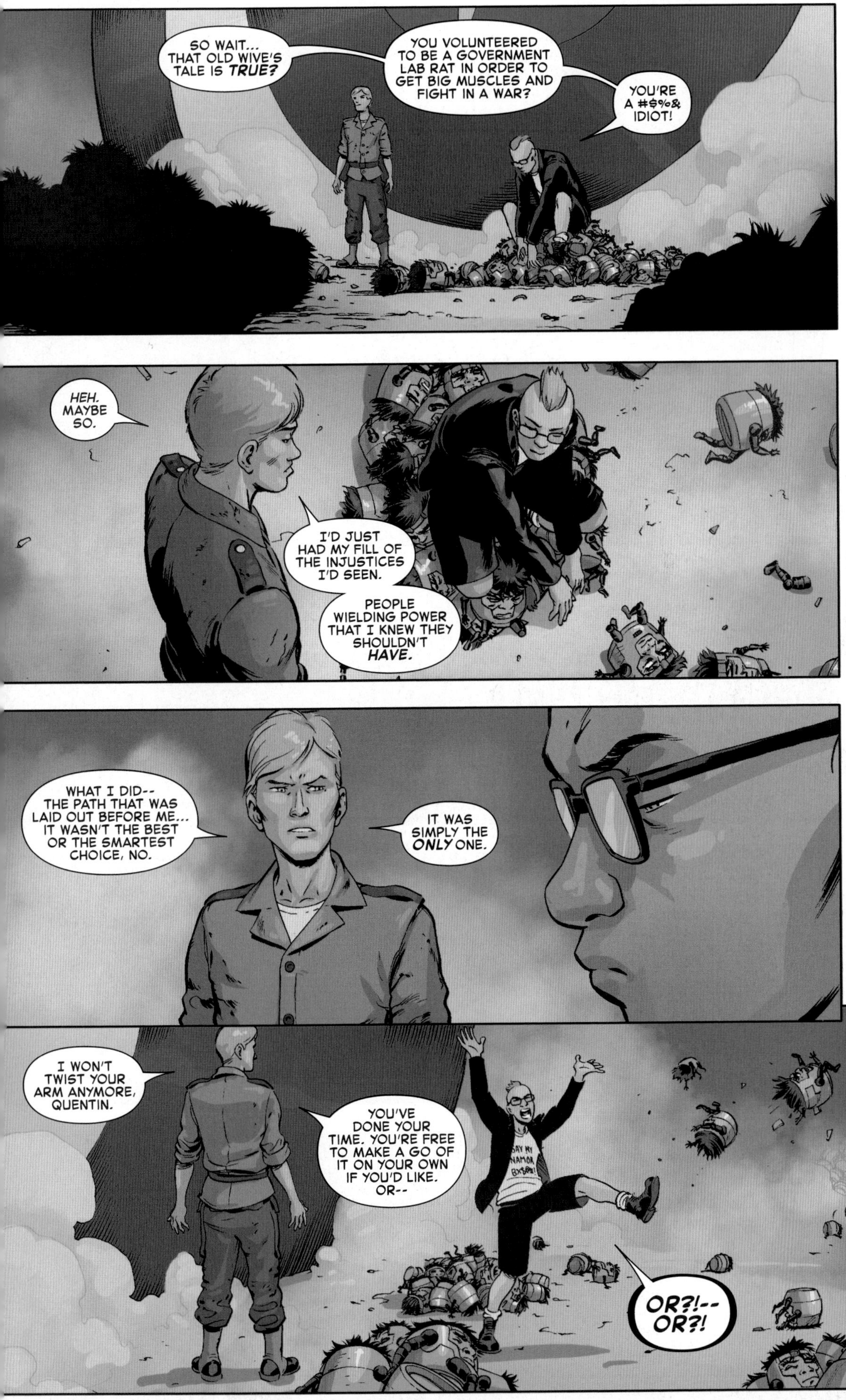
SO WAIT... THAT OLD WIVE'S TALE IS TRUE?
YOU VOLUNTEERED TO BE A GOVERNMENT LAB RAT IN ORDER TO GET BIG MUSCLES AND FIGHT IN A WAR?
YOU'RE A #$%& IDIOT!
HEH. MAYBE SO.
I'D JUST HAD MY FILL OF THE INJUSTICES I'D SEEN.
PEOPLE WIELDING POWER THAT I KNEW THEY SHOULDN'T HAVE.
WHAT I DID-- THE PATH THAT WAS LAID OUT BEFORE ME... IT WASN'T THE BEST OR THE SMARTEST CHOICE, NO.
IT WAS SIMPLY THE ONLY ONE.
I WON'T TWIST YOUR ARM ANYMORE, QUENTIN.
YOU'VE DONE YOUR TIME. YOU'RE FREE TO MAKE A GO OF IT ON YOUR OWN IF YOU'D LIKE. OR--
OR?!-- OR?!

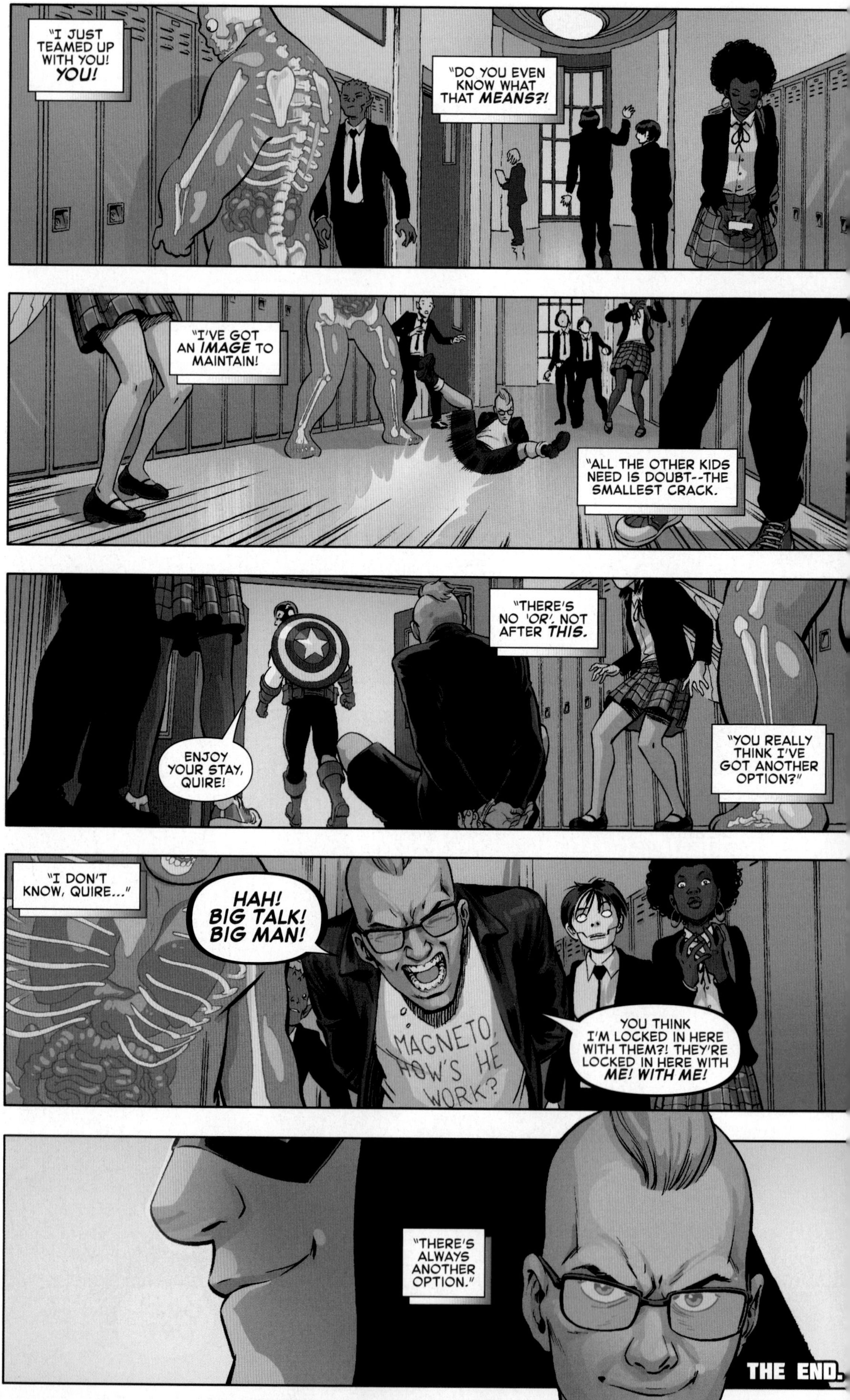
"I JUST TEAMED UP WITH YOU! YOU!
"DO YOU EVEN KNOW WHAT THAT MEANS?!
"I'VE GOT AN IMAGE TO MAINTAIN!
"ALL THE OTHER KIDS NEED IS DOUBT--THE SMALLEST CRACK.
ENJOY YOUR STAY, QUIRE!
"THERE'S NO 'OR'. NOT AFTER THIS.
"YOU REALLY THINK I'VE GOT ANOTHER OPTION?"
"I DON'T KNOW, QUIRE..."
HAH! BIG TALK! BIG MAN!
MAGNETO, HOW'S HE WORK?
YOU THINK I'M LOCKED IN HERE WITH THEM?! THEY'RE LOCKED IN HERE WITH ME! WITH ME!
"THERE'S ALWAYS ANOTHER OPTION."
THE END.

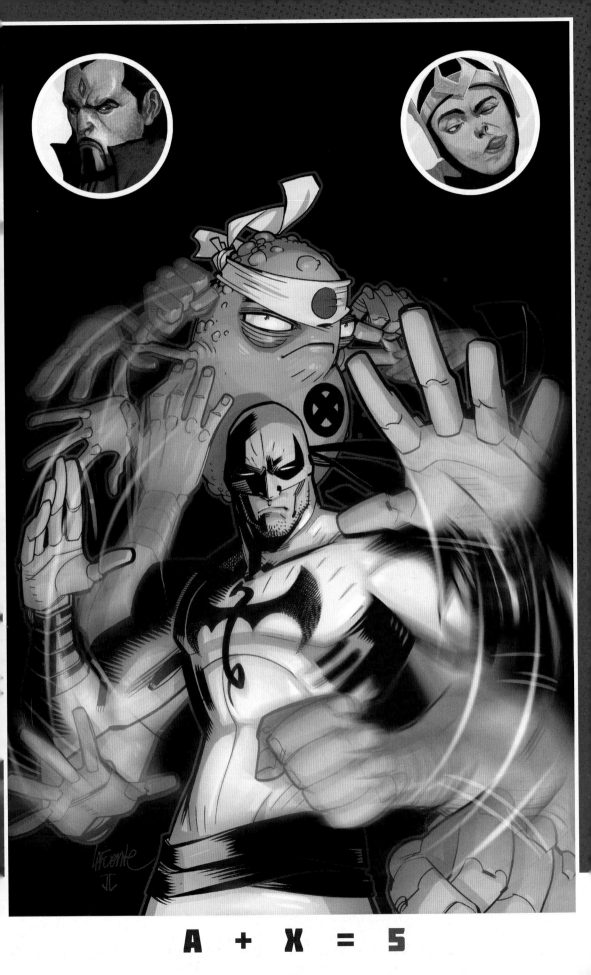

A + X = 5

**A: NO! It's the ABSOLUTE EPITOME of comic books! It's A+X, the comic that makes adding FUN by addin AVENGERS and X-MEN into AWESOME TEAM-UP STORIES instead of adding LAME OLD NUMBERS!**

**Q: Oh, okay—so this issue is a big team-up issue?**

**A: NO WAY! EVERY issue is a big team-up issue with A+X! Heck—every issue is TWO big team-up issues, because we have TWO HERO PLUSSING STORIES in EVERY ISSUE!**

**Q: That sounds fun! What's in this issue?**

**A: First up, we have unparalleled martial artist Avenger IRON FIST, teaming up with the most powerful X-Ma to ever wear the X...DOOP!**

**Q: I think I get the Iron Fist guy, but...what's a Doop?**

**A: He's this little green FLOATY guy who talks WEIRD and who we DON'T KNOW MUCH ABOUT!**

**Q: Oh...all right. What's the second story?**

**A: Oh-ho-ho-HO! We pulled a trick on that one! For that story, we team up the very first Avengers VILLAIN, the Asgardian God of Mischief LOKI, with the classic X-Foe and genetic manipulator, MISTER SINISTER! See how we CHANGE THINGS UP?**

**Q: Yes, I see what you did there. Can I read the book now?**

**A: YOU KNOW IT!**

# A+X

## IRON FIST + DOOP

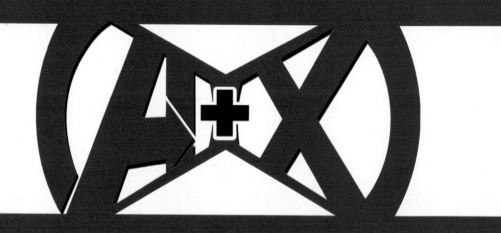

KATHRYN IMMONEN, WRITER
DAVID LAFUENTE, ARTIST
JIM CAMPBELL, COLOR ARTIST
VC'S CLAYTON COWLES, LETTERER

## LOKI + Mister Sinister

KIERON GILLEN, WRITER
JOE BENNETT, PENCILER
MARK MORALES, INKER
JIM CHARALAMPIDIS, COLORIST
VC'S CLAYTON COWLES, LETTERER


JORDAN D. WHITE, ASSOCIATE EDITOR
NICK LOWE, EDITOR
AXEL ALONSO, EDITOR IN CHIEF
JOE QUESADA, CHIEF CREATIVE OFFICER
DAN BUCKLEY, PUBLISHER
ALAN FINE, EXECUTIVE PRODUCER

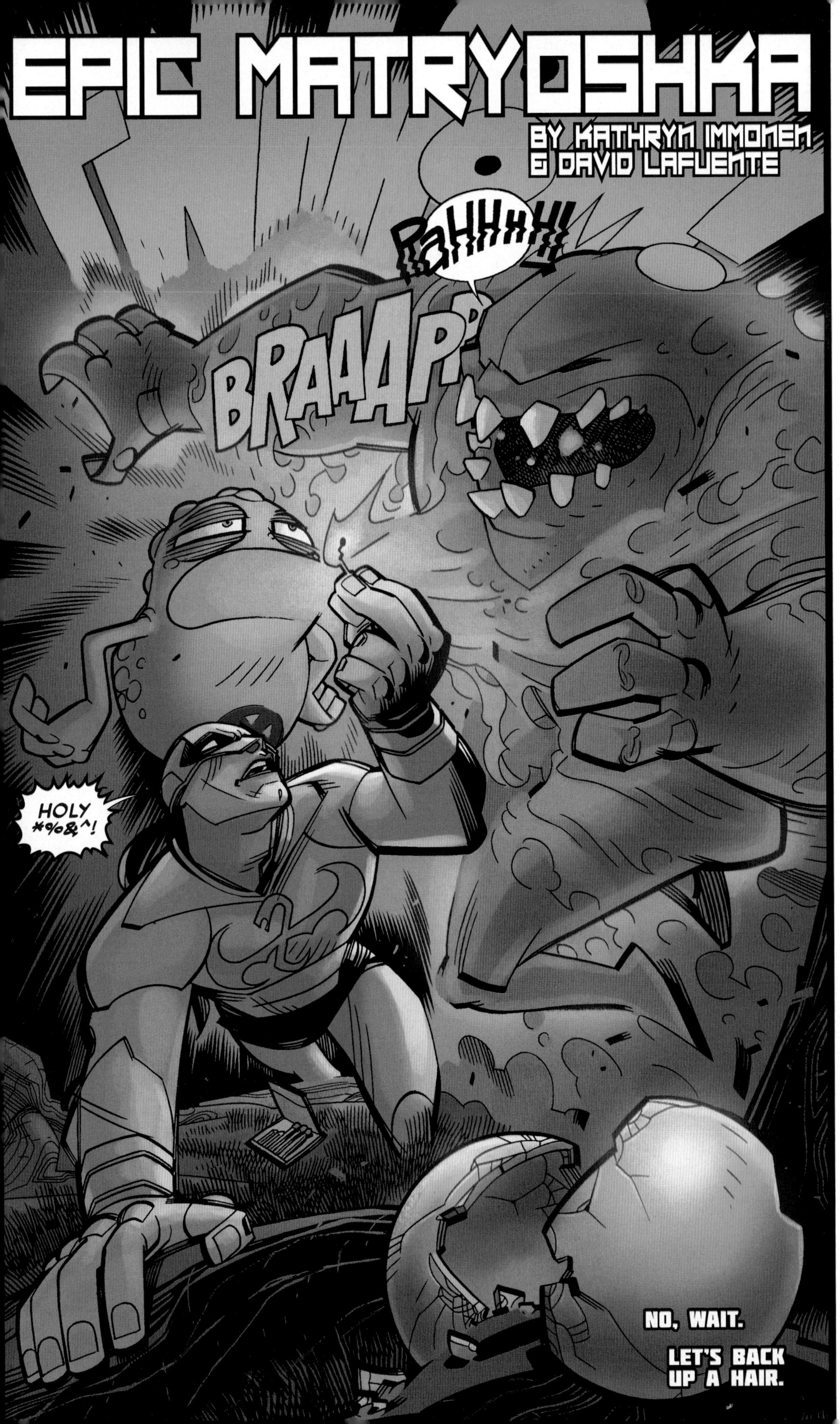

EPIC MATRYOSHKA
BY KATHRYN IMMONEN
& DAVID LAFUENTE
PAHHHHH!!
BRAAAP
HOLY *%&^!
NO, WAIT.
LET'S BACK UP A HAIR.

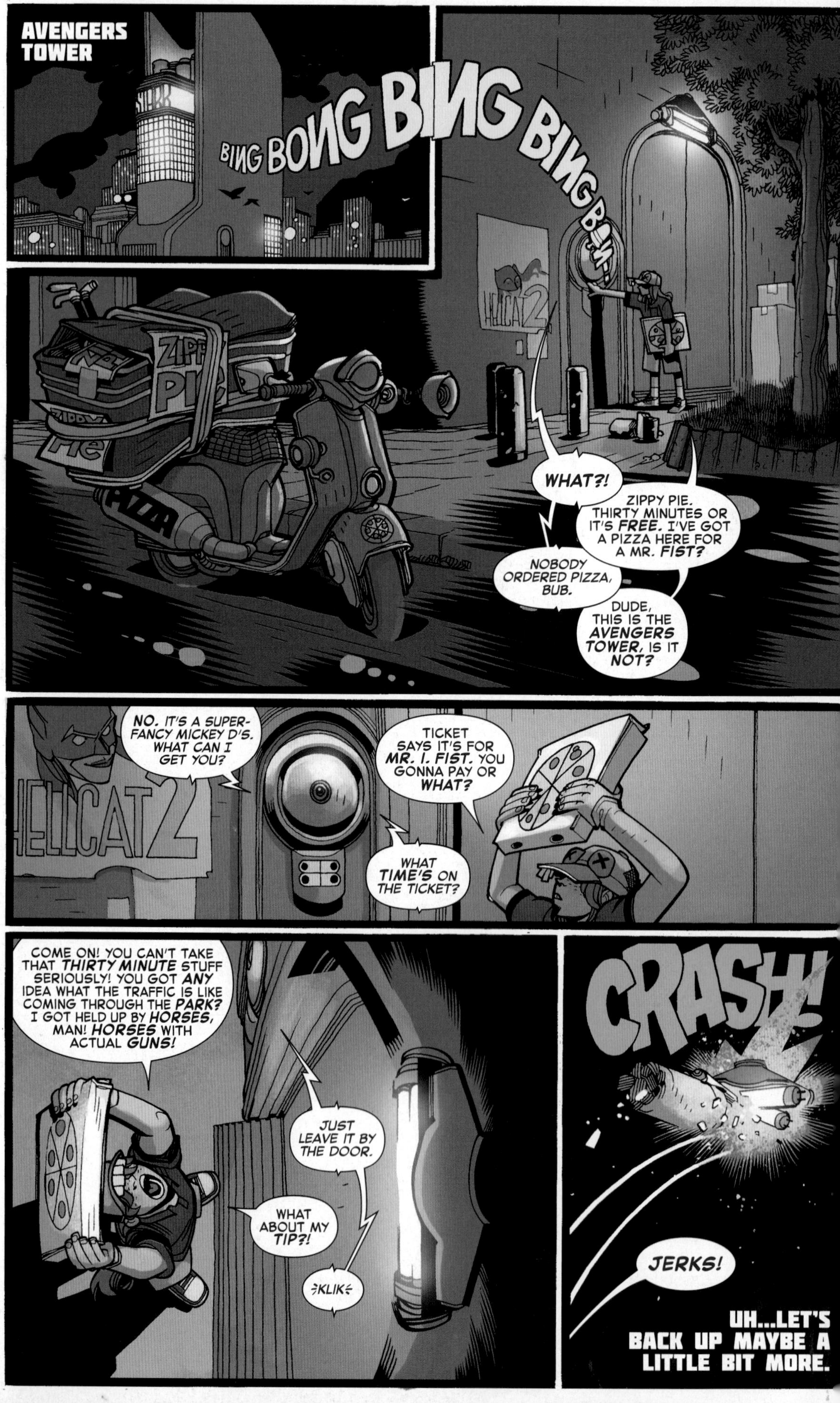
AVENGERS TOWER
BING BONG BING BING BING BONG
WHAT?!
ZIPPY PIE. THIRTY MINUTES OR IT'S FREE. I'VE GOT A PIZZA HERE FOR A MR. FIST?
NOBODY ORDERED PIZZA, BUB.
DUDE, THIS IS THE AVENGERS TOWER, IS IT NOT?
NO. IT'S A SUPER-FANCY MICKEY D'S. WHAT CAN I GET YOU?
TICKET SAYS IT'S FOR MR. I. FIST. YOU GONNA PAY OR WHAT?
WHAT TIME'S ON THE TICKET?
COME ON! YOU CAN'T TAKE THAT THIRTY MINUTE STUFF SERIOUSLY! YOU GOT ANY IDEA WHAT THE TRAFFIC IS LIKE COMING THROUGH THE PARK? I GOT HELD UP BY HORSES, MAN! HORSES WITH ACTUAL GUNS!
JUST LEAVE IT BY THE DOOR.
WHAT ABOUT MY TIP?!
KLIK
CRASH!
JERKS!
UH...LET'S BACK UP MAYBE A LITTLE BIT MORE.

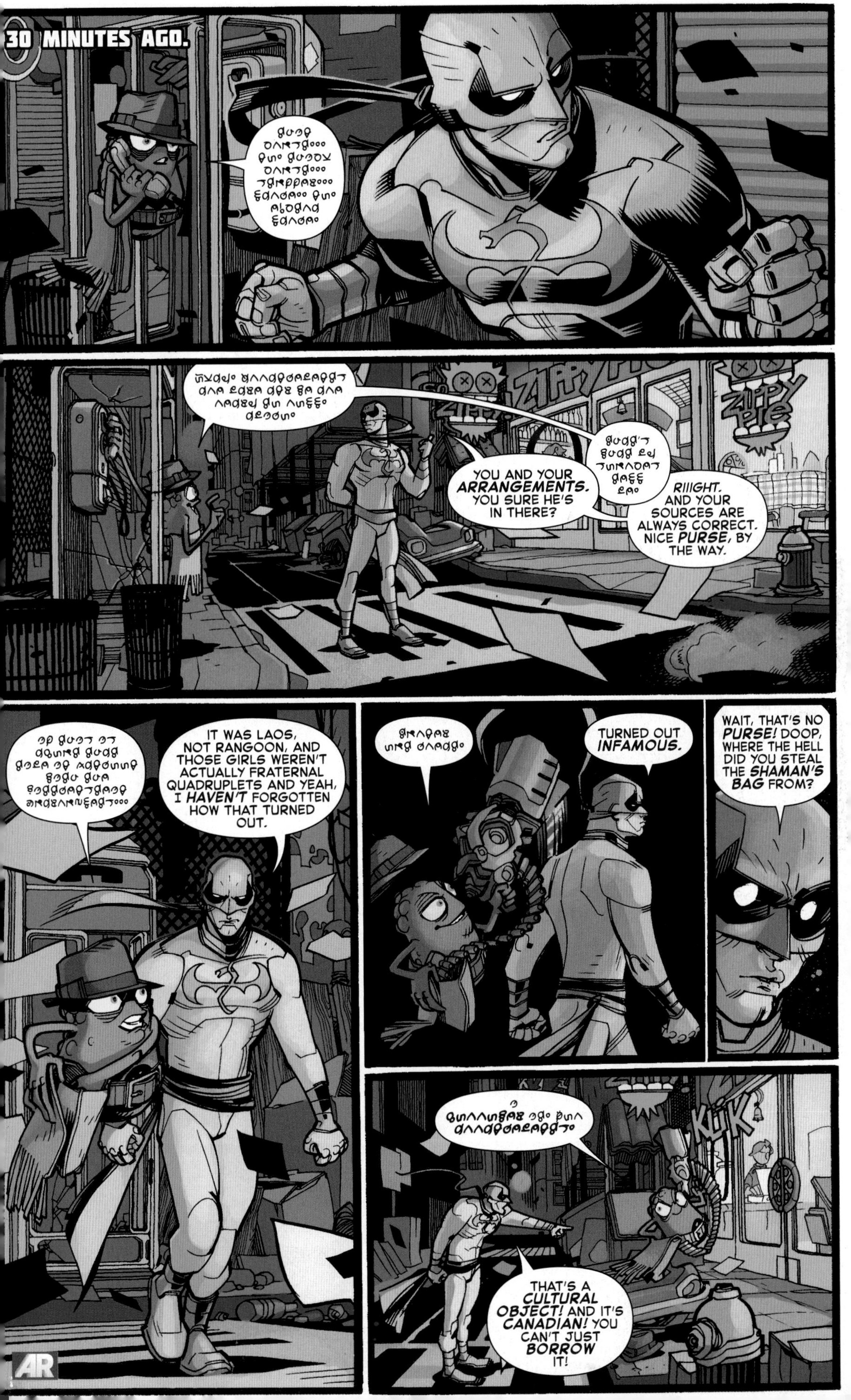
30 MINUTES AGO.
YOU AND YOUR ARRANGEMENTS. YOU SURE HE'S IN THERE?
RIIIGHT. AND YOUR SOURCES ARE ALWAYS CORRECT. NICE PURSE, BY THE WAY.
IT WAS LAOS, NOT RANGOON, AND THOSE GIRLS WEREN'T ACTUALLY FRATERNAL QUADRUPLETS AND YEAH, I HAVEN'T FORGOTTEN HOW THAT TURNED OUT.
TURNED OUT INFAMOUS.
WAIT, THAT'S NO PURSE! DOOP, WHERE THE HELL DID YOU STEAL THE SHAMAN'S BAG FROM?
KLIK
THAT'S A CULTURAL OBJECT! AND IT'S CANADIAN! YOU CAN'T JUST BORROW IT!

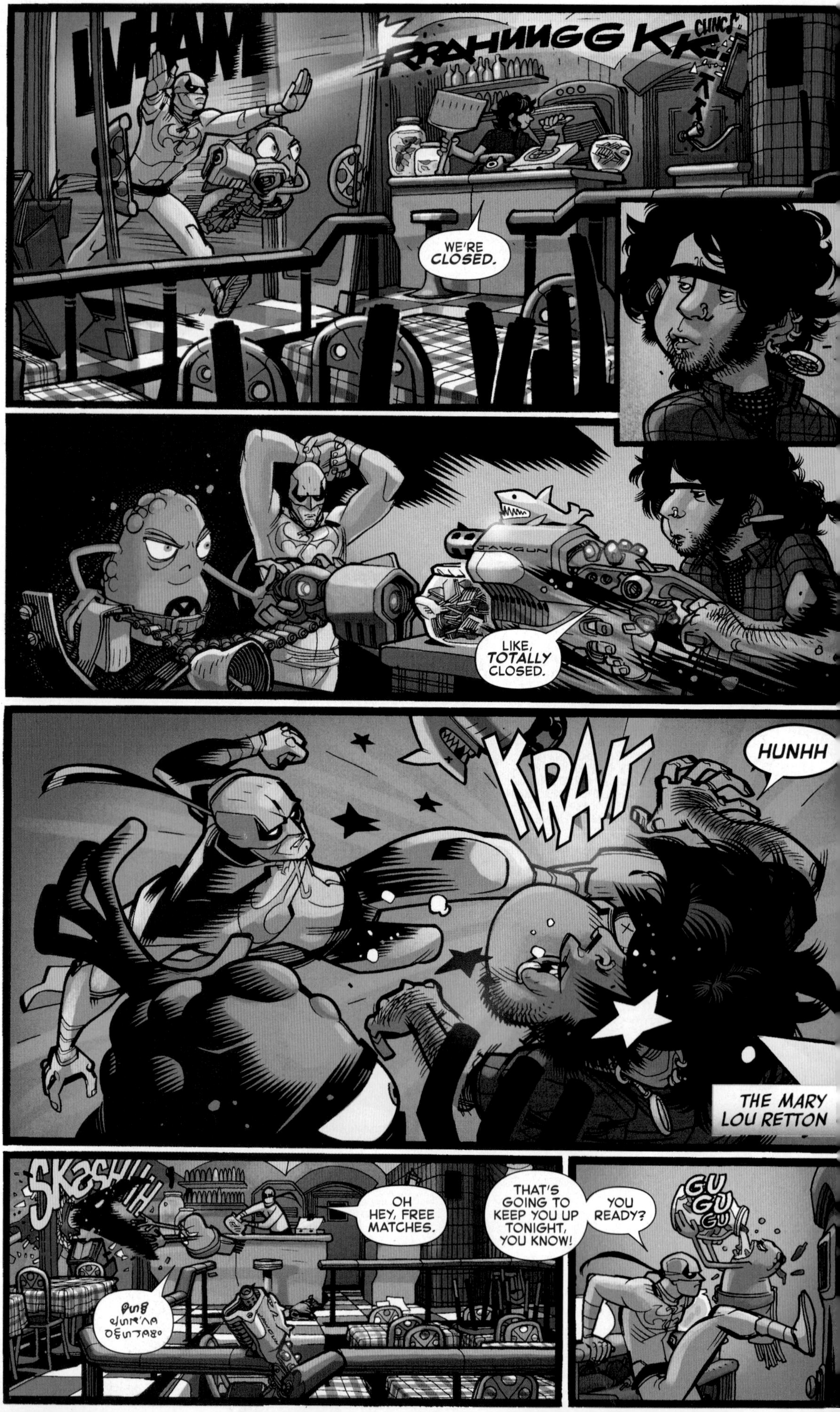
WHAM
RRAHHNGG KK
CLINC!
WE'RE CLOSED.
LIKE, TOTALLY CLOSED.
KRAK
HUNHH
THE MARY LOU RETTON
SKASHHH
OH HEY, FREE MATCHES.
THAT'S GOING TO KEEP YOU UP TONIGHT, YOU KNOW!
YOU READY?
GU GU GU

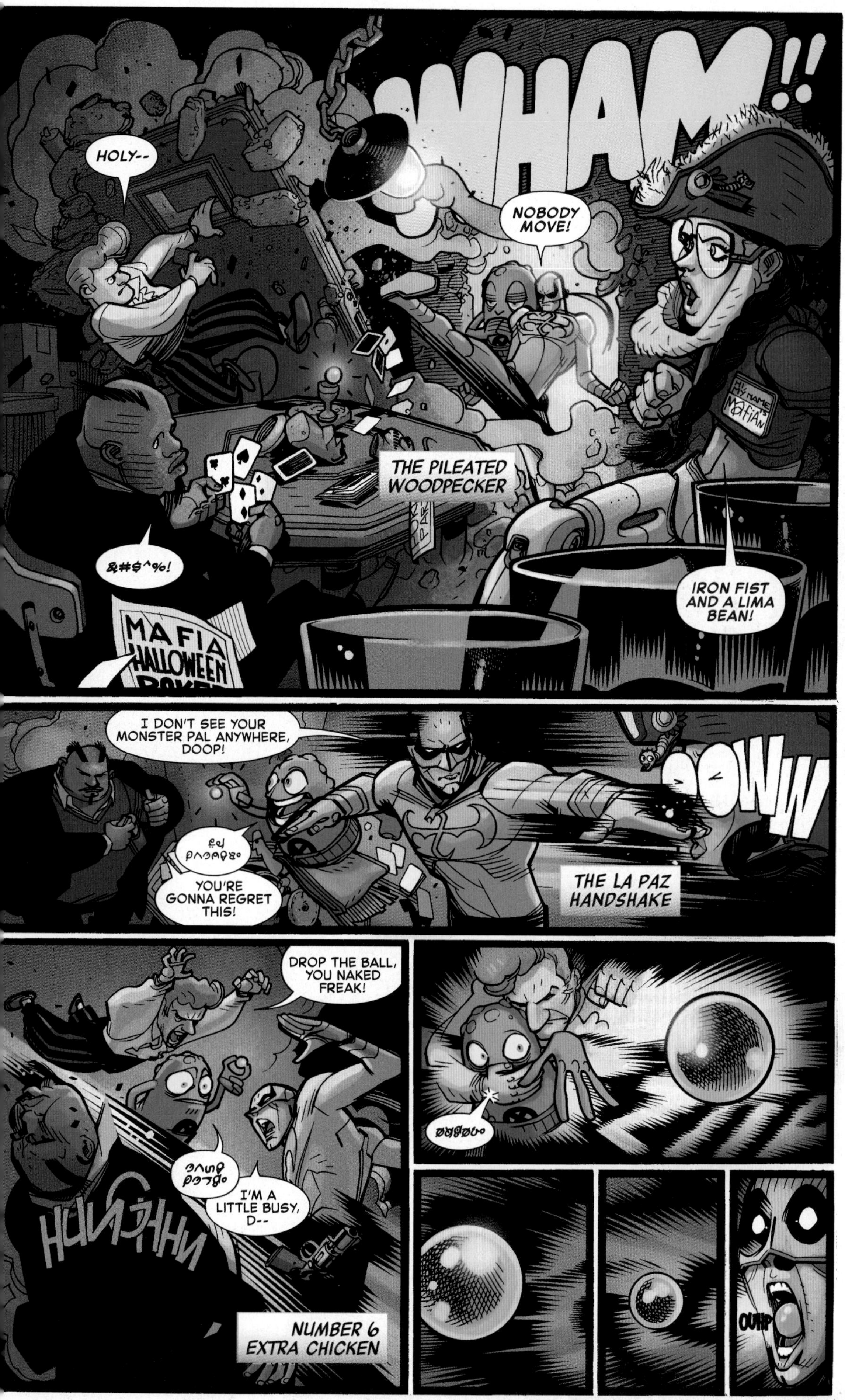
WHAM!!
HOLY--
NOBODY MOVE!
THE PILEATED WOODPECKER
&#$^%!
IRON FIST AND A LIMA BEAN!
MAFIA HALLOWEEN POKER
I DON'T SEE YOUR MONSTER PAL ANYWHERE, DOOP!
YOU'RE GONNA REGRET THIS!
THE LA PAZ HANDSHAKE
DROP THE BALL, YOU NAKED FREAK!
I'M A LITTLE BUSY, D--
NUMBER 6 EXTRA CHICKEN
OUHP

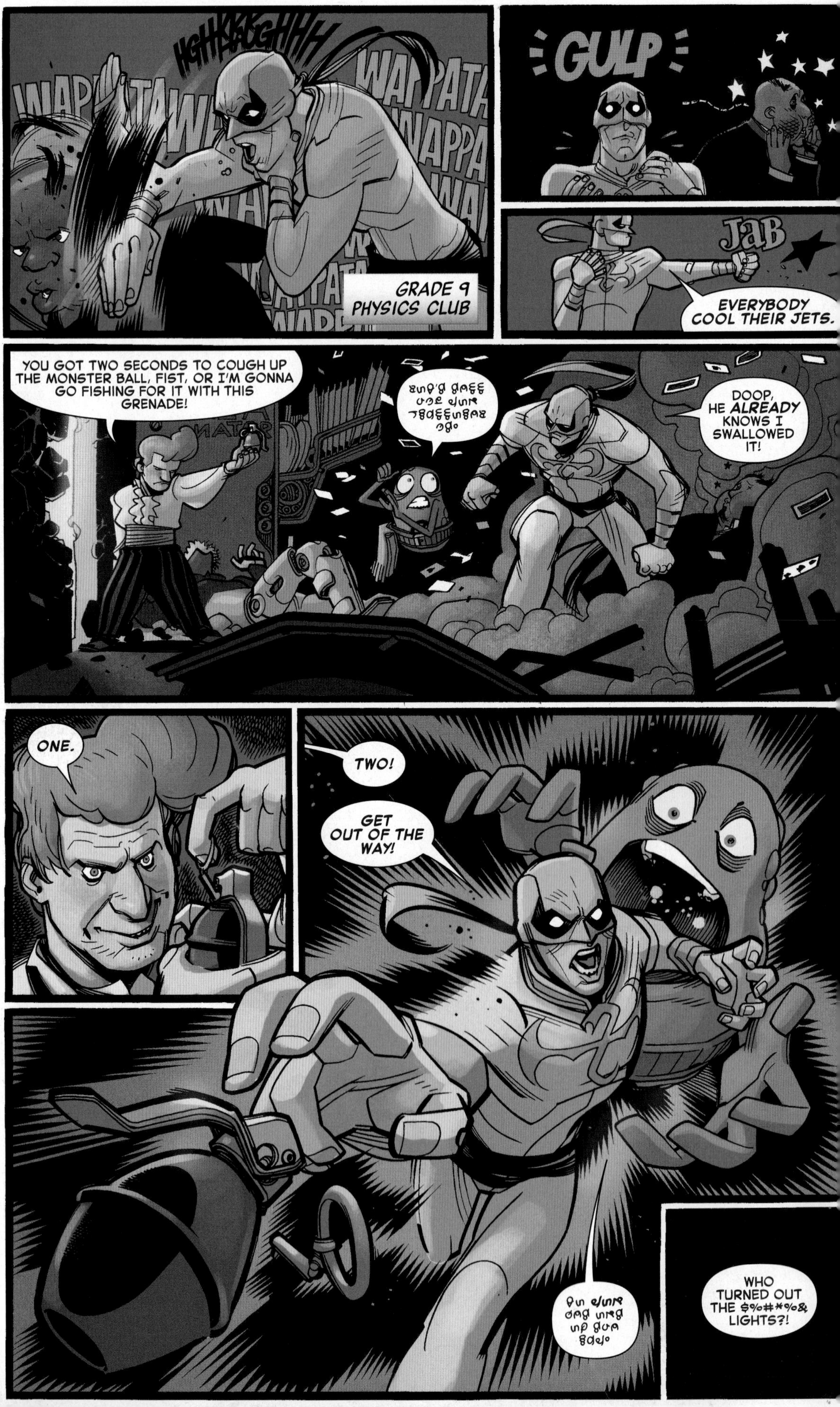

GRADE 9
PHYSICS CLUB
GULP
JaB
EVERYBODY COOL THEIR JETS.
YOU GOT TWO SECONDS TO COUGH UP THE MONSTER BALL, FIST, OR I'M GONNA GO FISHING FOR IT WITH THIS GRENADE!
DOOP, HE ALREADY KNOWS I SWALLOWED IT!
ONE.
TWO!
GET OUT OF THE WAY!
WHO TURNED OUT THE $%#*%& LIGHTS?!

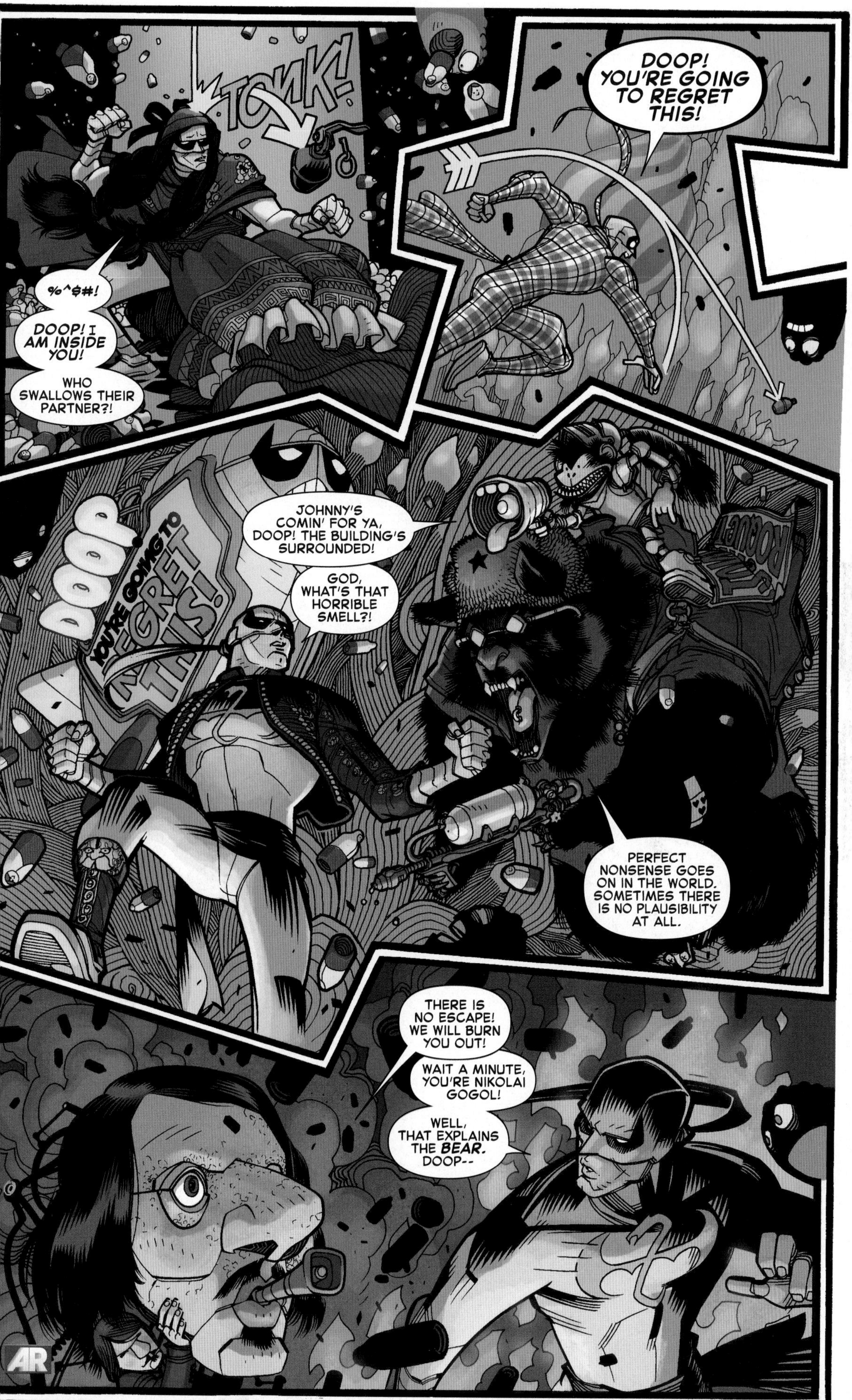
TONK!
%^$#!
DOOP! I AM INSIDE YOU!
WHO SWALLOWS THEIR PARTNER?!
DOOP! YOU'RE GOING TO REGRET THIS!
DOOP
YOU'RE GOING TO REGRET THIS!
JOHNNY'S COMIN' FOR YA, DOOP! THE BUILDING'S SURROUNDED!
GOD, WHAT'S THAT HORRIBLE SMELL?!
PERFECT NONSENSE GOES ON IN THE WORLD. SOMETIMES THERE IS NO PLAUSIBILITY AT ALL.
THERE IS NO ESCAPE! WE WILL BURN YOU OUT!
WAIT A MINUTE, YOU'RE NIKOLAI GOGOL!
WELL, THAT EXPLAINS THE BEAR. DOOP--

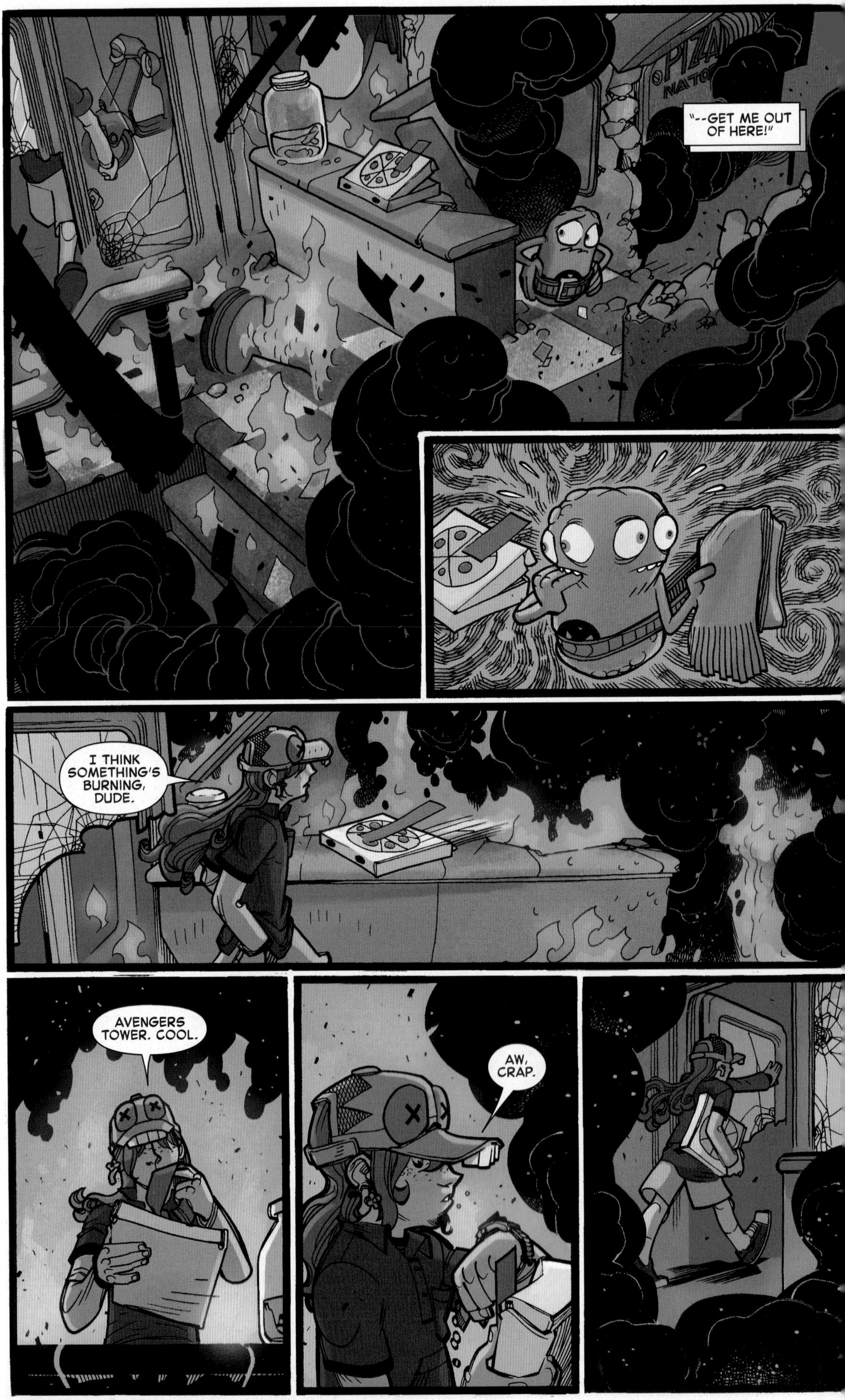

"--GET ME OUT OF HERE!"
I THINK SOMETHING'S BURNING, DUDE.
AVENGERS TOWER. COOL.
AW, CRAP.

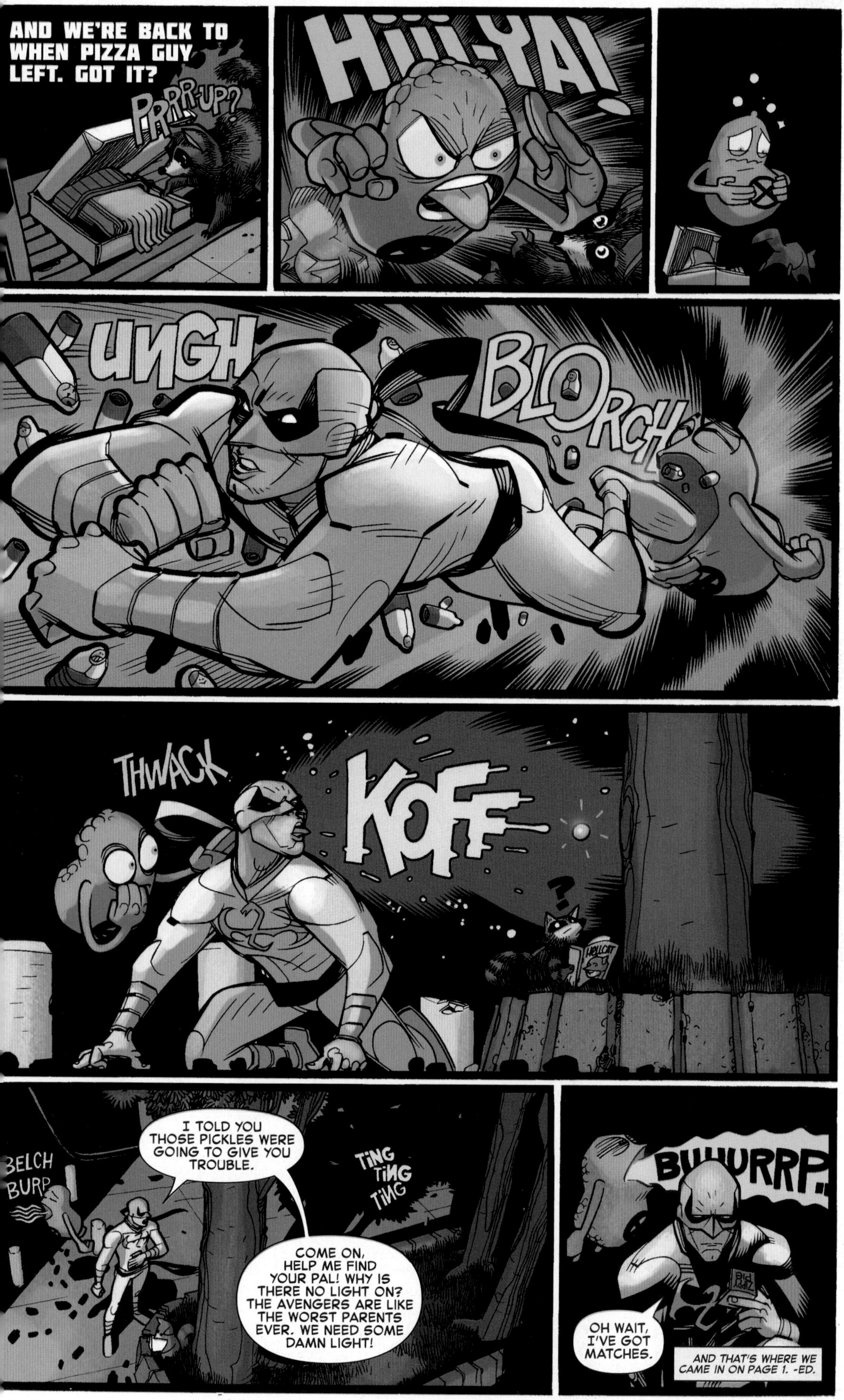
AND WE'RE BACK TO WHEN PIZZA GUY LEFT. GOT IT?
PRRR-UP?
HIII-YA!
UNGH
BLORCH
THWACK
KOFF
?
BELCH
BURP
I TOLD YOU THOSE PICKLES WERE GOING TO GIVE YOU TROUBLE.
TING TING TING
COME ON, HELP ME FIND YOUR PAL! WHY IS THERE NO LIGHT ON? THE AVENGERS ARE LIKE THE WORST PARENTS EVER. WE NEED SOME DAMN LIGHT!
BUUURRP..
OH WAIT, I'VE GOT MATCHES.
AND THAT'S WHERE WE CAME IN ON PAGE 1. -ED.

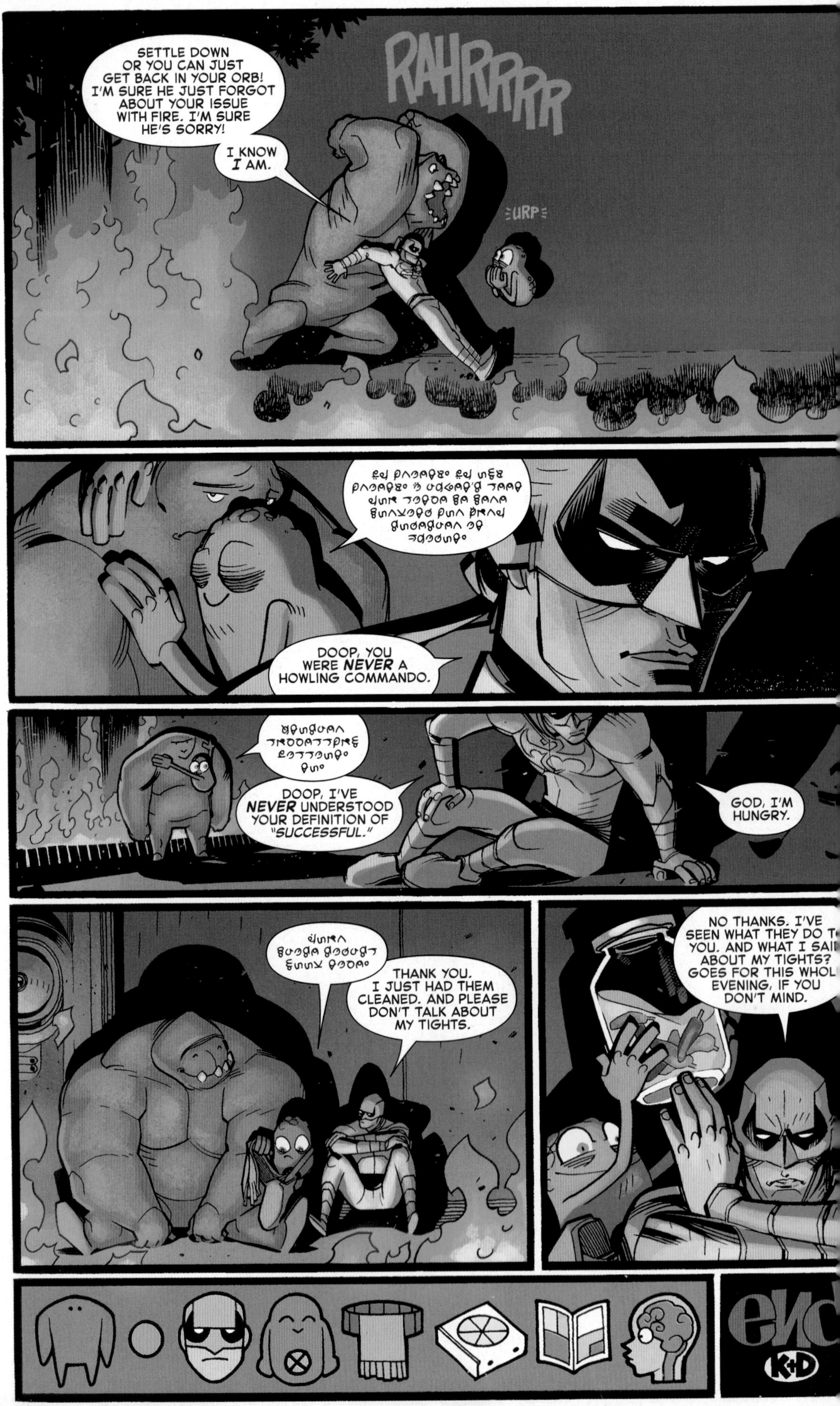
RAHRRRRR
SETTLE DOWN OR YOU CAN JUST GET BACK IN YOUR ORB! I'M SURE HE JUST FORGOT ABOUT YOUR ISSUE WITH FIRE. I'M SURE HE'S SORRY!
I KNOW I AM.
URP
DOOP, YOU WERE NEVER A HOWLING COMMANDO.
DOOP, I'VE NEVER UNDERSTOOD YOUR DEFINITION OF "SUCCESSFUL."
GOD, I'M HUNGRY.
THANK YOU. I JUST HAD THEM CLEANED. AND PLEASE DON'T TALK ABOUT MY TIGHTS.
NO THANKS. I'VE SEEN WHAT THEY DO T YOU. AND WHAT I SAI ABOUT MY TIGHTS? GOES FOR THIS WHOL EVENING, IF YOU DON'T MIND.
end
K+D

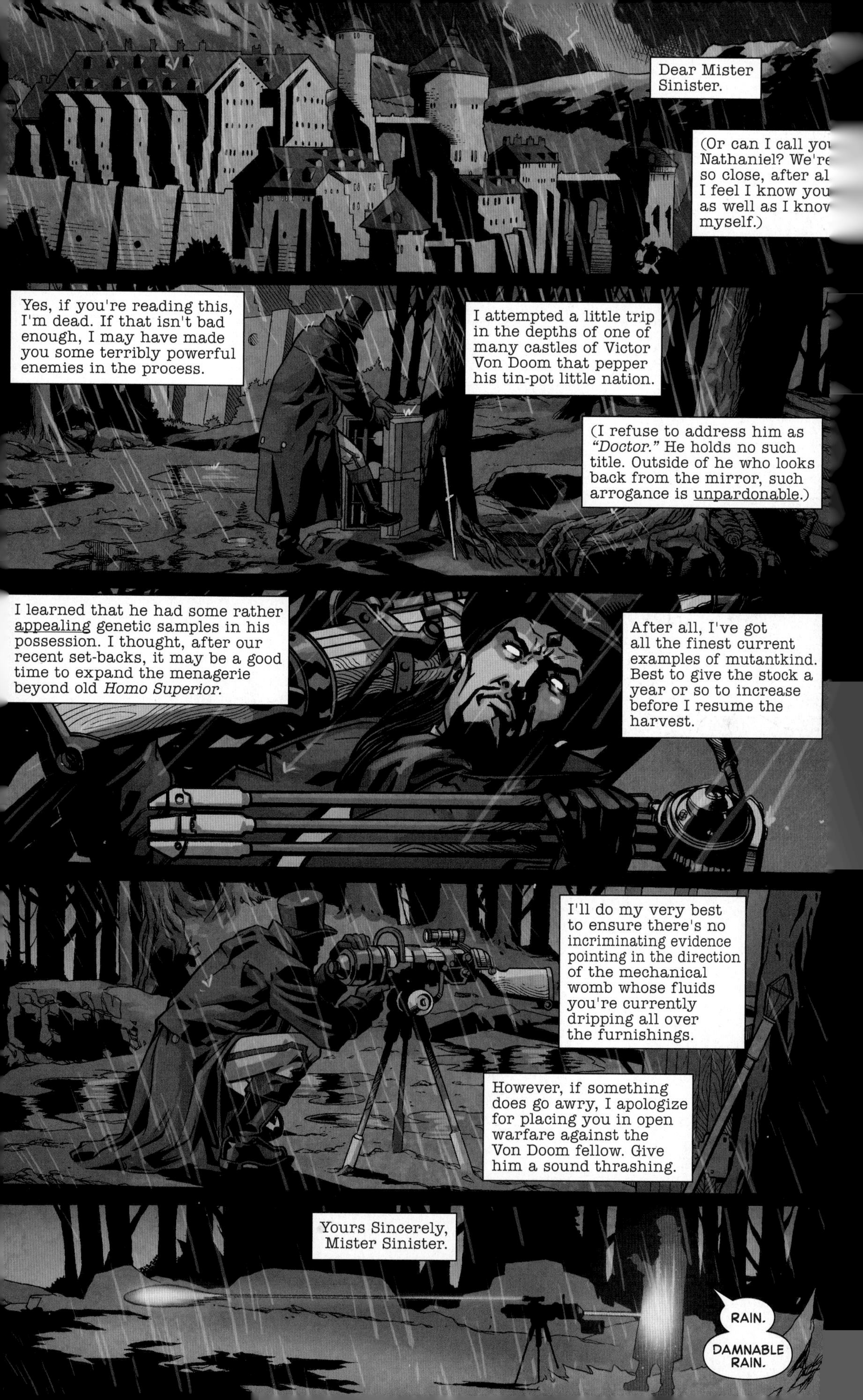
Dear Mister Sinister.
(Or can I call you Nathaniel? We're so close, after all. I feel I know you as well as I know myself.)
Yes, if you're reading this, I'm dead. If that isn't bad enough, I may have made you some terribly powerful enemies in the process.
I attempted a little trip in the depths of one of many castles of Victor Von Doom that pepper his tin-pot little nation.
(I refuse to address him as "Doctor." He holds no such title. Outside of he who looks back from the mirror, such arrogance is unpardonable.)
I learned that he had some rather appealing genetic samples in his possession. I thought, after our recent set-backs, it may be a good time to expand the menagerie beyond old Homo Superior.
After all, I've got all the finest current examples of mutantkind. Best to give the stock a year or so to increase before I resume the harvest.
I'll do my very best to ensure there's no incriminating evidence pointing in the direction of the mechanical womb whose fluids you're currently dripping all over the furnishings.
However, if something does go awry, I apologize for placing you in open warfare against the Von Doom fellow. Give him a sound thrashing.
Yours Sincerely, Mister Sinister.
RAIN.
DAMNABLE RAIN.

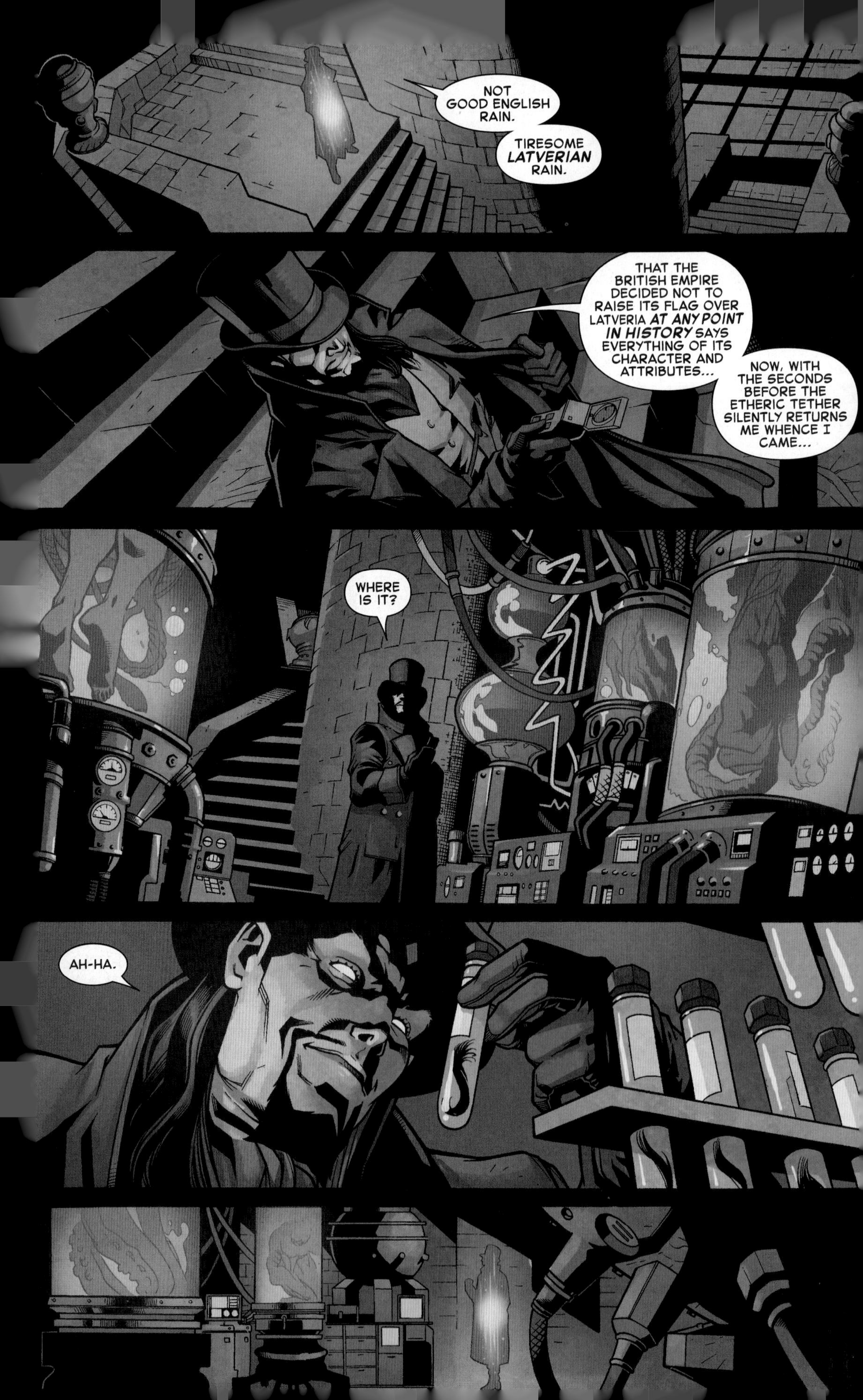
NOT GOOD ENGLISH RAIN.
TIRESOME *LATVERIAN* RAIN.
THAT THE BRITISH EMPIRE DECIDED NOT TO RAISE ITS FLAG OVER LATVERIA ***AT ANY POINT IN HISTORY*** SAYS EVERYTHING OF ITS CHARACTER AND ATTRIBUTES...
NOW, WITH THE SECONDS BEFORE THE ETHERIC TETHER SILENTLY RETURNS ME WHENCE I CAME...
WHERE IS IT?
AH-HA.

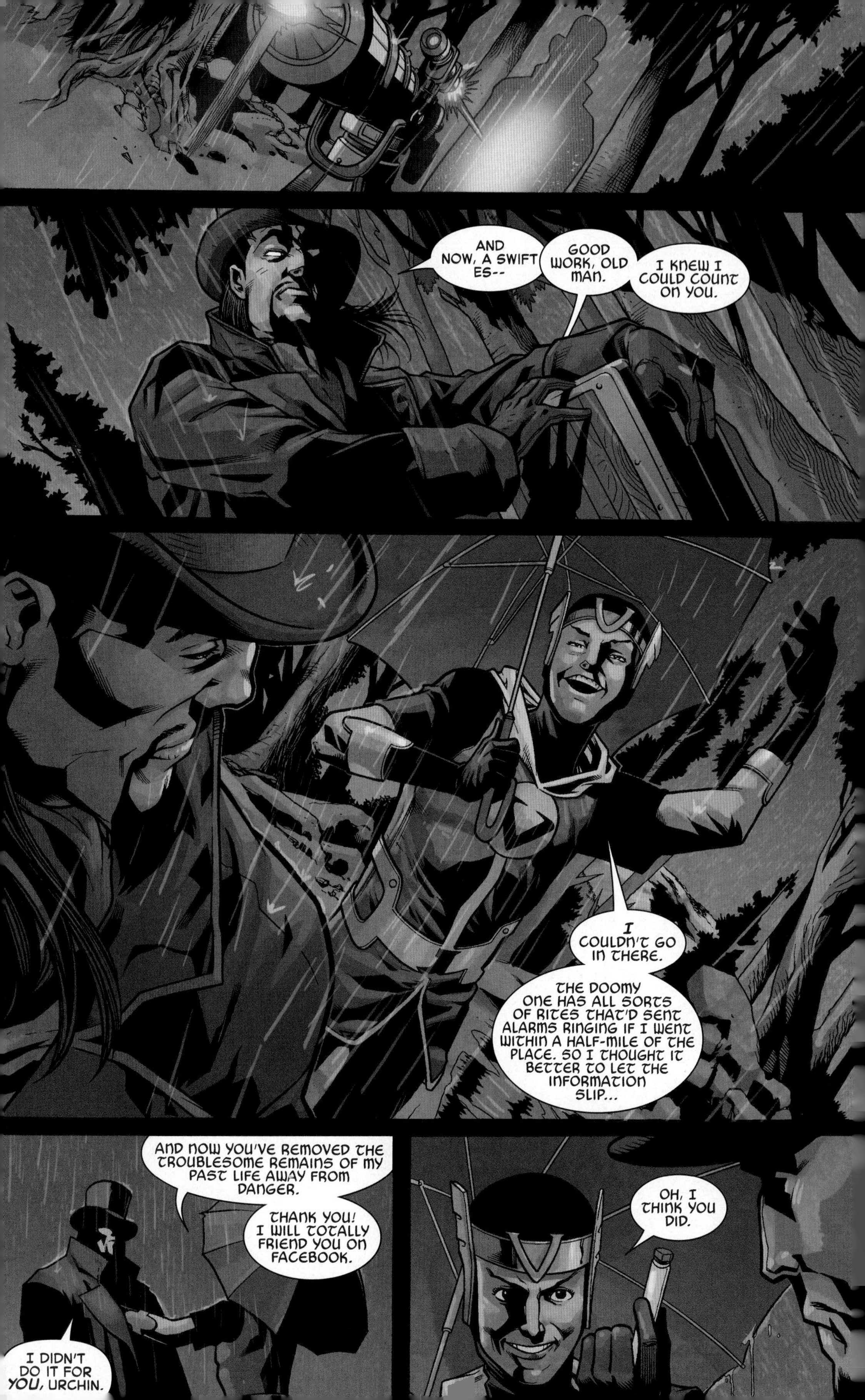
AND NOW, A SWIFT ES--
GOOD WORK, OLD MAN.
I KNEW I COULD COUNT ON YOU.
I COULDN'T GO IN THERE.
THE DOOMY ONE HAS ALL SORTS OF RITES THAT'D SENT ALARMS RINGING IF I WENT WITHIN A HALF-MILE OF THE PLACE. SO I THOUGHT IT BETTER TO LET THE INFORMATION SLIP...
AND NOW YOU'VE REMOVED THE TROUBLESOME REMAINS OF MY PAST LIFE AWAY FROM DANGER.
THANK YOU! I WILL TOTALLY FRIEND YOU ON FACEBOOK.
I DIDN'T DO IT FOR YOU, URCHIN.
OH, I THINK YOU DID.

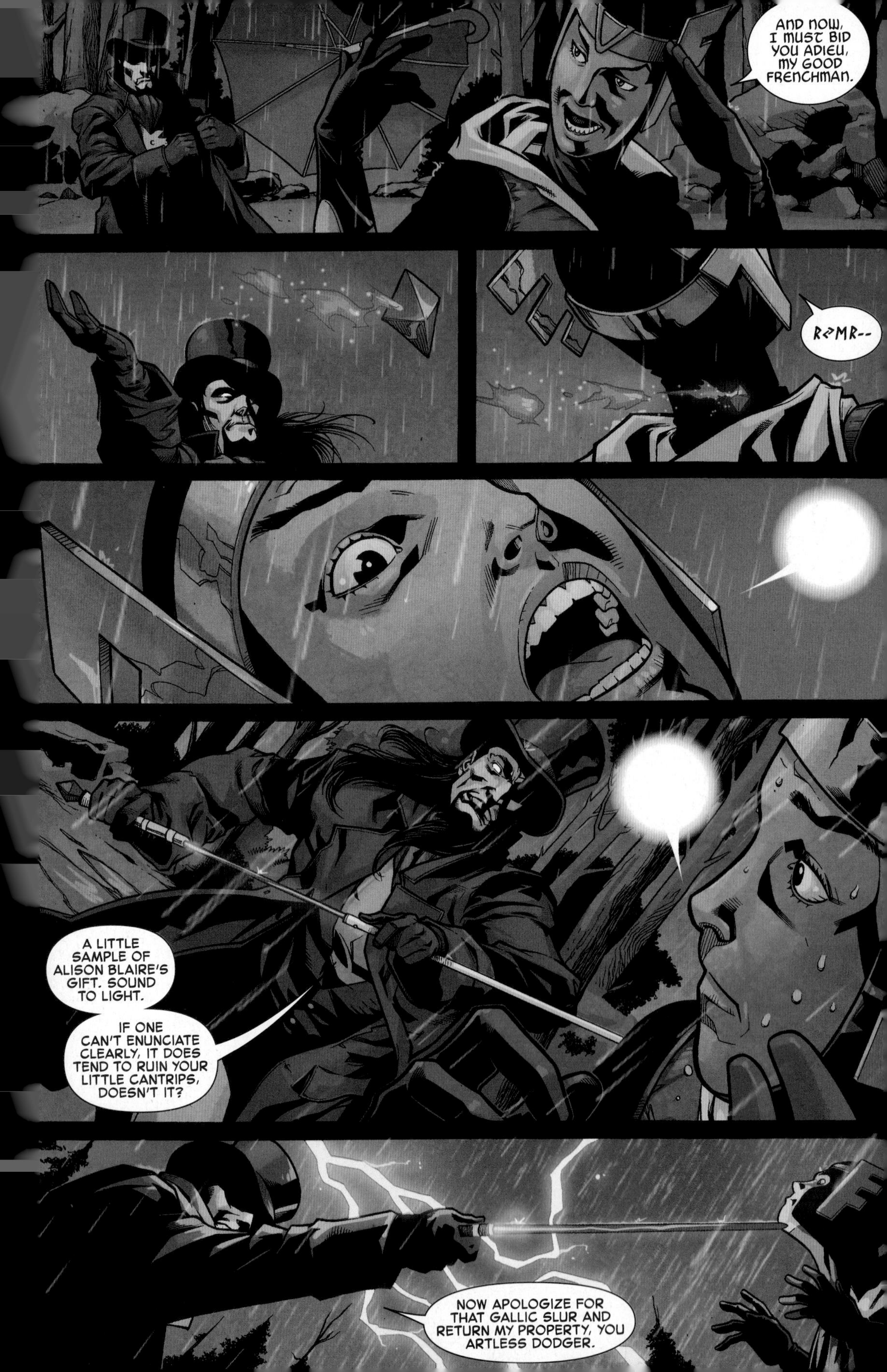
AND NOW, I MUST BID YOU ADIEU, MY GOOD FRENCHMAN.
RZMR--
A LITTLE SAMPLE OF ALISON BLAIRE'S GIFT. SOUND TO LIGHT.
IF ONE CAN'T ENUNCIATE CLEARLY, IT DOES TEND TO RUIN YOUR LITTLE CANTRIPS, DOESN'T IT?
NOW APOLOGIZE FOR THAT GALLIC SLUR AND RETURN MY PROPERTY, YOU ARTLESS DODGER.

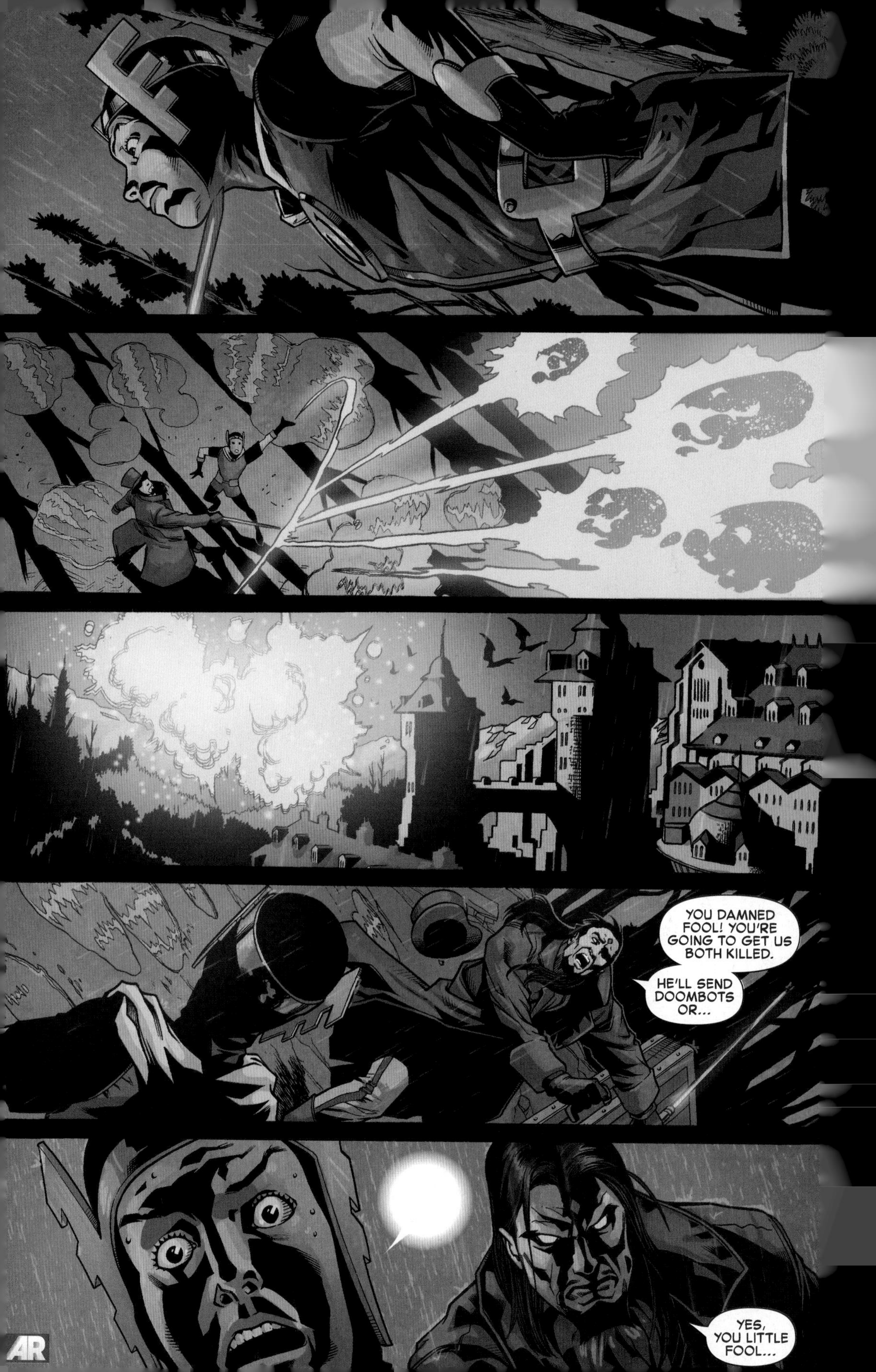
YOU DAMNED FOOL! YOU'RE GOING TO GET US BOTH KILLED.
HE'LL SEND DOOMBOTS OR...
YES, YOU LITTLE FOOL...
AR

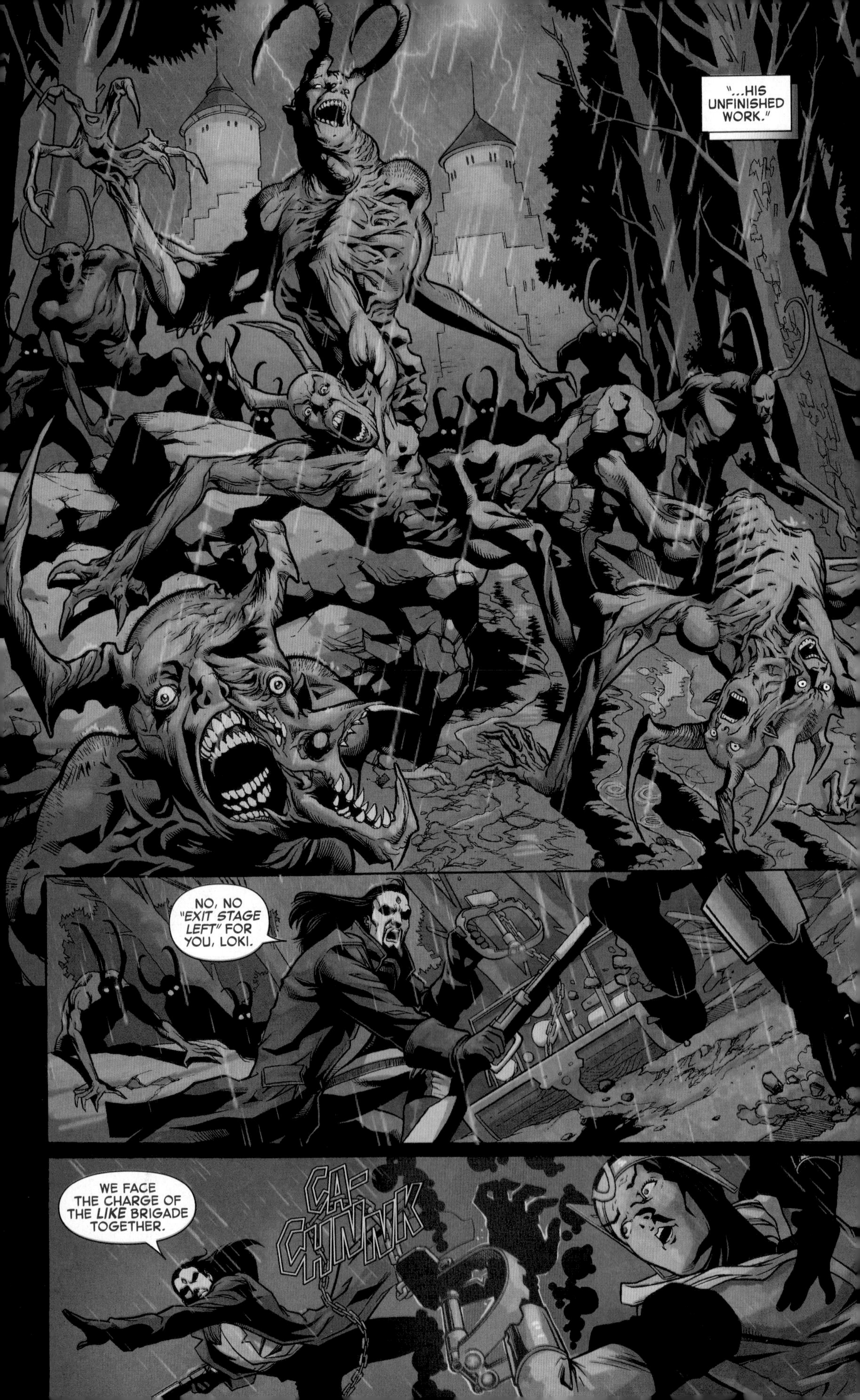
"...HIS UNFINISHED WORK."
NO, NO "EXIT STAGE LEFT" FOR YOU, LOKI.
WE FACE THE CHARGE OF THE LIKE BRIGADE TOGETHER.
CA-CHNNK

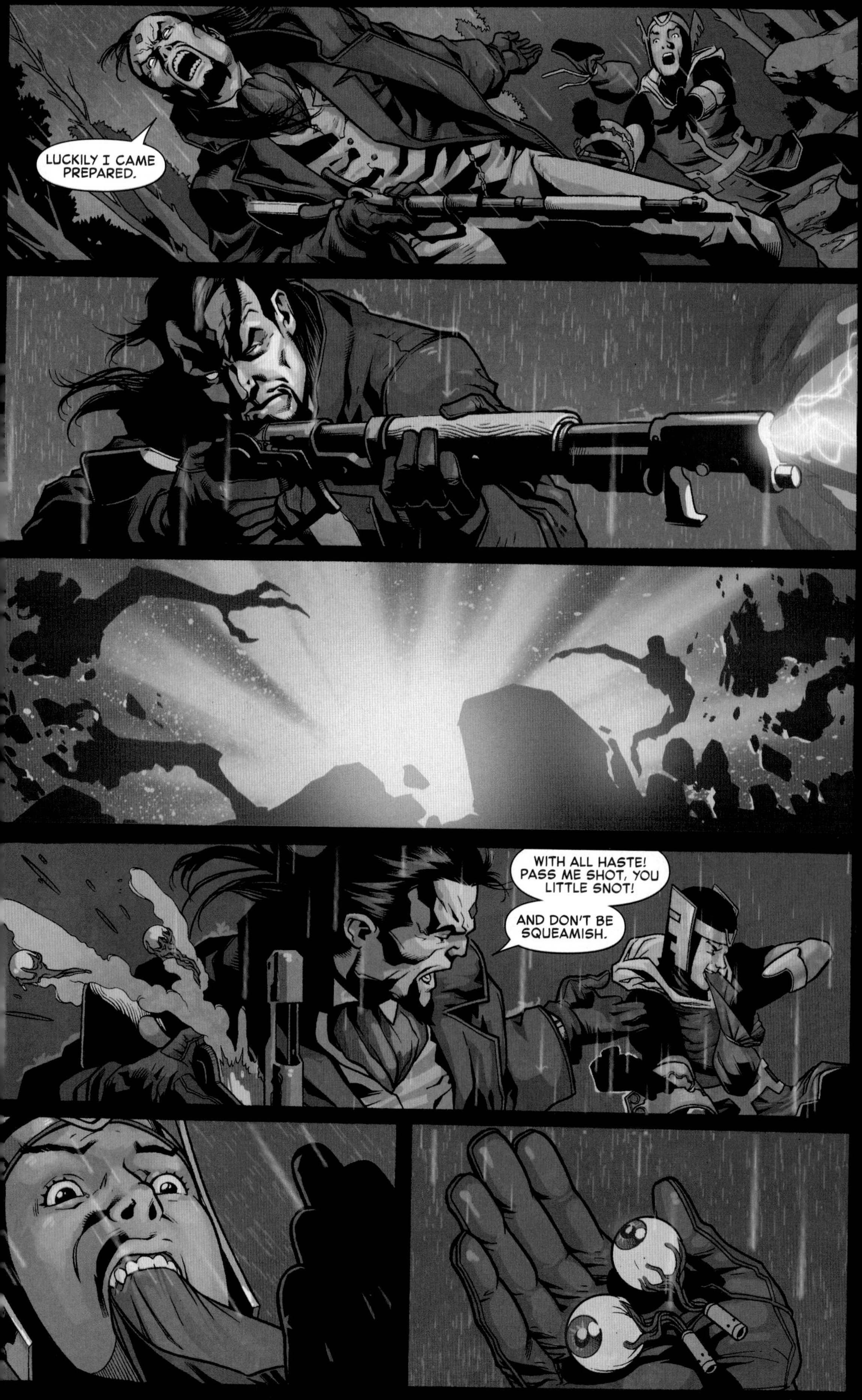
LUCKILY I CAME PREPARED.
WITH ALL HASTE! PASS ME SHOT, YOU LITTLE SNOT!
AND DON'T BE SQUEAMISH.

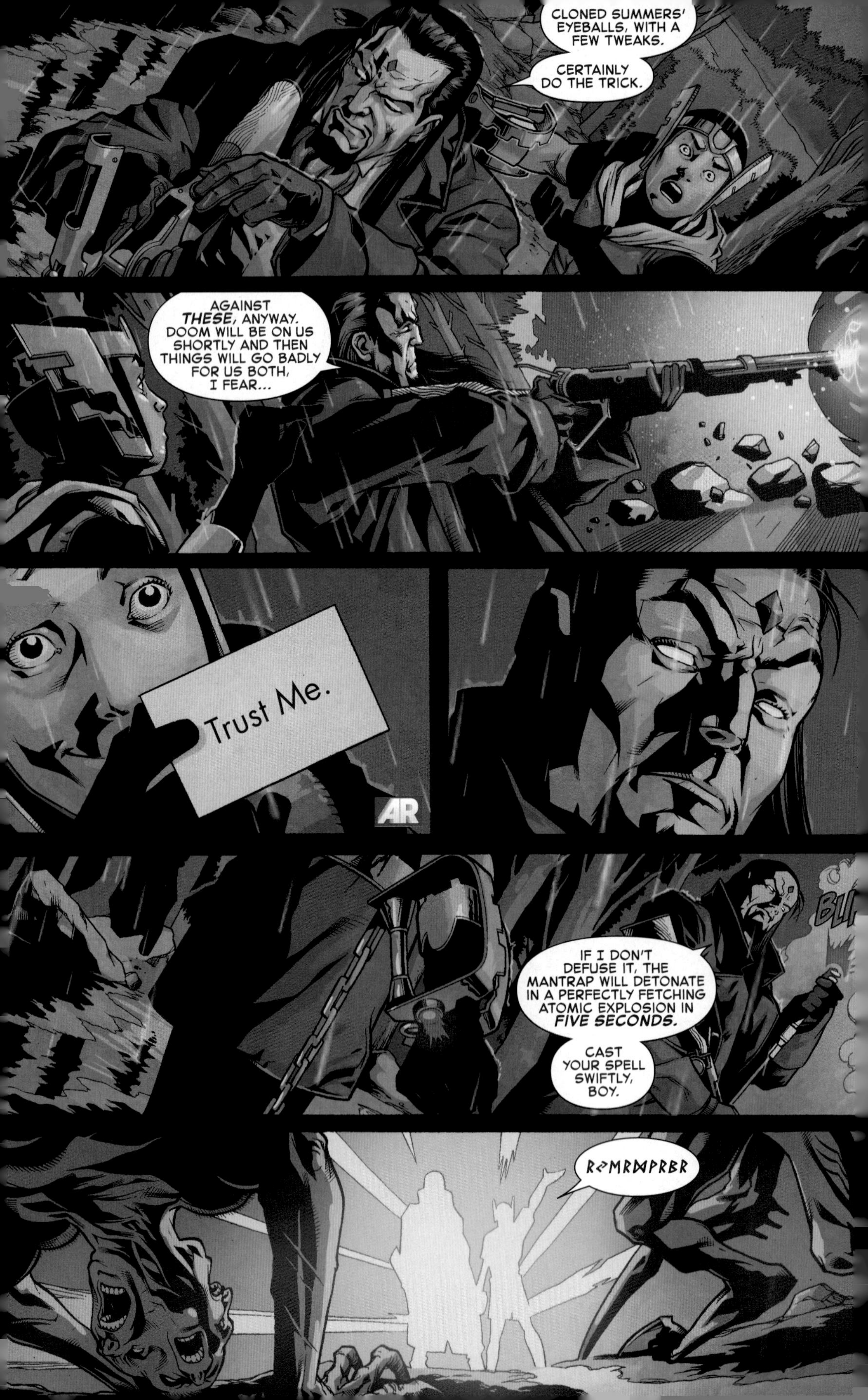
CLONED SUMMERS' EYEBALLS, WITH A FEW TWEAKS.
CERTAINLY DO THE TRICK.
AGAINST THESE, ANYWAY. DOOM WILL BE ON US SHORTLY AND THEN THINGS WILL GO BADLY FOR US BOTH, I FEAR...
Trust Me.
IF I DON'T DEFUSE IT, THE MANTRAP WILL DETONATE IN A PERFECTLY FETCHING ATOMIC EXPLOSION IN FIVE SECONDS.
CAST YOUR SPELL SWIFTLY, BOY.

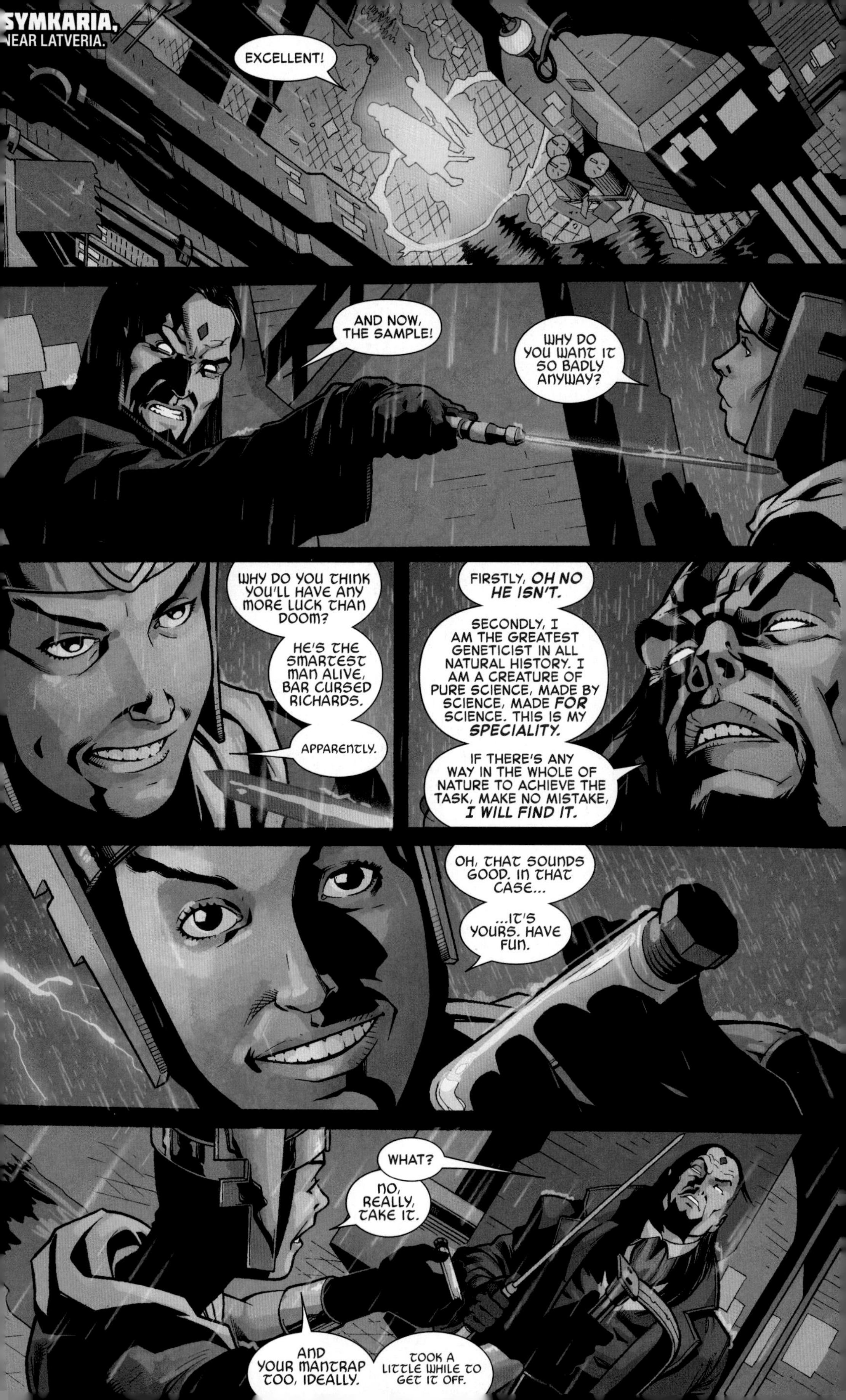
SYMKARIA,
NEAR LATVERIA.
EXCELLENT!
AND NOW, THE SAMPLE!
WHY DO YOU WANT IT SO BADLY ANYWAY?
WHY DO YOU THINK YOU'LL HAVE ANY MORE LUCK THAN DOOM?
HE'S THE SMARTEST MAN ALIVE, BAR CURSED RICHARDS.
APPARENTLY.
FIRSTLY, OH NO HE ISN'T.
SECONDLY, I AM THE GREATEST GENETICIST IN ALL NATURAL HISTORY. I AM A CREATURE OF PURE SCIENCE, MADE BY SCIENCE, MADE FOR SCIENCE. THIS IS MY SPECIALITY.
IF THERE'S ANY WAY IN THE WHOLE OF NATURE TO ACHIEVE THE TASK, MAKE NO MISTAKE, I WILL FIND IT.
OH, THAT SOUNDS GOOD. IN THAT CASE...
...IT'S YOURS. HAVE FUN.
WHAT?
NO, REALLY, TAKE IT.
AND YOUR MANTRAP TOO, IDEALLY.
TOOK A LITTLE WHILE TO GET IT OFF.

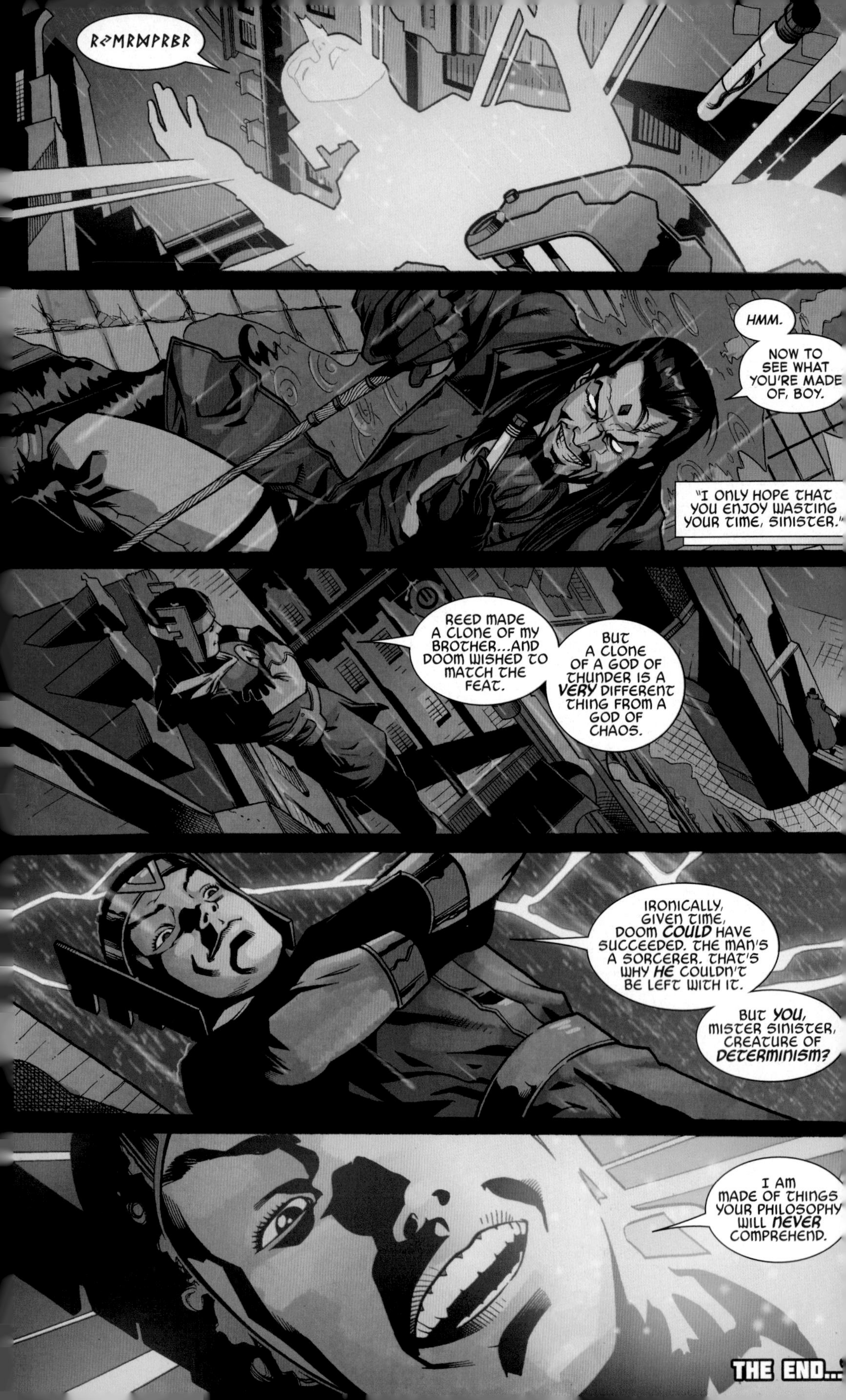

HMM.
NOW TO SEE WHAT YOU'RE MADE OF, BOY.
"I ONLY HOPE THAT YOU ENJOY WASTING YOUR TIME, SINISTER."
REED MADE A CLONE OF MY BROTHER...AND DOOM WISHED TO MATCH THE FEAT.
BUT A CLONE OF A GOD OF THUNDER IS A VERY DIFFERENT THING FROM A GOD OF CHAOS.
IRONICALLY, GIVEN TIME, DOOM COULD HAVE SUCCEEDED. THE MAN'S A SORCERER. THAT'S WHY HE COULDN'T BE LEFT WITH IT.
BUT YOU, MISTER SINISTER, CREATURE OF DETERMINISM?
I AM MADE OF THINGS YOUR PHILOSOPHY WILL NEVER COMPREHEND.
THE END...?

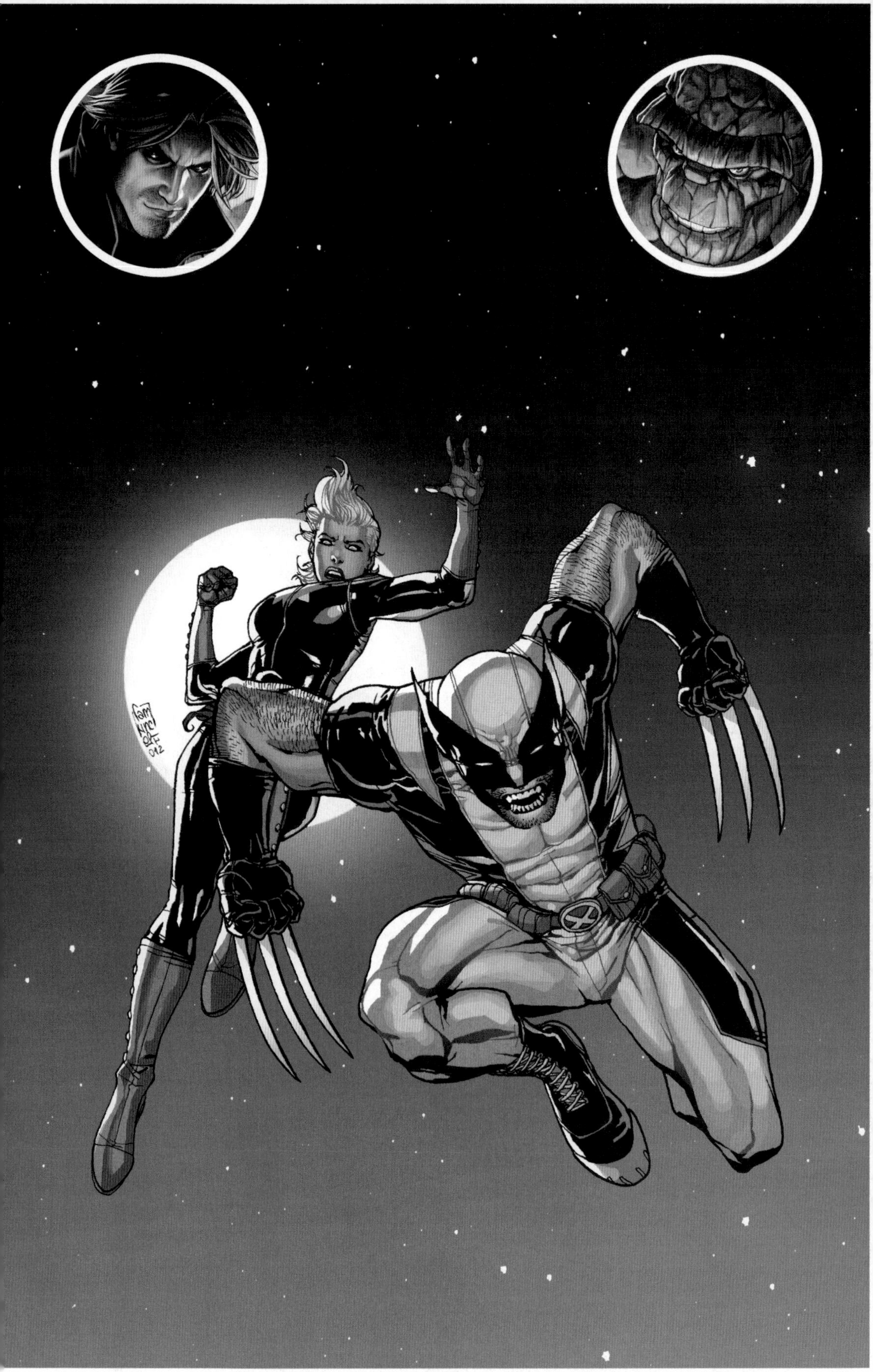

A + X = 6

A: DON'T EAT! Read A+X instead!

Q: I don't know—I was thinking about celery sticks with peanut butter on top, maybe?

A: That actually sounds PRETTY GOOD! But how about this SUPER HERO SANDWICH? Take one AVENGER, add one X-MAN, and TOSS them in a STICKY SITUATION.

Q: Sounds more like a gross salad than a sandwich, but I'm intrigued. What kind of flavors are we talking about?

A: How about CAJUN with a HIGH MINERAL CONTENT? THE THING, the Fantastic Four's punch-throwing pilot with ROCK-LIKE SKIN is mixing it up with GAMBIT, the X-Men's SUPER-THIEF who can excite molecules in objects until they EXPLODE!

Q: Okay, I'm on board! I'll just—

A: HOLD IT RIGHT THERE! A+X is a SMÖRGÅSBORD, not a SUPERMARKET SAMPLE. We're also serving a mélange of WOLVERINE, the mutant with a crazy HEALING FACTOR and ADAMANTIUM CLAWS, and all-around SUPER-lady CAPTAIN MARVEL.

Q: Hmm…I wonder if I'll be confused. Did Captain Marvel figure out that thing with her brain yet?

A: Do you have to meet the COW to enjoy the NACHO CHEESE?! Just READ.

Q: Wait a minute—does the comic taste like cheese?

A: There's only ONE WAY to FIND OUT.

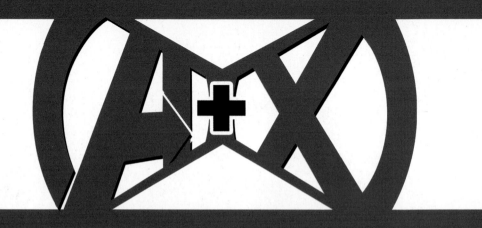

# CAPTAIN MARVEL + WOLVERINE

PETER **DAVID** — WRITER

GIUSEPPE **CAMUNCOLI** — ARTISTS WITH MICHELE **BENEVENTO**

DAN **BROWN** & ANDRES **MOSSA** — COLORISTS

VC'S CLAYTON **COWLES** — LETTERER

JENNIFER M. **SMITH** — ASST. EDITOR

JEANINE **SCHAEFER** — EDITOR

# THE THING + GAMBIT

MIKE **COSTA** — WRITER

STEFANO **CASELLI** — ARTIST

ANDRES **MOSSA** — COLORIST

VC'S CLAYTON **COWLES** — LETTERER

JORDAN D. **WHITE** — ASSOC. EDITOR

NICK **LOWE** — EDITOR

AXEL **ALONSO** — EDITOR IN CHIEF

JOE **QUESADA** — CHIEF CREATIVE OFFICER

DAN **BUCKLEY** — PUBLISHER

ALAN **FINE** — EXECUTIVE PRODUCER

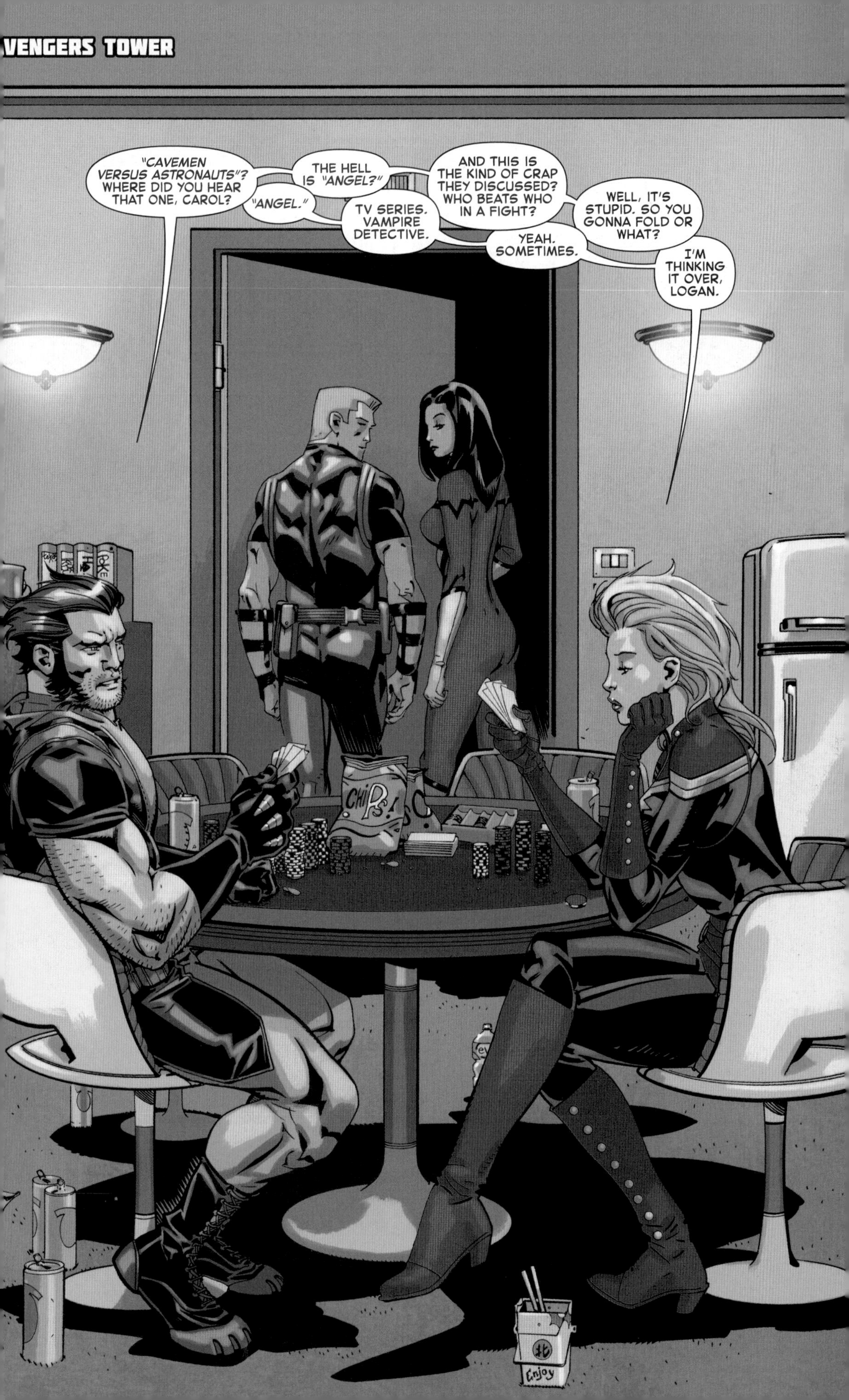
VENGERS TOWER
"CAVEMEN VERSUS ASTRONAUTS"? WHERE DID YOU HEAR THAT ONE, CAROL?
"ANGEL."
THE HELL IS "ANGEL?"
TV SERIES. VAMPIRE DETECTIVE.
AND THIS IS THE KIND OF CRAP THEY DISCUSSED? WHO BEATS WHO IN A FIGHT?
YEAH. SOMETIMES.
WELL, IT'S STUPID. SO YOU GONNA FOLD OR WHAT?
I'M THINKING IT OVER, LOGAN.
CHIPS!
Enjoy

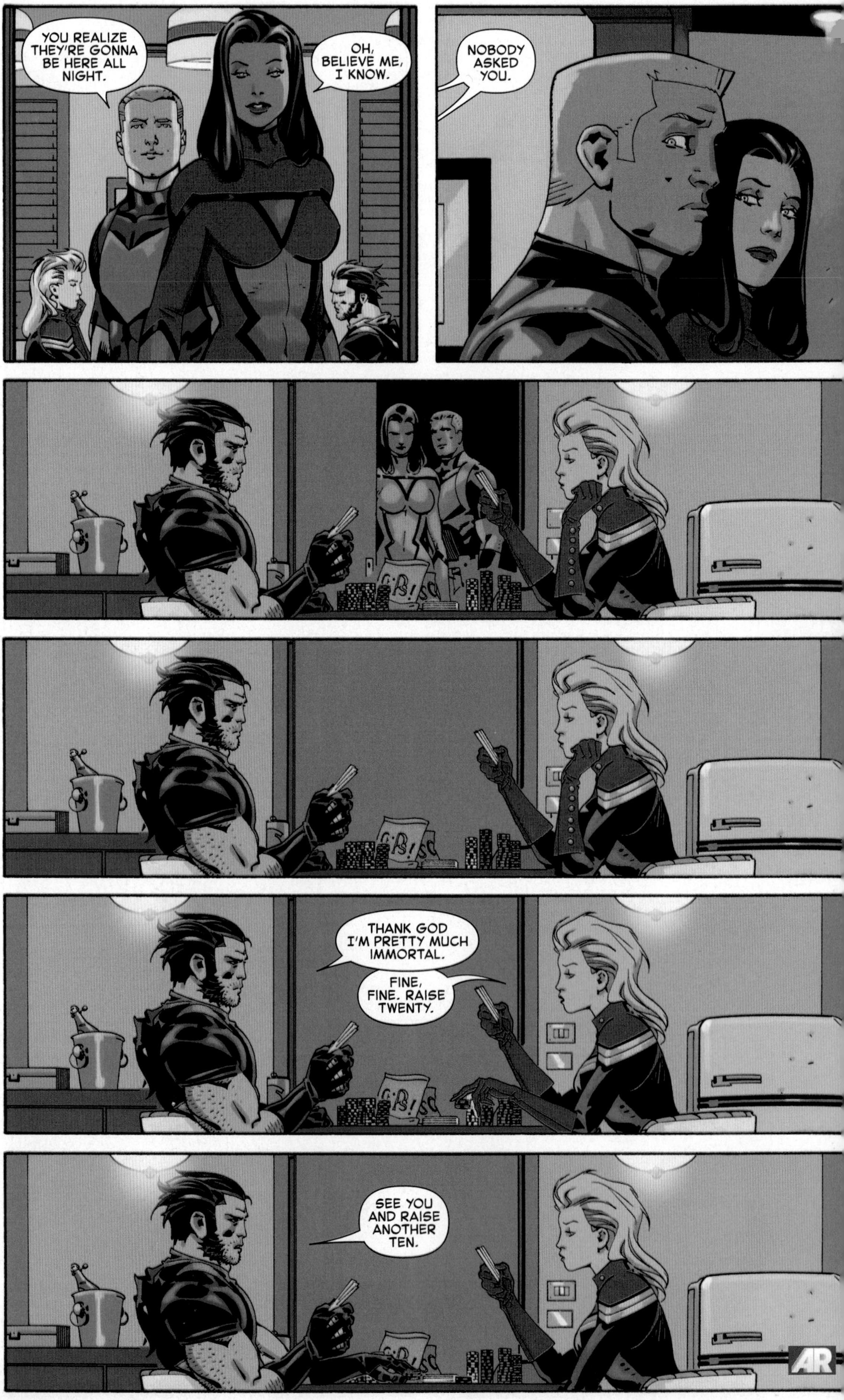
YOU REALIZE THEY'RE GONNA BE HERE ALL NIGHT.
OH, BELIEVE ME, I KNOW.
NOBODY ASKED YOU.
THANK GOD I'M PRETTY MUCH IMMORTAL.
FINE, FINE. RAISE TWENTY.
SEE YOU AND RAISE ANOTHER TEN.

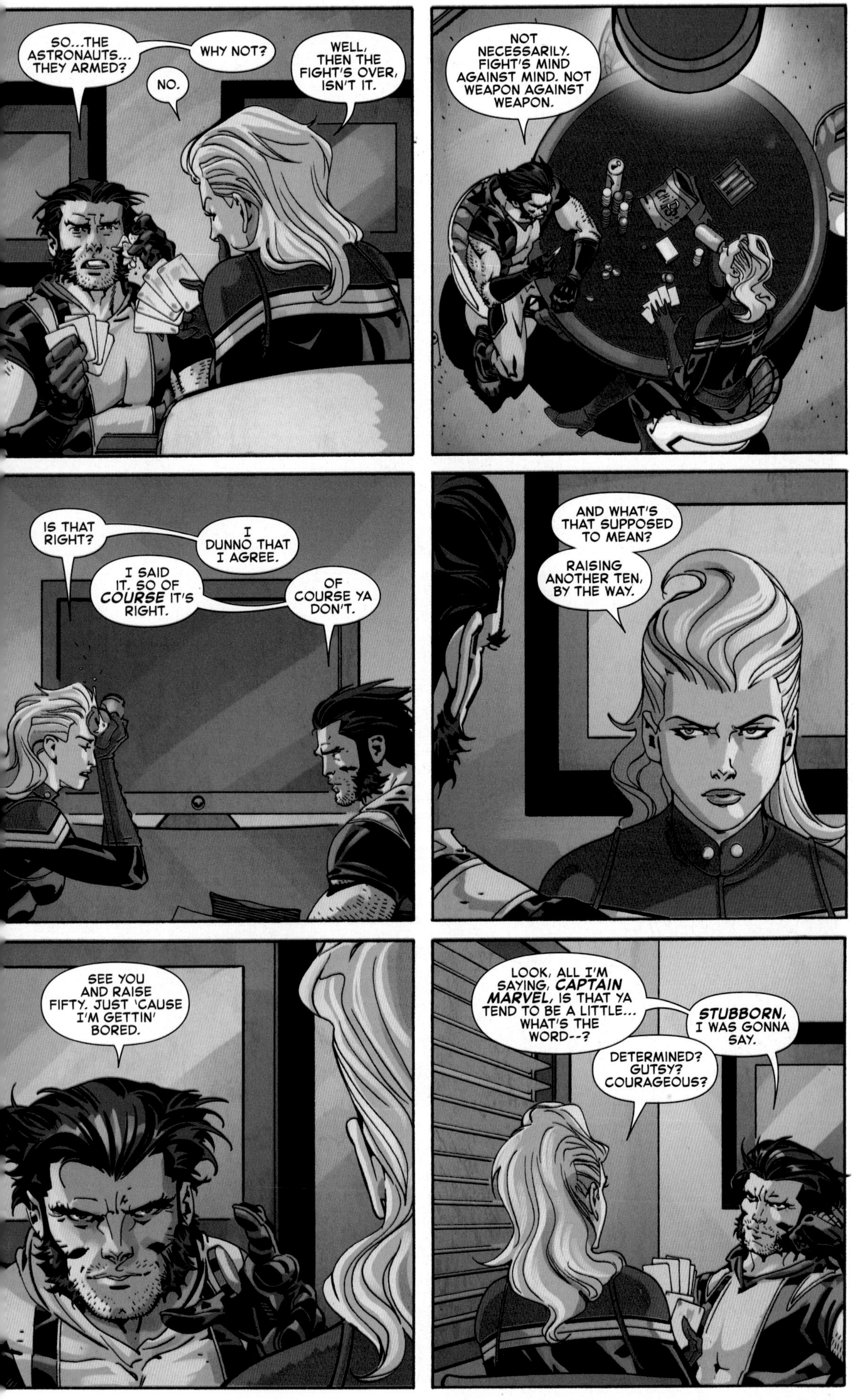
SO...THE ASTRONAUTS... THEY ARMED?
NO.
WHY NOT?
WELL, THEN THE FIGHT'S OVER, ISN'T IT.
NOT NECESSARILY. FIGHT'S MIND AGAINST MIND. NOT WEAPON AGAINST WEAPON.
IS THAT RIGHT?
I DUNNO THAT I AGREE.
I SAID IT. SO OF COURSE IT'S RIGHT.
OF COURSE YA DON'T.
AND WHAT'S THAT SUPPOSED TO MEAN?
RAISING ANOTHER TEN, BY THE WAY.
SEE YOU AND RAISE FIFTY. JUST 'CAUSE I'M GETTIN' BORED.
LOOK, ALL I'M SAYING, CAPTAIN MARVEL, IS THAT YA TEND TO BE A LITTLE... WHAT'S THE WORD--?
DETERMINED? GUTSY? COURAGEOUS?
STUBBORN, I WAS GONNA SAY.

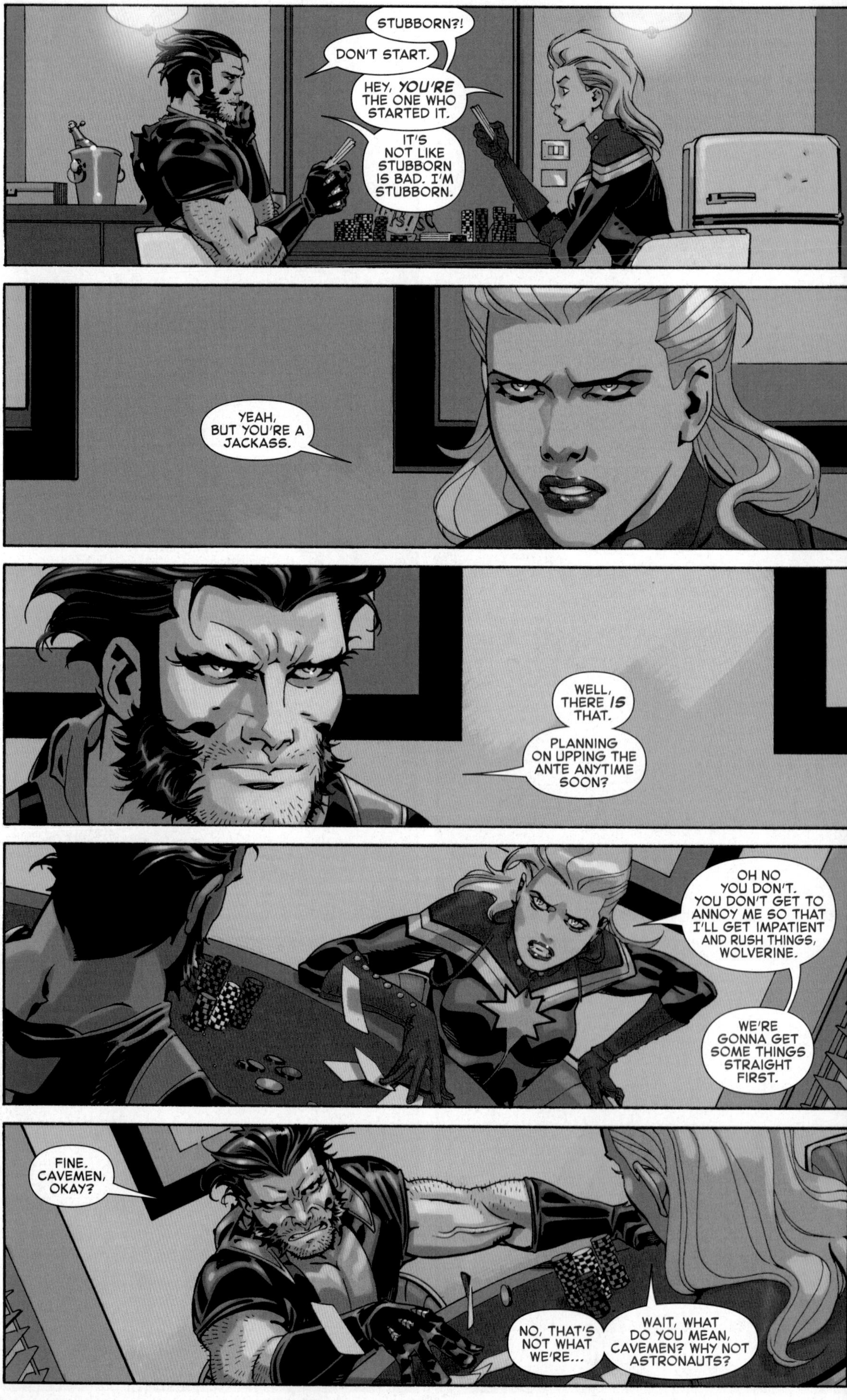
STUBBORN?!
DON'T START.
HEY, YOU'RE THE ONE WHO STARTED IT.
IT'S NOT LIKE STUBBORN IS BAD. I'M STUBBORN.
YEAH, BUT YOU'RE A JACKASS.
WELL, THERE IS THAT.
PLANNING ON UPPING THE ANTE ANYTIME SOON?
OH NO YOU DON'T. YOU DON'T GET TO ANNOY ME SO THAT I'LL GET IMPATIENT AND RUSH THINGS, WOLVERINE.
WE'RE GONNA GET SOME THINGS STRAIGHT FIRST.
FINE. CAVEMEN, OKAY?
NO, THAT'S NOT WHAT WE'RE...
WAIT, WHAT DO YOU MEAN, CAVEMEN? WHY NOT ASTRONAUTS?

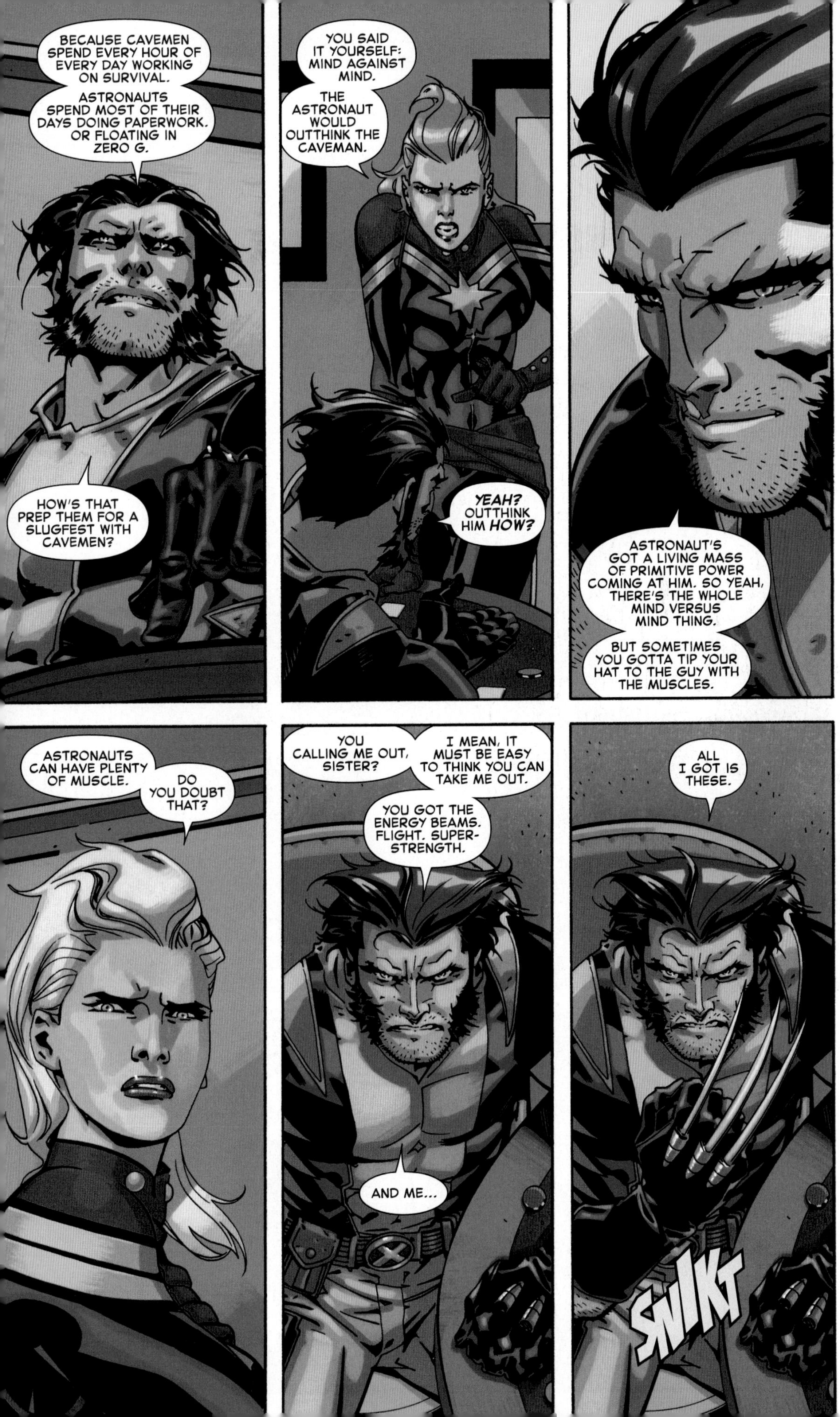
BECAUSE CAVEMEN SPEND EVERY HOUR OF EVERY DAY WORKING ON SURVIVAL.
ASTRONAUTS SPEND MOST OF THEIR DAYS DOING PAPERWORK. OR FLOATING IN ZERO G.
HOW'S THAT PREP THEM FOR A SLUGFEST WITH CAVEMEN?
YOU SAID IT YOURSELF: MIND AGAINST MIND.
THE ASTRONAUT WOULD OUTTHINK THE CAVEMAN.
YEAH? OUTTHINK HIM HOW?
ASTRONAUT'S GOT A LIVING MASS OF PRIMITIVE POWER COMING AT HIM. SO YEAH, THERE'S THE WHOLE MIND VERSUS MIND THING.
BUT SOMETIMES YOU GOTTA TIP YOUR HAT TO THE GUY WITH THE MUSCLES.
ASTRONAUTS CAN HAVE PLENTY OF MUSCLE.
DO YOU DOUBT THAT?
YOU CALLING ME OUT, SISTER?
I MEAN, IT MUST BE EASY TO THINK YOU CAN TAKE ME OUT.
YOU GOT THE ENERGY BEAMS. FLIGHT. SUPER-STRENGTH.
AND ME...
ALL I GOT IS THESE.
SNIKT

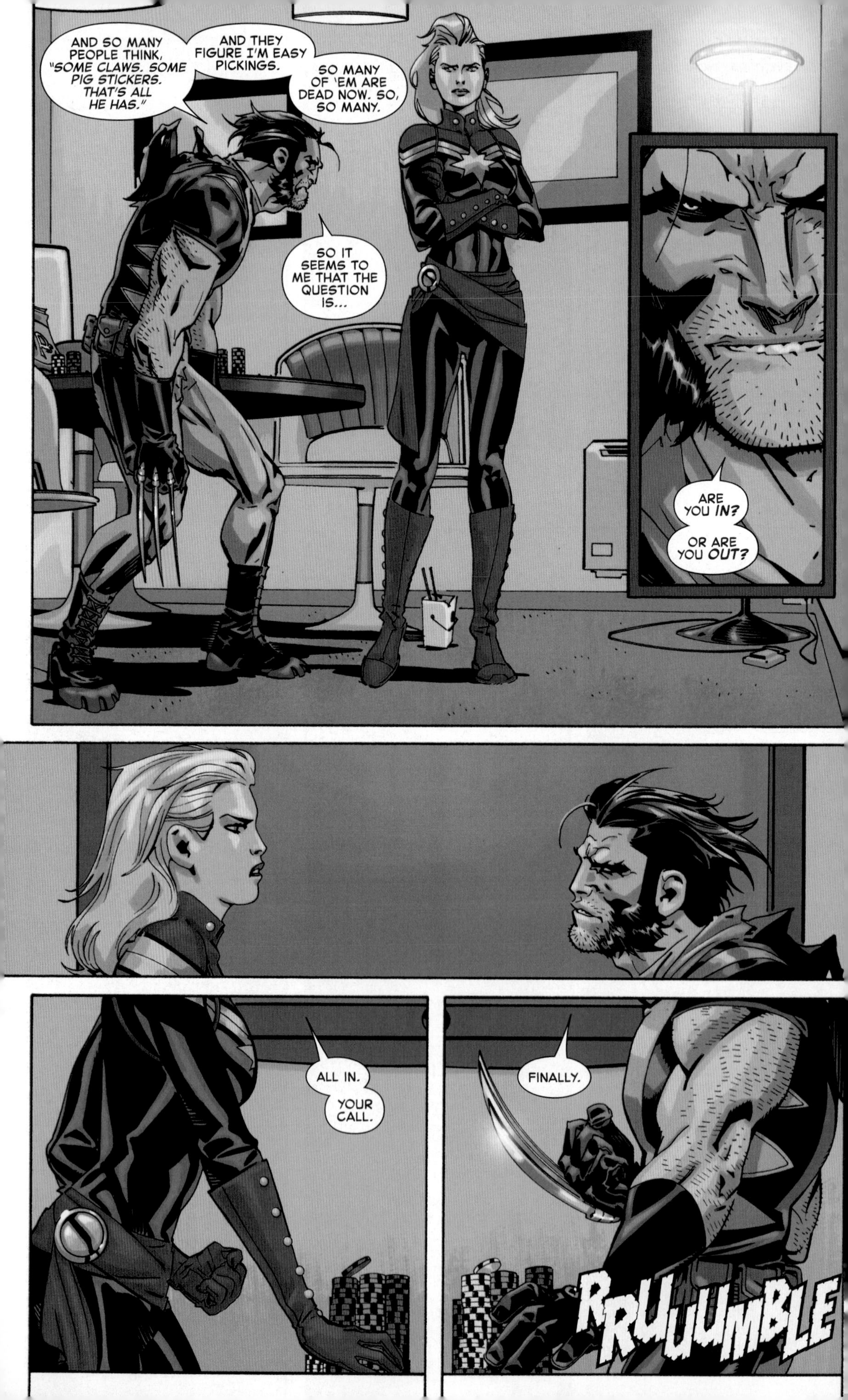
AND SO MANY PEOPLE THINK, "SOME CLAWS. SOME PIG STICKERS. THAT'S ALL HE HAS."
AND THEY FIGURE I'M EASY PICKINGS.
SO MANY OF 'EM ARE DEAD NOW. SO, SO MANY.
SO IT SEEMS TO ME THAT THE QUESTION IS...
ARE YOU *IN?*
OR ARE YOU *OUT?*
ALL IN.
YOUR CALL.
FINALLY.
RRUUUMBLE

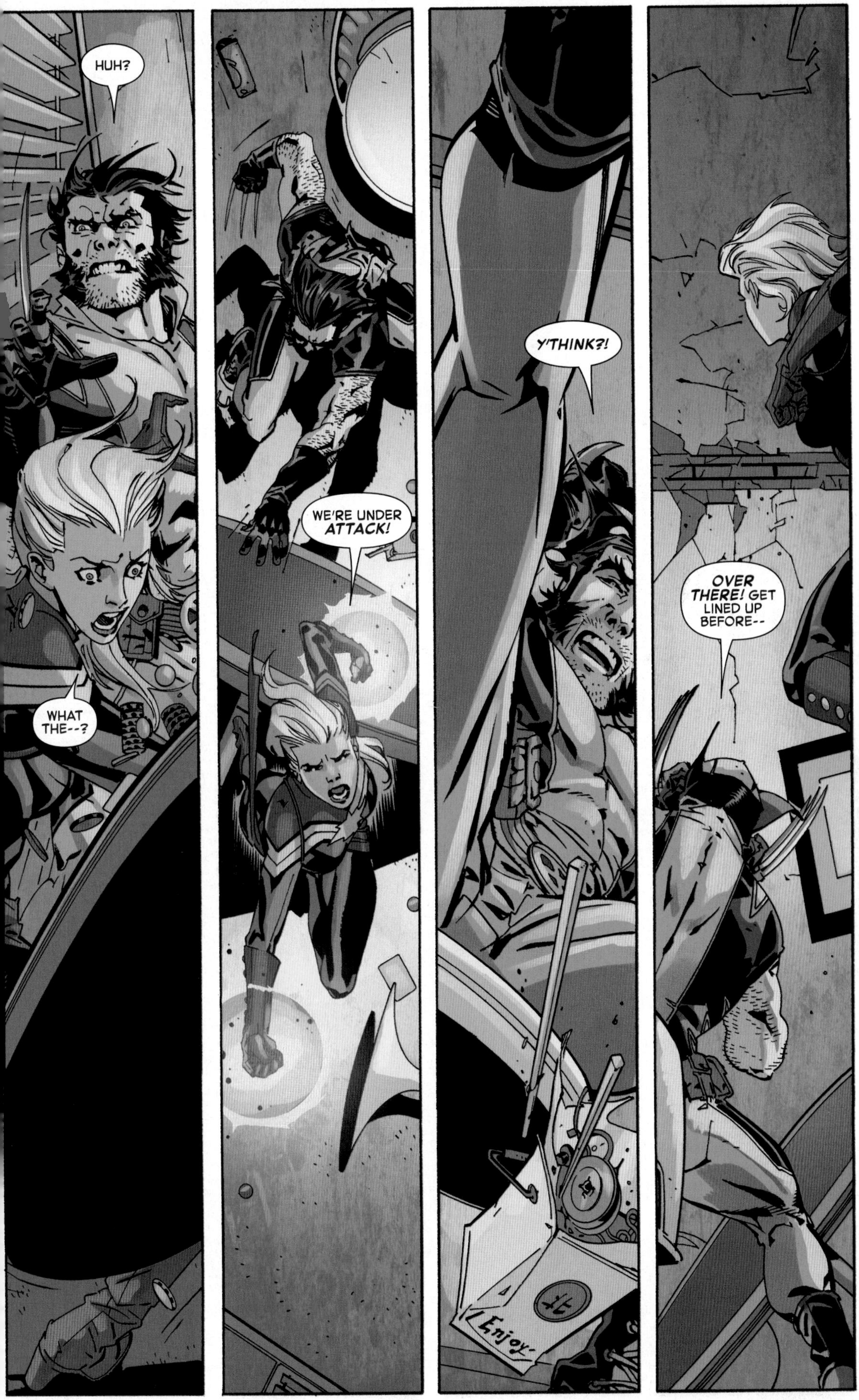
HUH?
WHAT THE--?
WE'RE UNDER ATTACK!
Y'THINK?!
OVER THERE! GET LINED UP BEFORE--
Enjoy-

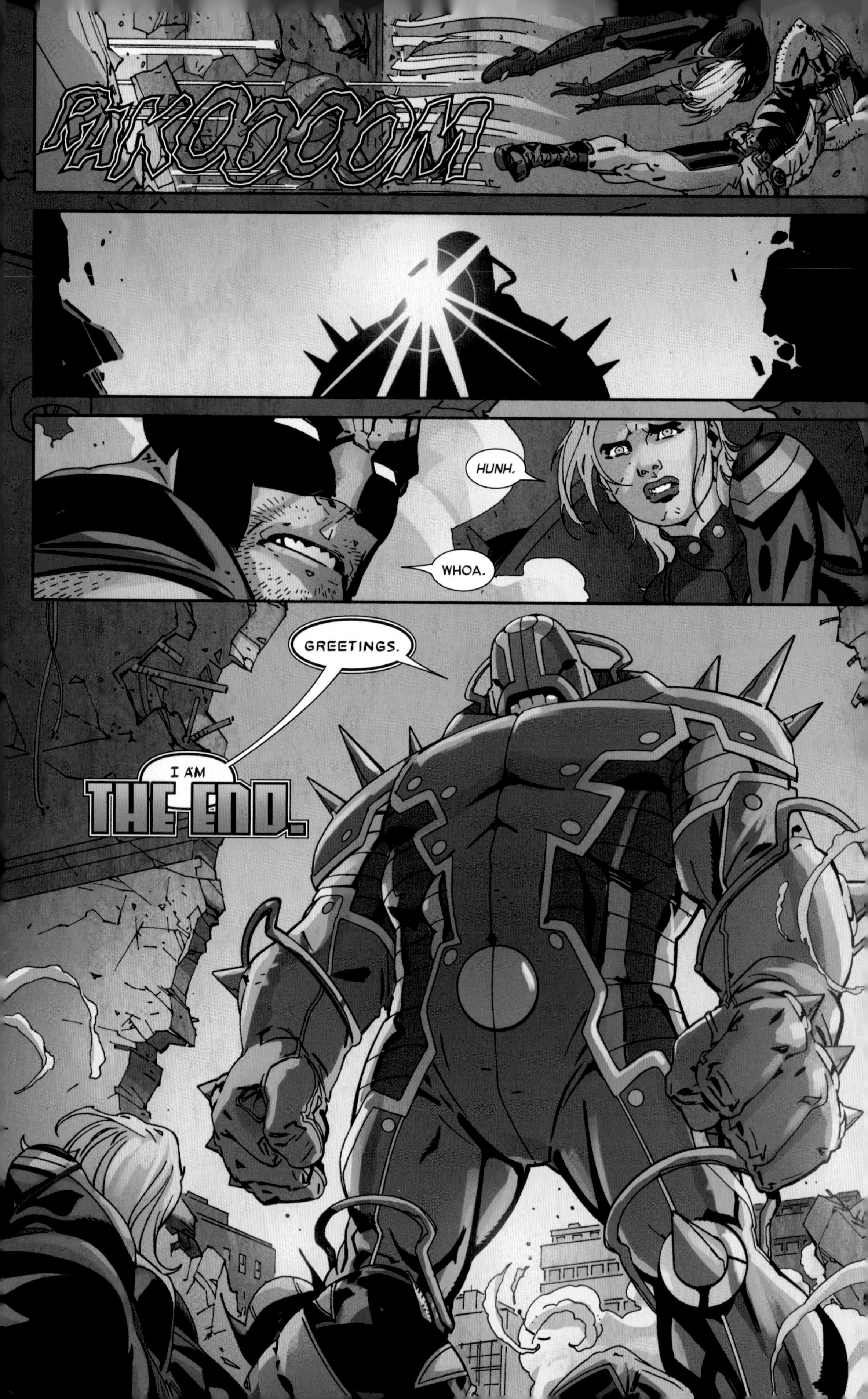

KRAKOOOOM
HUNH.
WHOA.
GREETINGS.
I AM
THE END.

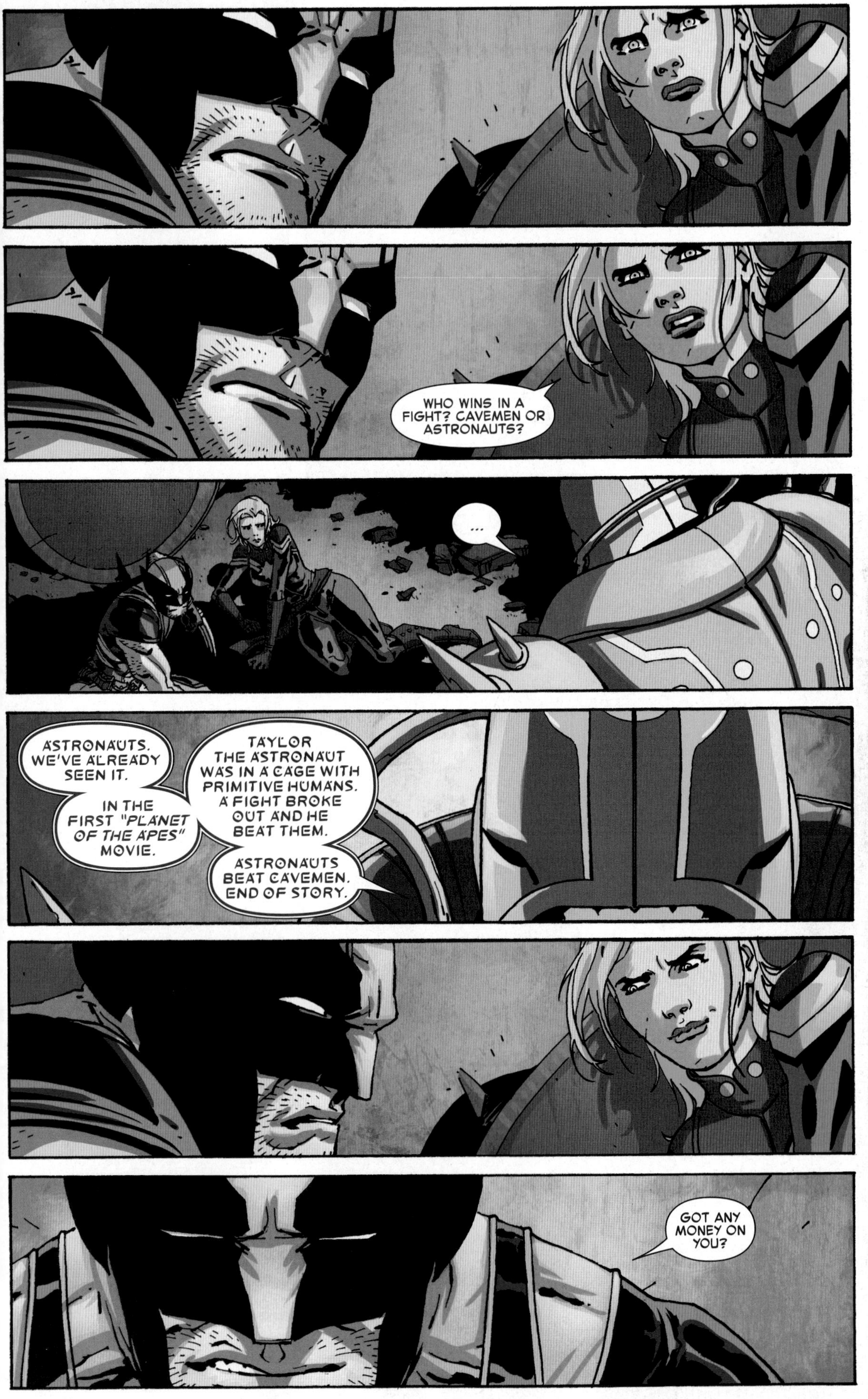
WHO WINS IN A FIGHT? CAVEMEN OR ASTRONAUTS?
...
ASTRONAUTS. WE'VE ALREADY SEEN IT.
IN THE FIRST "PLANET OF THE APES" MOVIE.
TAYLOR THE ASTRONAUT WAS IN A CAGE WITH PRIMITIVE HUMANS. A FIGHT BROKE OUT AND HE BEAT THEM.
ASTRONAUTS BEAT CAVEMEN. END OF STORY.
GOT ANY MONEY ON YOU?

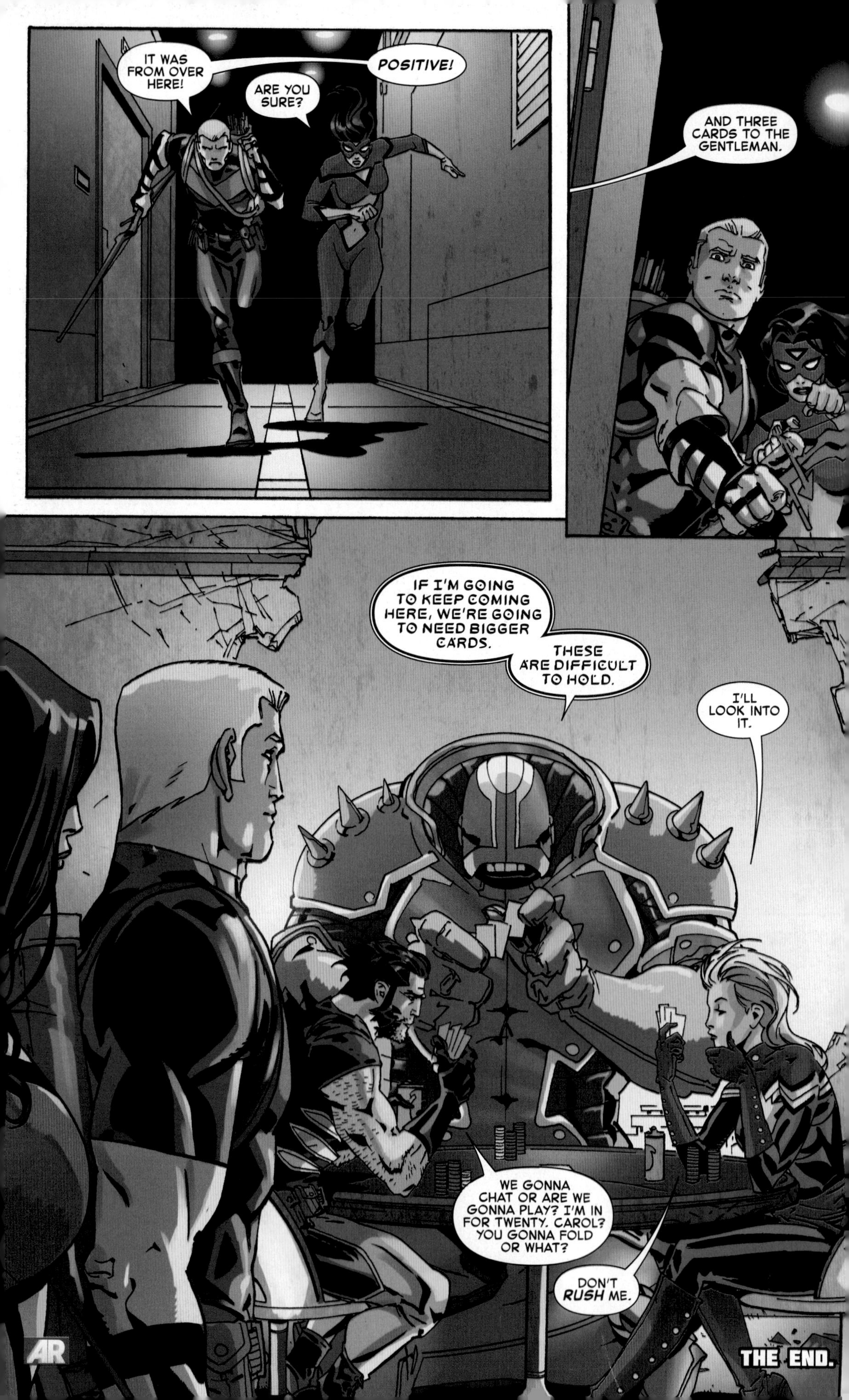
IT WAS FROM OVER HERE!
ARE YOU SURE?
POSITIVE!
AND THREE CARDS TO THE GENTLEMAN.
IF I'M GOING TO KEEP COMING HERE, WE'RE GOING TO NEED BIGGER CARDS.
THESE ARE DIFFICULT TO HOLD.
I'LL LOOK INTO IT.
WE GONNA CHAT OR ARE WE GONNA PLAY? I'M IN FOR TWENTY. CAROL? YOU GONNA FOLD OR WHAT?
DON'T RUSH ME.
THE END.

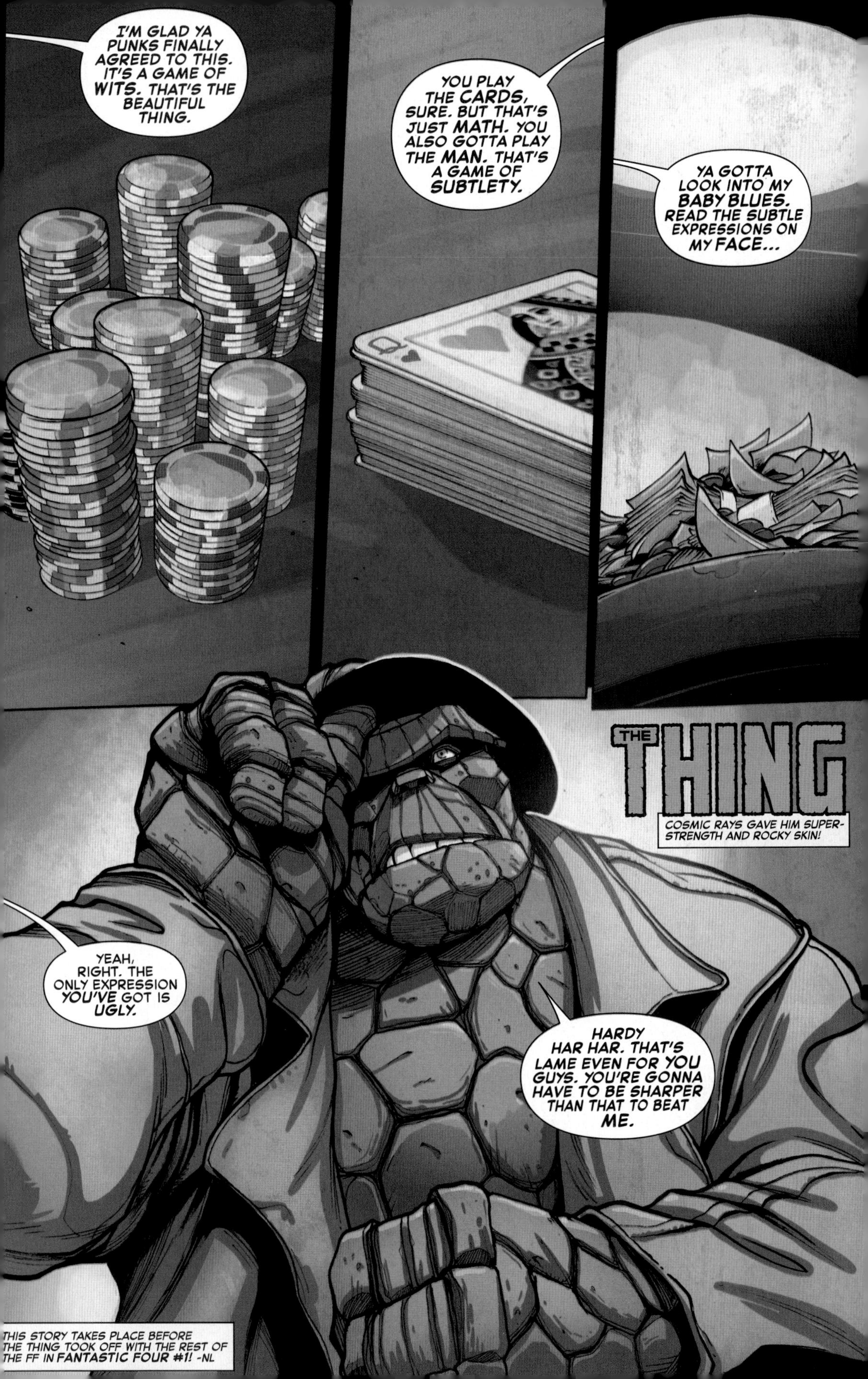
I'M GLAD YA PUNKS FINALLY AGREED TO THIS. IT'S A GAME OF WITS. THAT'S THE BEAUTIFUL THING.
YOU PLAY THE CARDS, SURE. BUT THAT'S JUST MATH. YOU ALSO GOTTA PLAY THE MAN. THAT'S A GAME OF SUBTLETY.
YA GOTTA LOOK INTO MY BABY BLUES. READ THE SUBTLE EXPRESSIONS ON MY FACE...
THE THING
COSMIC RAYS GAVE HIM SUPER-STRENGTH AND ROCKY SKIN!
YEAH, RIGHT. THE ONLY EXPRESSION YOU'VE GOT IS UGLY.
HARDY HAR HAR. THAT'S LAME EVEN FOR YOU GUYS. YOU'RE GONNA HAVE TO BE SHARPER THAN THAT TO BEAT ME.
THIS STORY TAKES PLACE BEFORE THE THING TOOK OFF WITH THE REST OF THE FF IN FANTASTIC FOUR #1! -NL

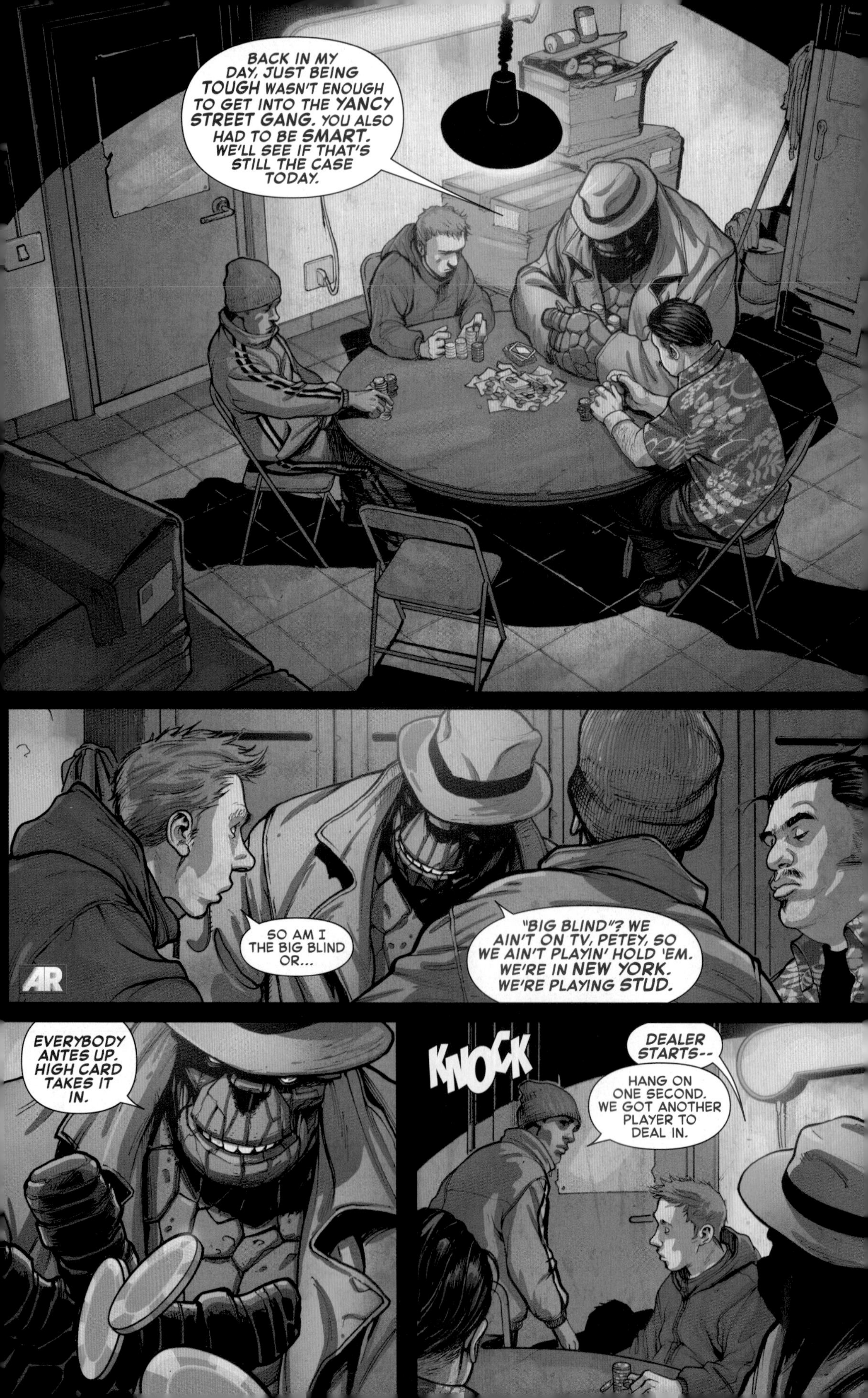
BACK IN MY DAY, JUST BEING TOUGH WASN'T ENOUGH TO GET INTO THE YANCY STREET GANG. YOU ALSO HAD TO BE SMART. WE'LL SEE IF THAT'S STILL THE CASE TODAY.
SO AM I THE BIG BLIND OR...
"BIG BLIND"? WE AIN'T ON TV, PETEY, SO WE AIN'T PLAYIN' HOLD 'EM. WE'RE IN NEW YORK. WE'RE PLAYING STUD.
EVERYBODY ANTES UP. HIGH CARD TAKES IT IN.
KNOCK
DEALER STARTS--
HANG ON ONE SECOND. WE GOT ANOTHER PLAYER TO DEAL IN.

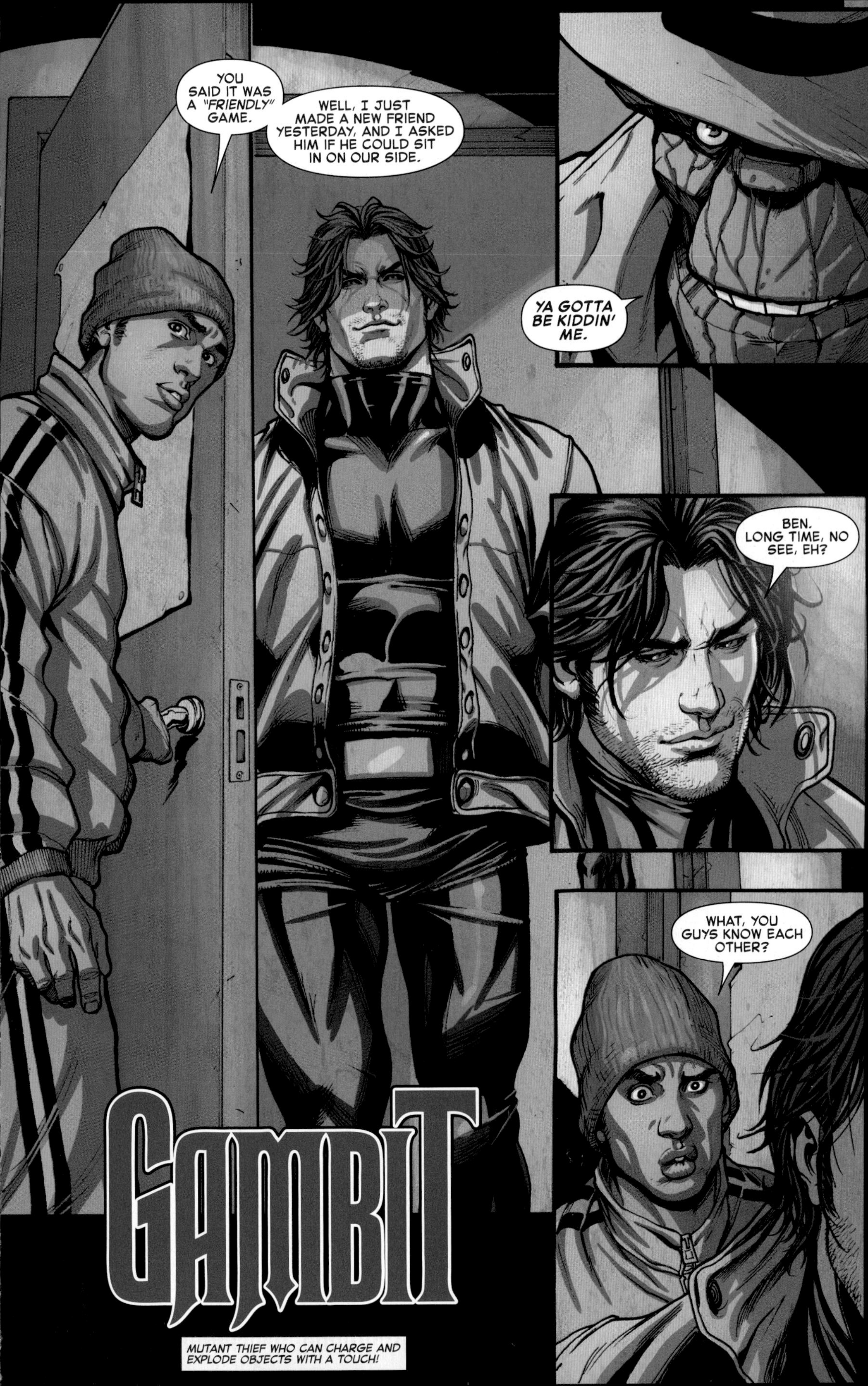
YOU SAID IT WAS A "FRIENDLY" GAME.
WELL, I JUST MADE A NEW FRIEND YESTERDAY, AND I ASKED HIM IF HE COULD SIT IN ON OUR SIDE.
YA GOTTA BE KIDDIN' ME.
BEN. LONG TIME, NO SEE, EH?
WHAT, YOU GUYS KNOW EACH OTHER?
GAMBIT
MUTANT THIEF WHO CAN CHARGE AND EXPLODE OBJECTS WITH A TOUCH!

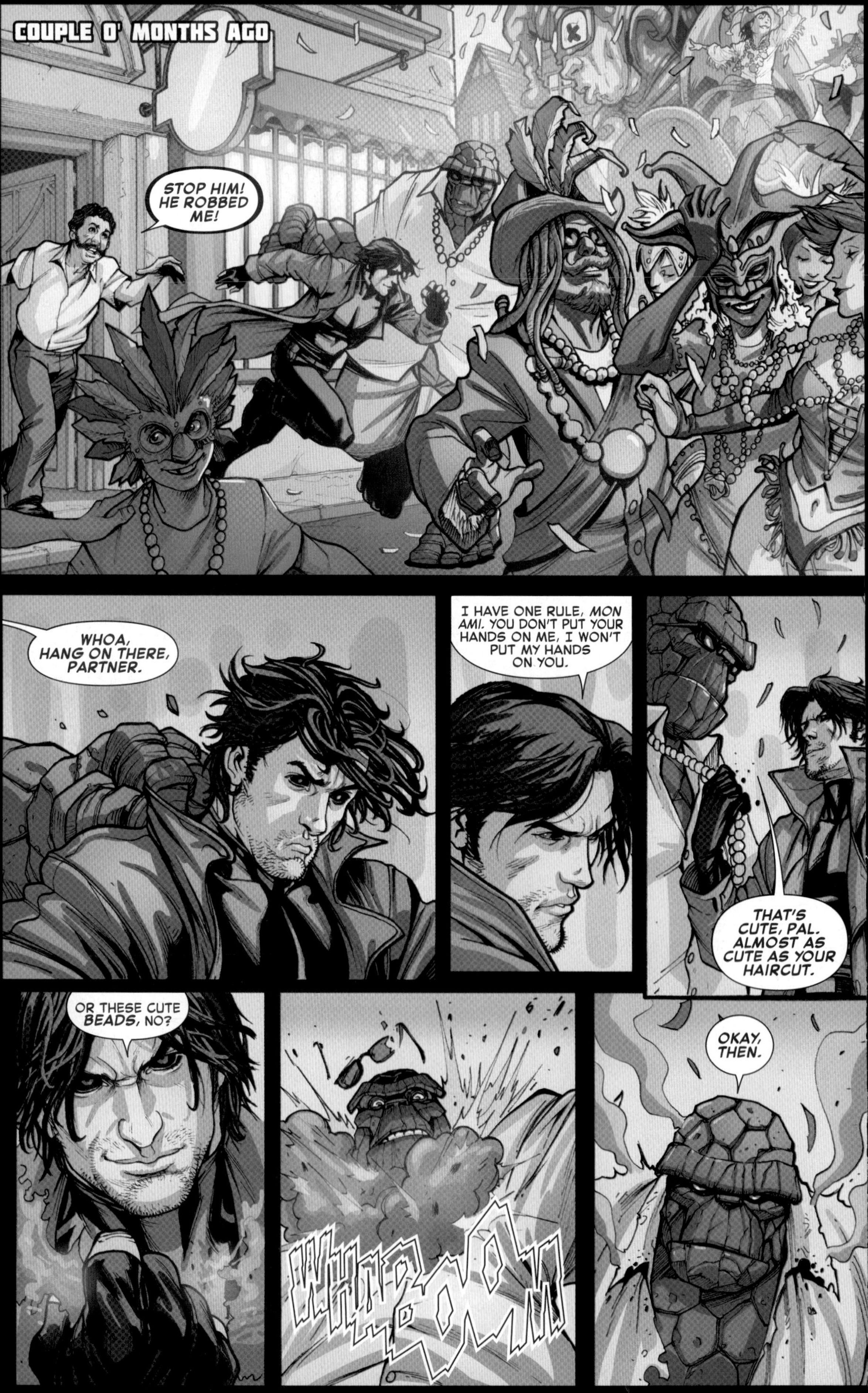
COUPLE O' MONTHS AGO
STOP HIM! HE ROBBED ME!
WHOA, HANG ON THERE, PARTNER.
I HAVE ONE RULE, MON AMI. YOU DON'T PUT YOUR HANDS ON ME, I WON'T PUT MY HANDS ON YOU.
THAT'S CUTE, PAL. ALMOST AS CUTE AS YOUR HAIRCUT.
OR THESE CUTE BEADS, NO?
OKAY, THEN.

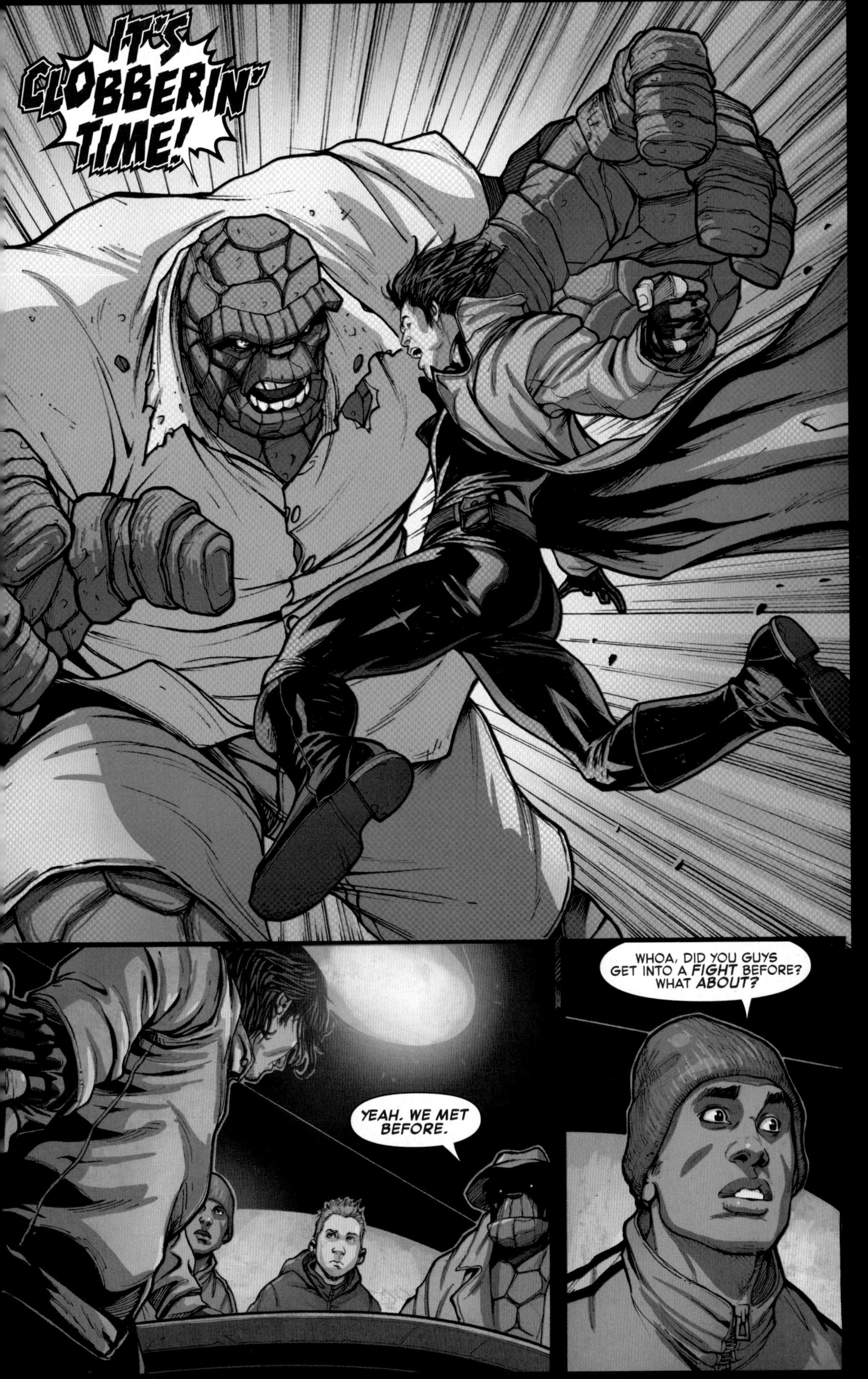
IT'S CLOBBERIN' TIME!
YEAH. WE MET BEFORE.
WHOA, DID YOU GUYS GET INTO A FIGHT BEFORE? WHAT ABOUT?

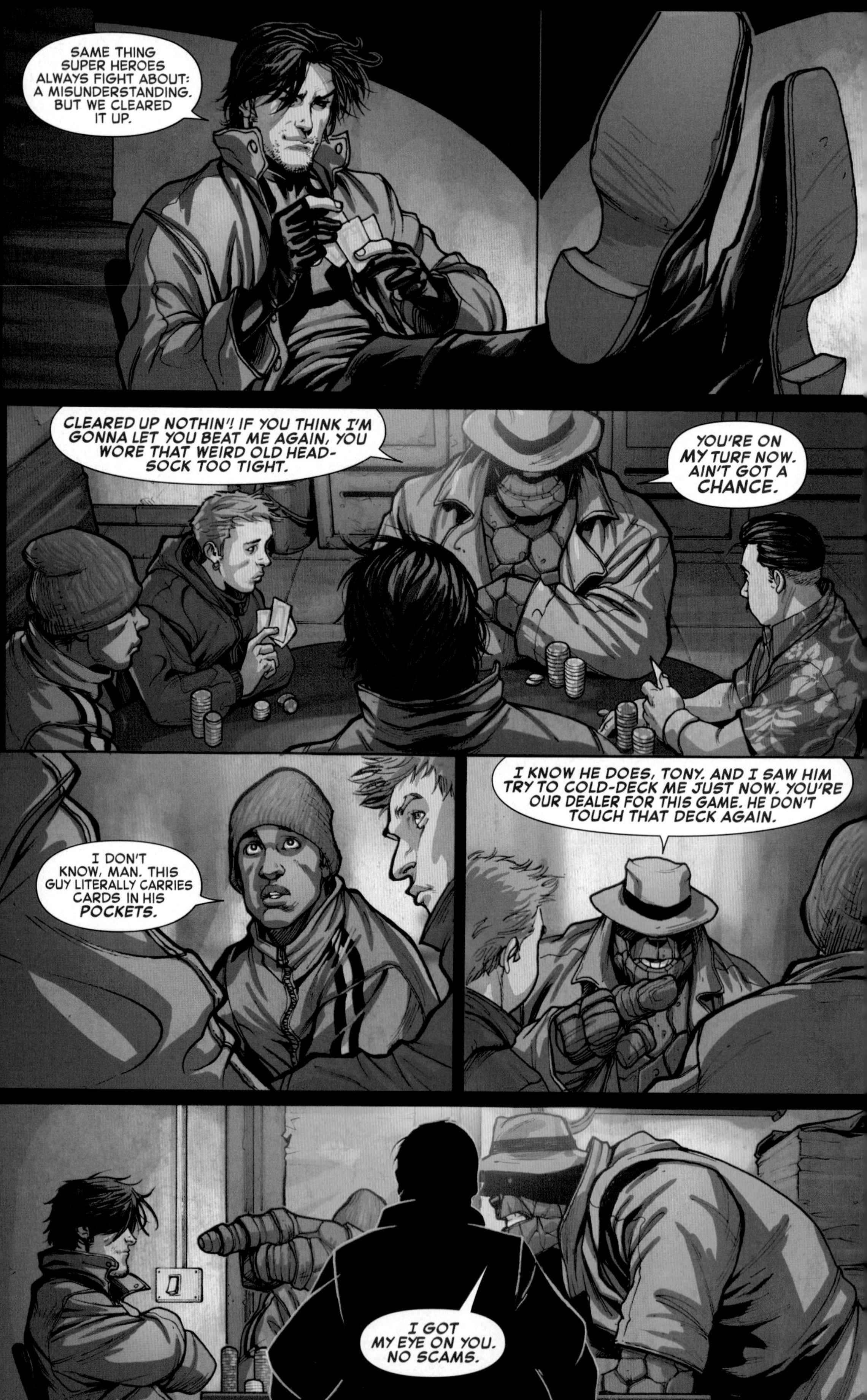
SAME THING SUPER HEROES ALWAYS FIGHT ABOUT: A MISUNDERSTANDING. BUT WE CLEARED IT UP.
CLEARED UP NOTHIN'! IF YOU THINK I'M GONNA LET YOU BEAT ME AGAIN, YOU WORE THAT WEIRD OLD HEAD-SOCK TOO TIGHT.
YOU'RE ON MY TURF NOW. AIN'T GOT A CHANCE.
I DON'T KNOW, MAN. THIS GUY LITERALLY CARRIES CARDS IN HIS POCKETS.
I KNOW HE DOES, TONY. AND I SAW HIM TRY TO COLD-DECK ME JUST NOW. YOU'RE OUR DEALER FOR THIS GAME. HE DON'T TOUCH THAT DECK AGAIN.
I GOT MY EYE ON YOU. NO SCAMS.

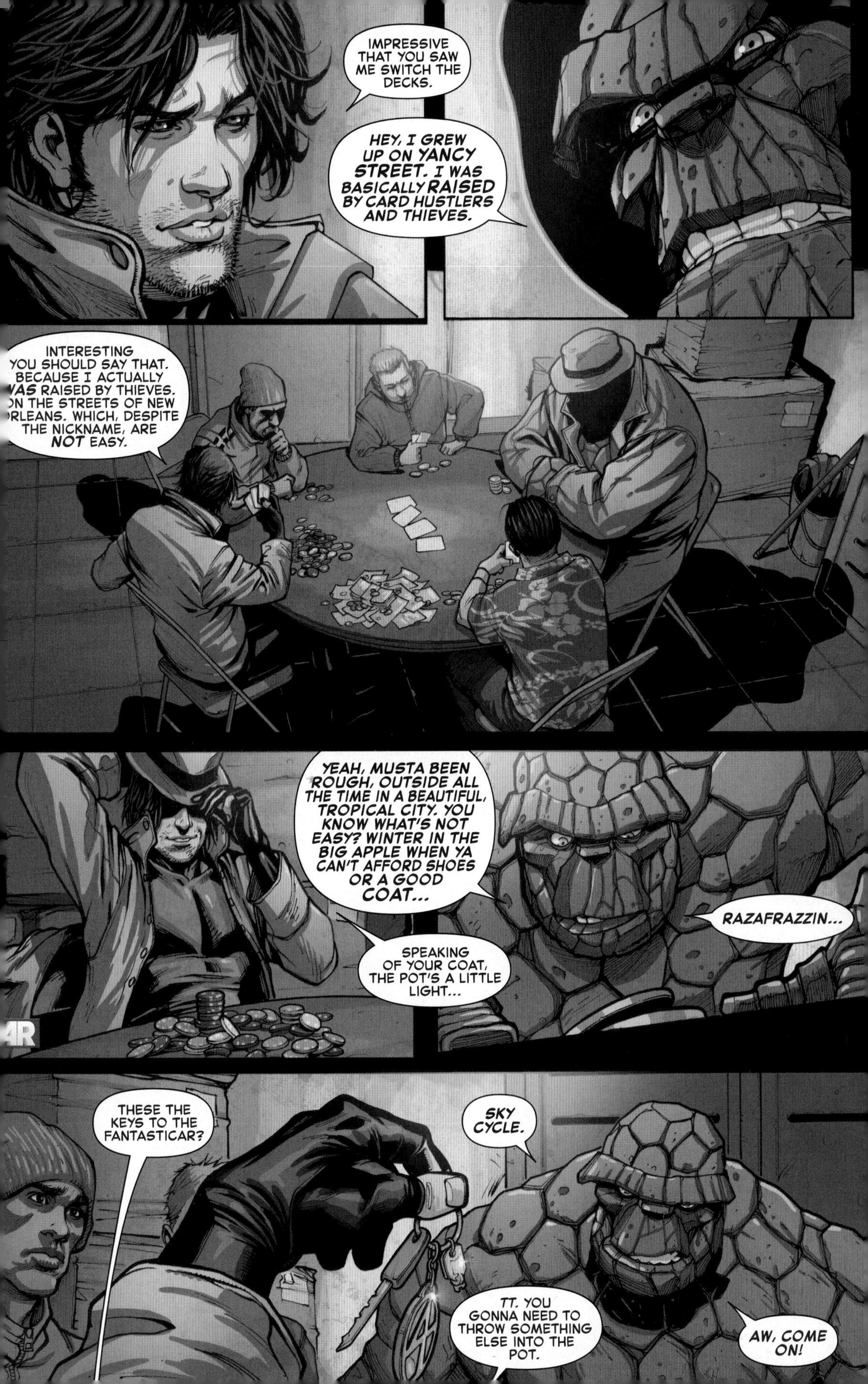
IMPRESSIVE THAT YOU SAW ME SWITCH THE DECKS.
HEY, I GREW UP ON YANCY STREET. I WAS BASICALLY RAISED BY CARD HUSTLERS AND THIEVES.
INTERESTING YOU SHOULD SAY THAT. BECAUSE I ACTUALLY WAS RAISED BY THIEVES. ON THE STREETS OF NEW ORLEANS. WHICH, DESPITE THE NICKNAME, ARE NOT EASY.
YEAH, MUSTA BEEN ROUGH, OUTSIDE ALL THE TIME IN A BEAUTIFUL, TROPICAL CITY. YOU KNOW WHAT'S NOT EASY? WINTER IN THE BIG APPLE WHEN YA CAN'T AFFORD SHOES OR A GOOD COAT...
SPEAKING OF YOUR COAT, THE POT'S A LITTLE LIGHT...
RAZAFRAZZIN...
THESE THE KEYS TO THE FANTASTICAR?
SKY CYCLE.
TT. YOU GONNA NEED TO THROW SOMETHING ELSE INTO THE POT.
AW, COME ON!

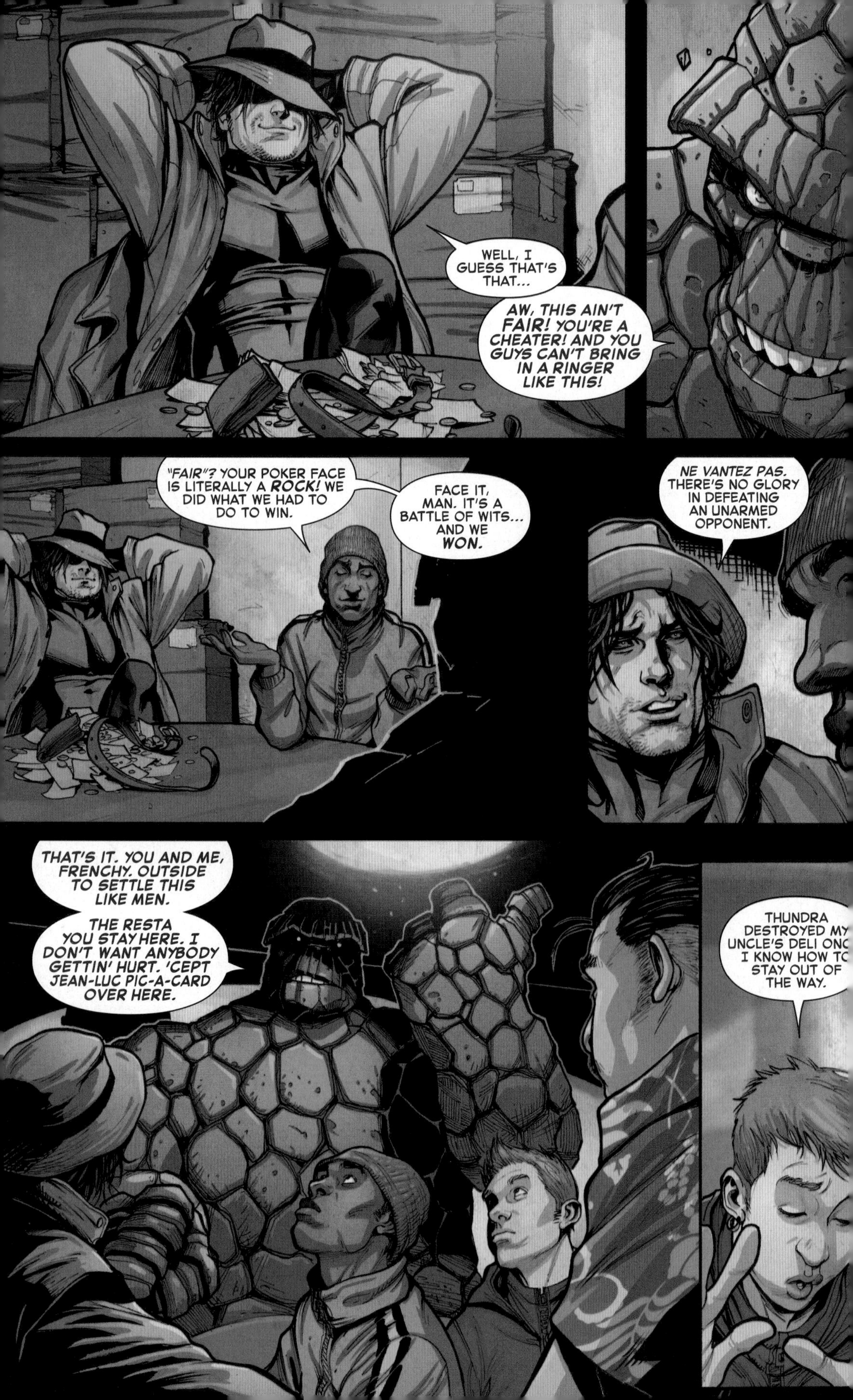

WELL, I GUESS THAT'S THAT...
AW, THIS AIN'T FAIR! YOU'RE A CHEATER! AND YOU GUYS CAN'T BRING IN A RINGER LIKE THIS!
"FAIR"? YOUR POKER FACE IS LITERALLY A ROCK! WE DID WHAT WE HAD TO DO TO WIN.
FACE IT, MAN. IT'S A BATTLE OF WITS... AND WE WON.
NE VANTEZ PAS. THERE'S NO GLORY IN DEFEATING AN UNARMED OPPONENT.
THAT'S IT. YOU AND ME, FRENCHY. OUTSIDE TO SETTLE THIS LIKE MEN.
THE RESTA YOU STAY HERE. I DON'T WANT ANYBODY GETTIN' HURT. 'CEPT JEAN-LUC PIC-A-CARD OVER HERE.
THUNDRA DESTROYED MY UNCLE'S DELI ONC I KNOW HOW TO STAY OUT OF THE WAY.

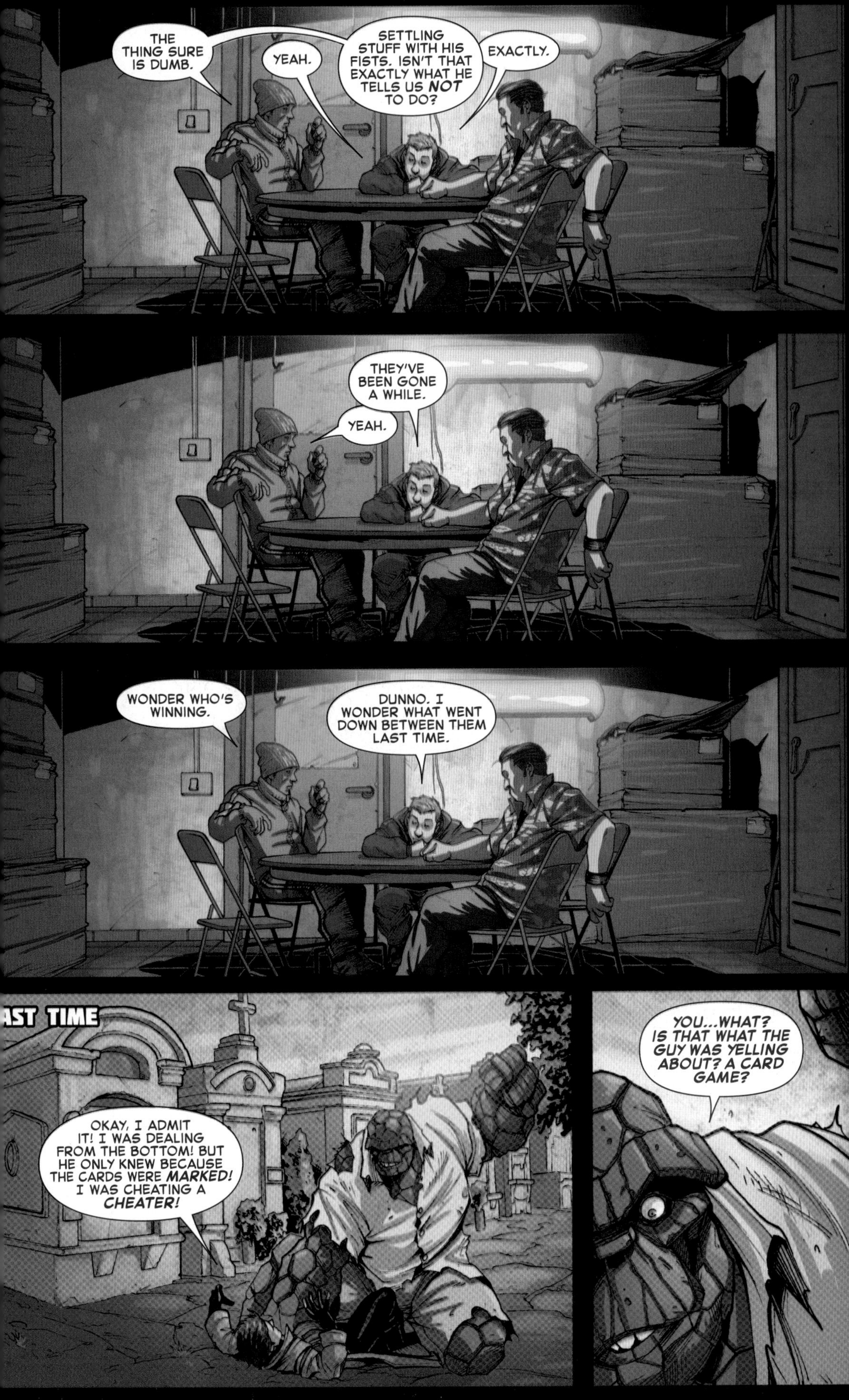
THE THING SURE IS DUMB.
YEAH.
SETTLING STUFF WITH HIS FISTS. ISN'T THAT EXACTLY WHAT HE TELLS US NOT TO DO?
EXACTLY.
THEY'VE BEEN GONE A WHILE.
YEAH.
WONDER WHO'S WINNING.
DUNNO. I WONDER WHAT WENT DOWN BETWEEN THEM LAST TIME.
AST TIME
OKAY, I ADMIT IT! I WAS DEALING FROM THE BOTTOM! BUT HE ONLY KNEW BECAUSE THE CARDS WERE MARKED! I WAS CHEATING A CHEATER!
YOU...WHAT? IS THAT WHAT THE GUY WAS YELLING ABOUT? A CARD GAME?

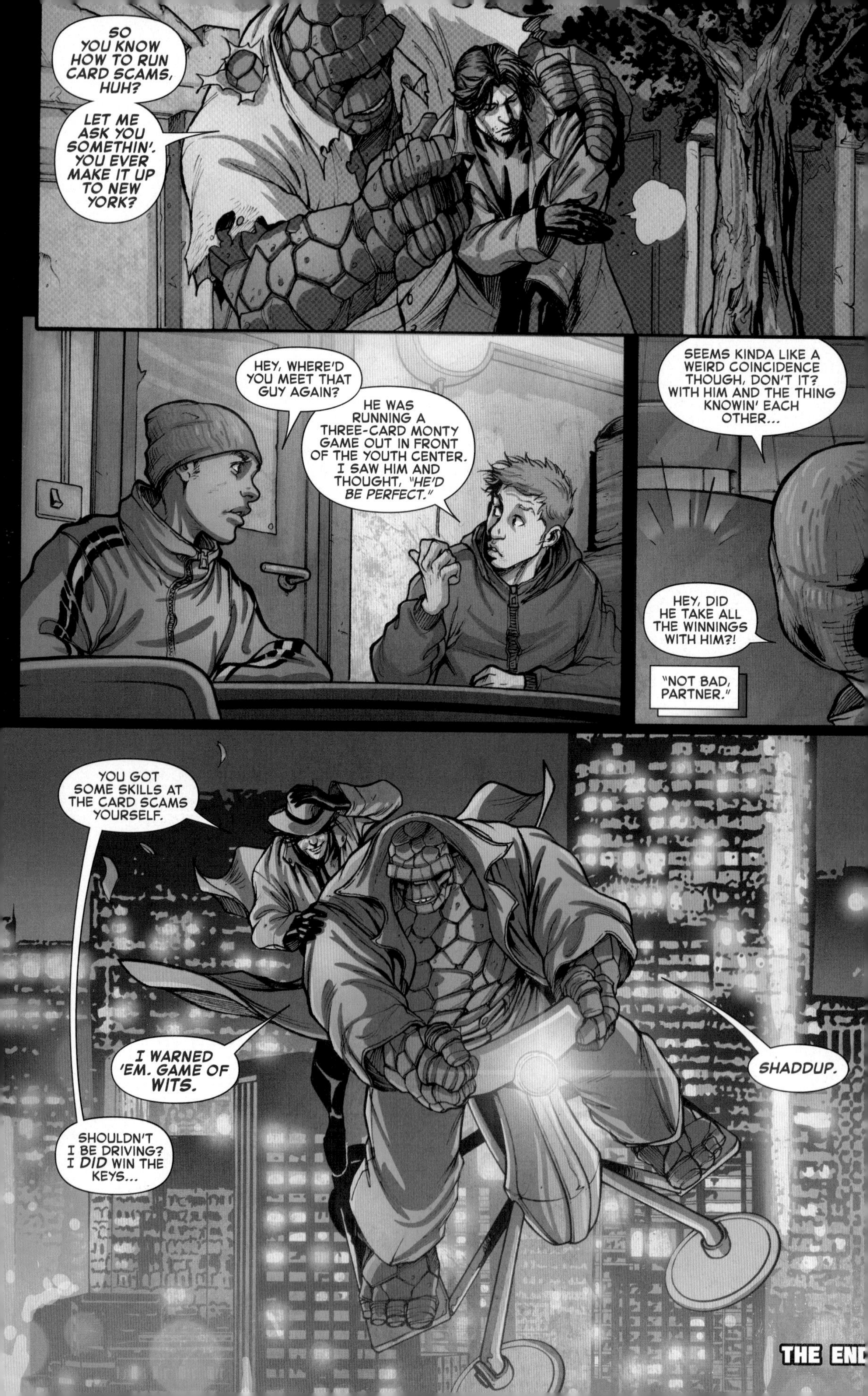
SO YOU KNOW HOW TO RUN CARD SCAMS, HUH?
LET ME ASK YOU SOMETHIN'. YOU EVER MAKE IT UP TO NEW YORK?
HEY, WHERE'D YOU MEET THAT GUY AGAIN?
HE WAS RUNNING A THREE-CARD MONTY GAME OUT IN FRONT OF THE YOUTH CENTER. I SAW HIM AND THOUGHT, "HE'D BE PERFECT."
SEEMS KINDA LIKE A WEIRD COINCIDENCE THOUGH, DON'T IT? WITH HIM AND THE THING KNOWIN' EACH OTHER...
HEY, DID HE TAKE ALL THE WINNINGS WITH HIM?!
"NOT BAD, PARTNER."
YOU GOT SOME SKILLS AT THE CARD SCAMS YOURSELF.
I WARNED 'EM. GAME OF WITS.
SHOULDN'T I BE DRIVING? I DID WIN THE KEYS...
SHADDUP.
THE END

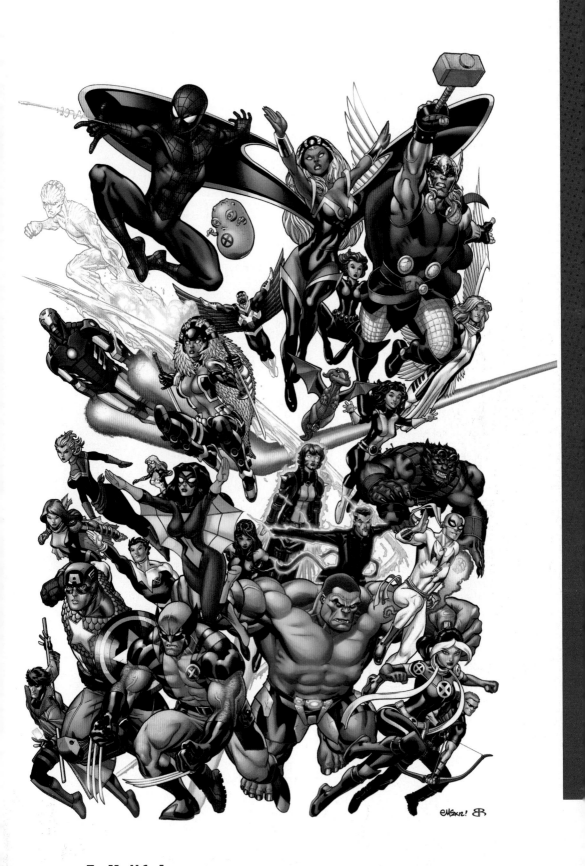

**A+X #1-4** COMBINED VARIANTS BY ED McGUINNESS & BRIAN REBER

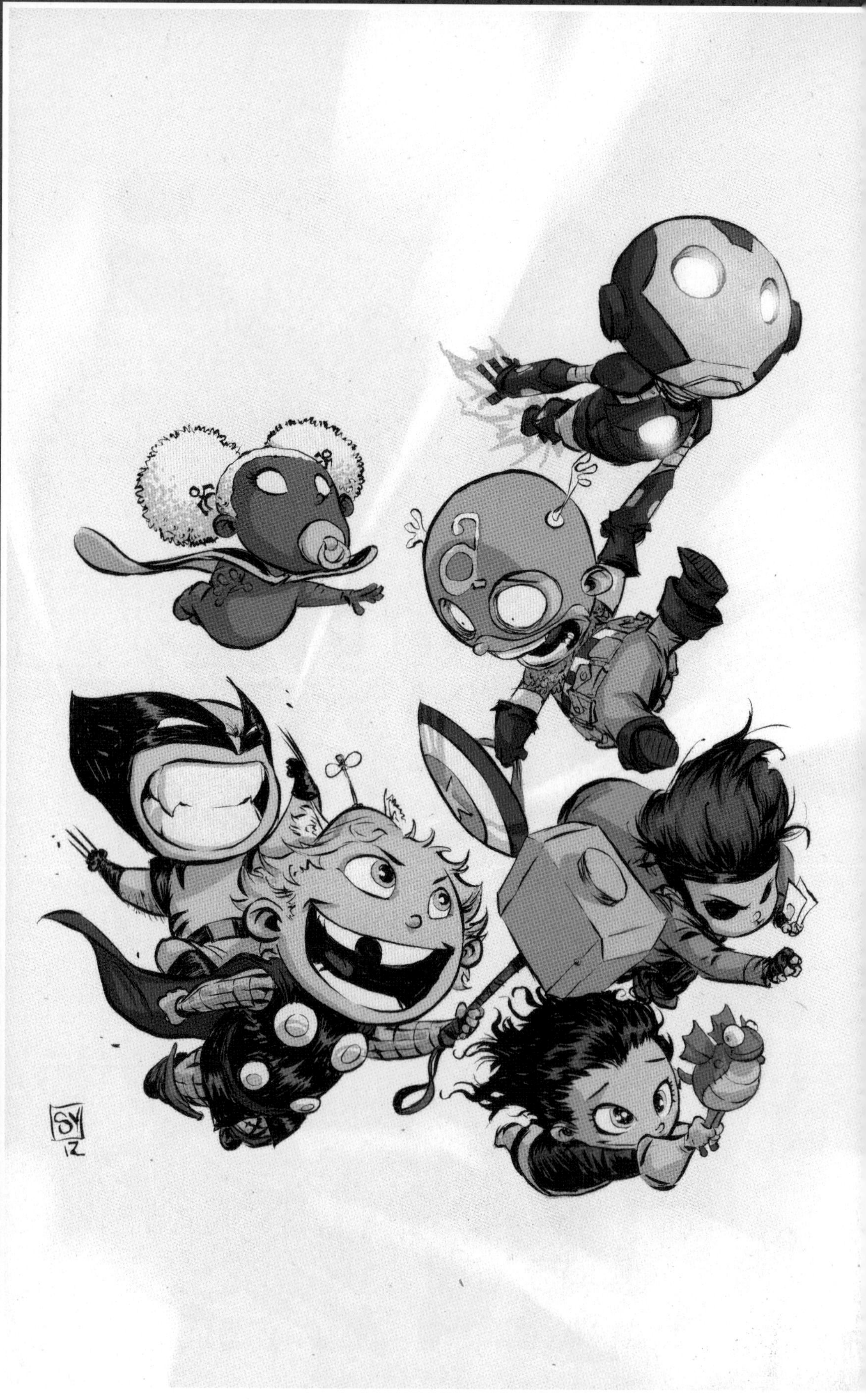
SY
12

**A+X #1** VARIANT BY SKOTTIE YOUNG

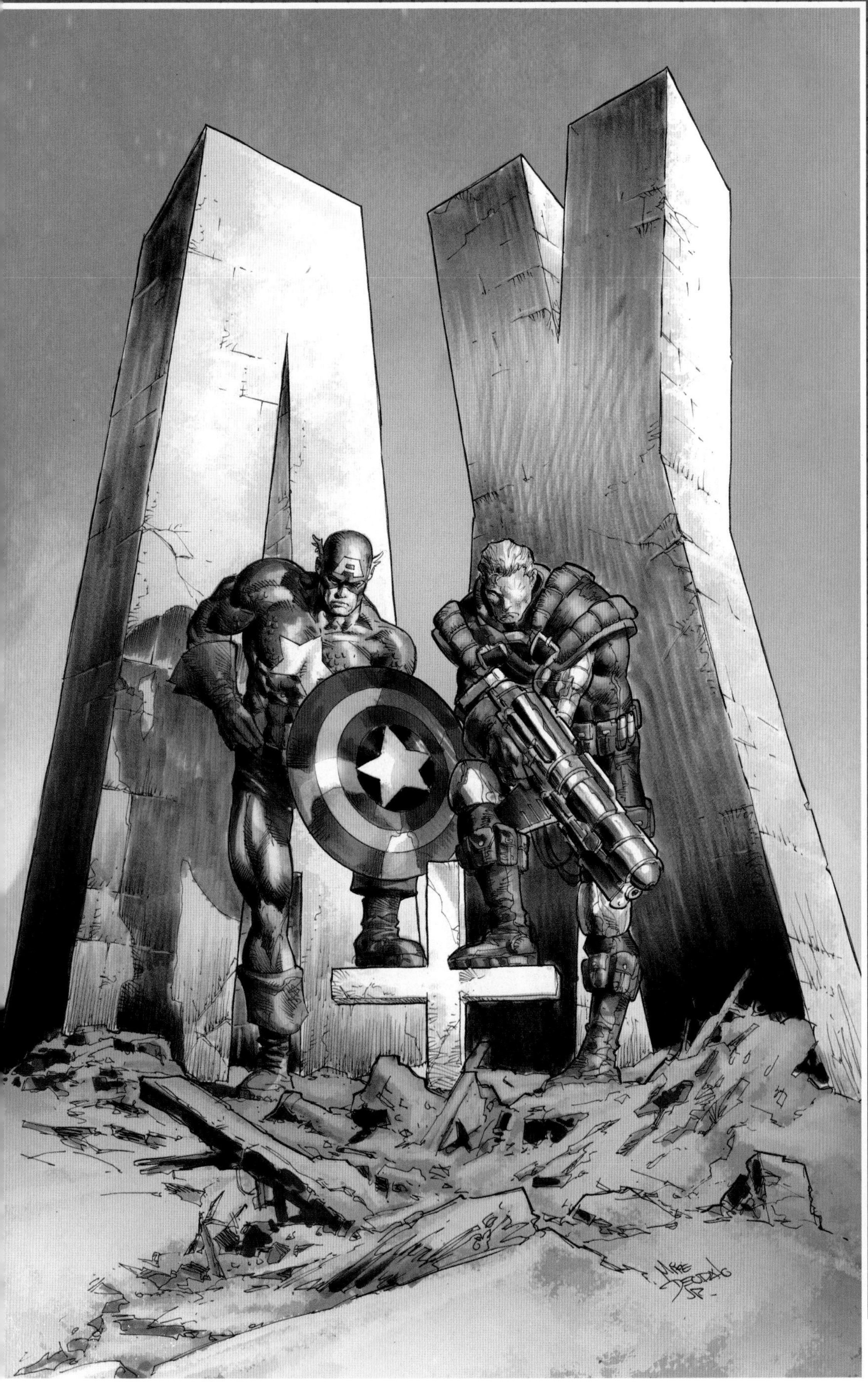
MIKE DEODATO JR.

**A+X #1** VARIANT BY MIKE DEODATO JR. & RAIN BEREDO

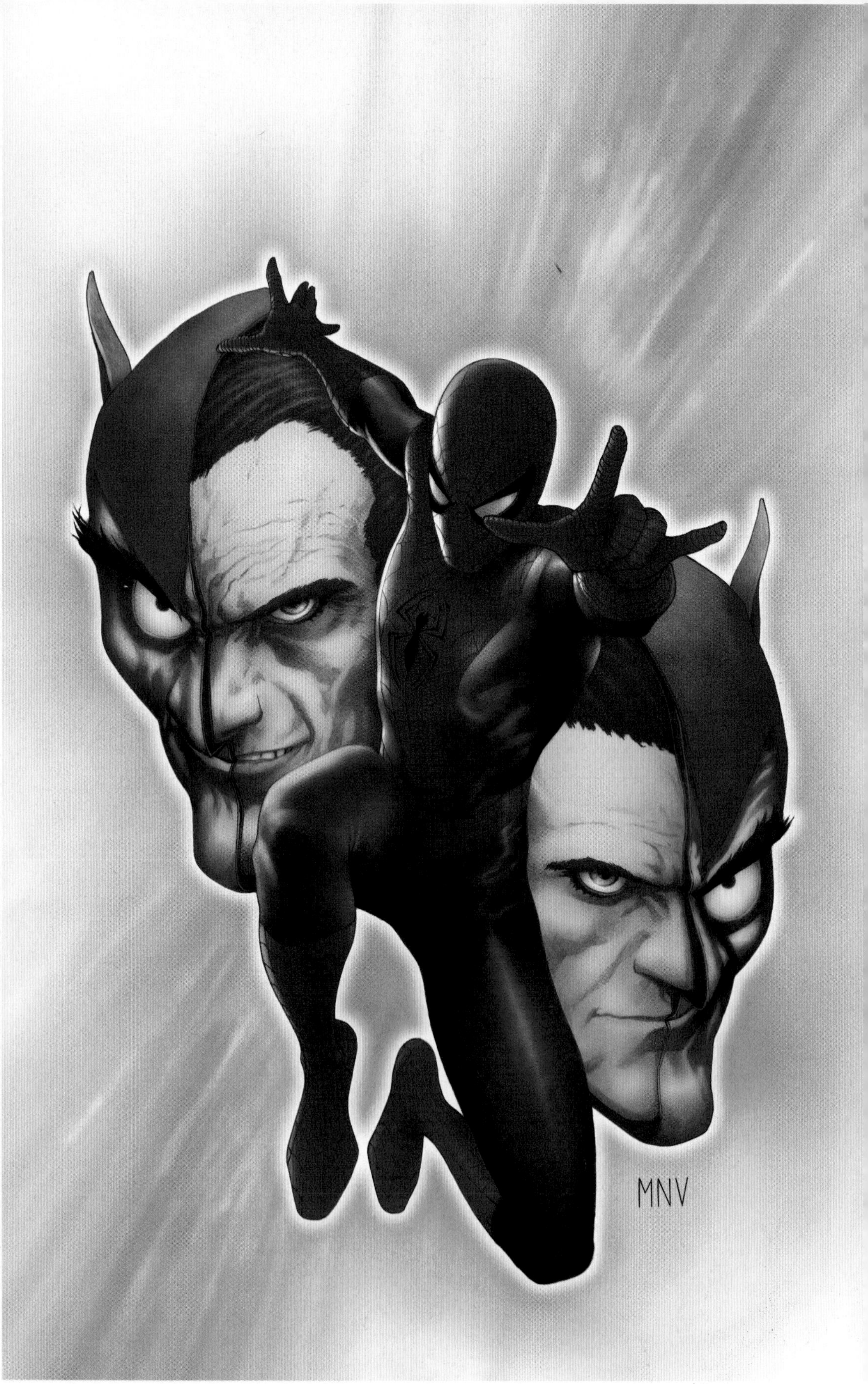
MNV

**A+X #1** ASM 50TH ANNIVERSARY VARIANT BY STEVE McNIVEN

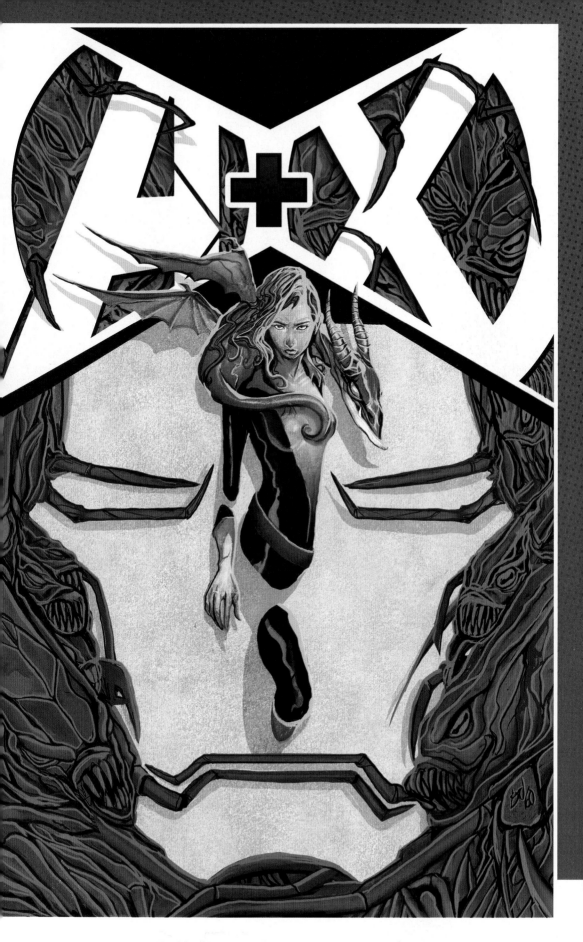

**A+X #2** VARIANT BY MIKE DEL MUNDO

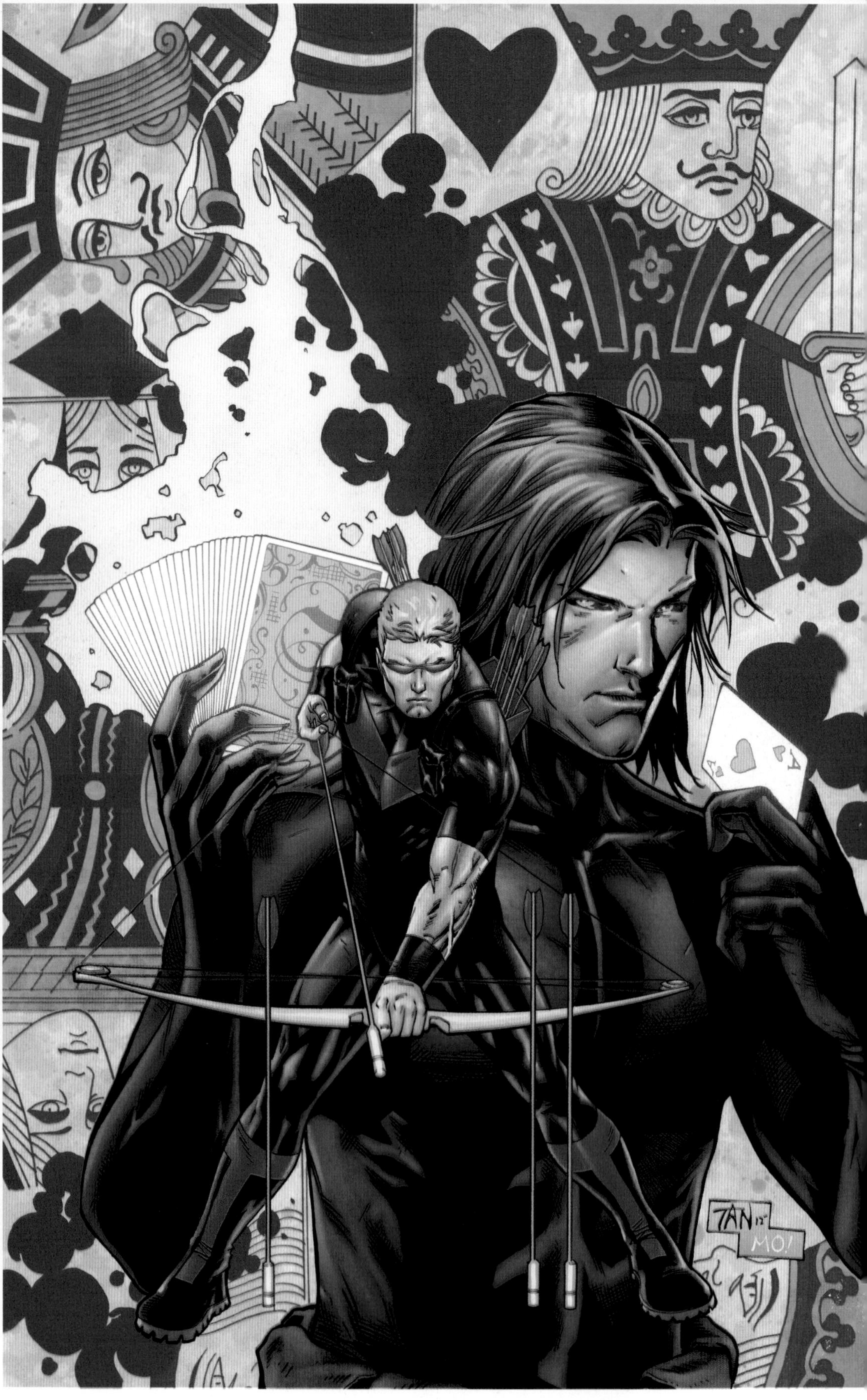
TAN
MO!

**A+X #3** VARIANT BY BILLY TAN & MORRY HOLLOWELL

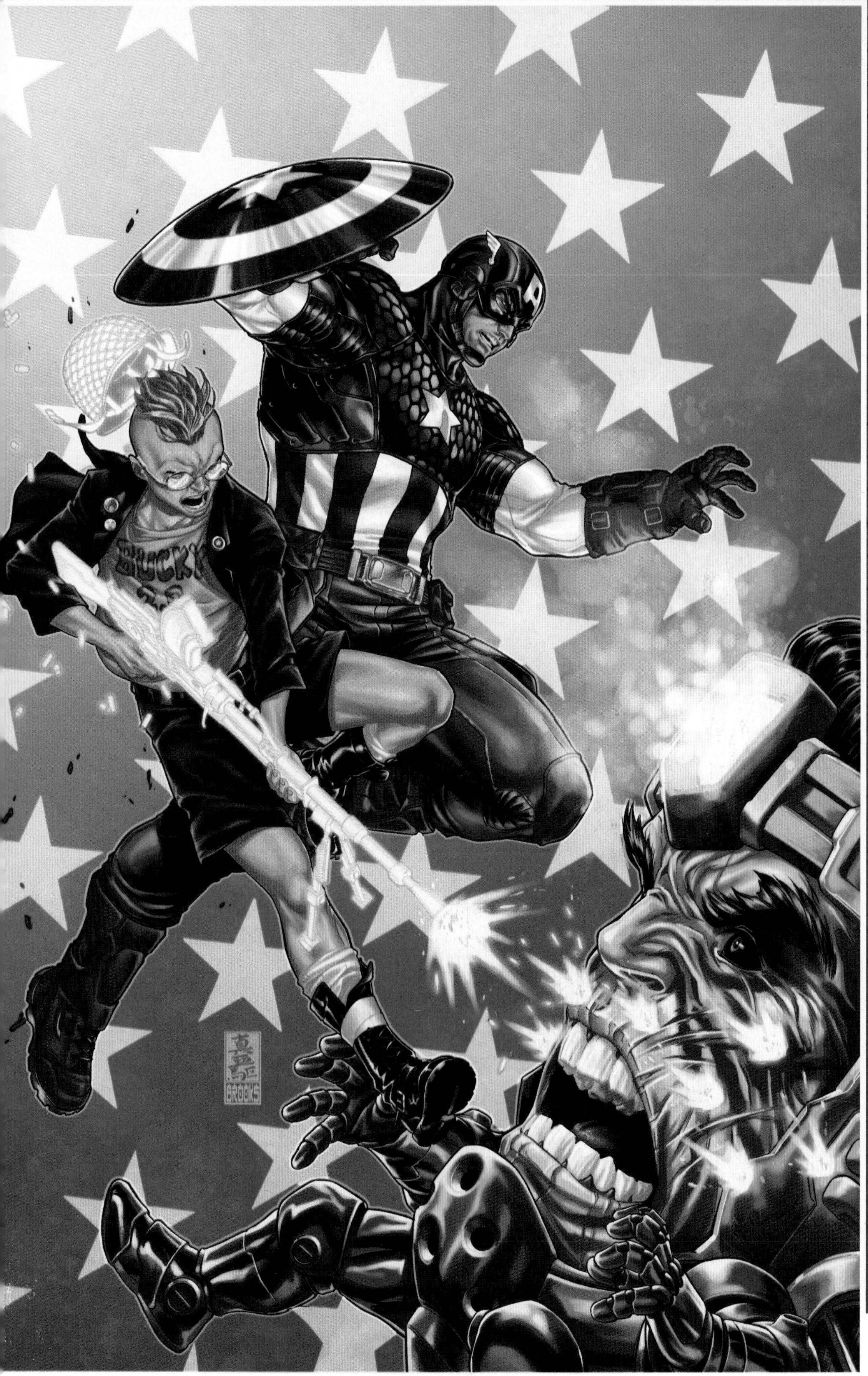
BROOKS

**A+X #4** VARIANT BY MARK BROOKS

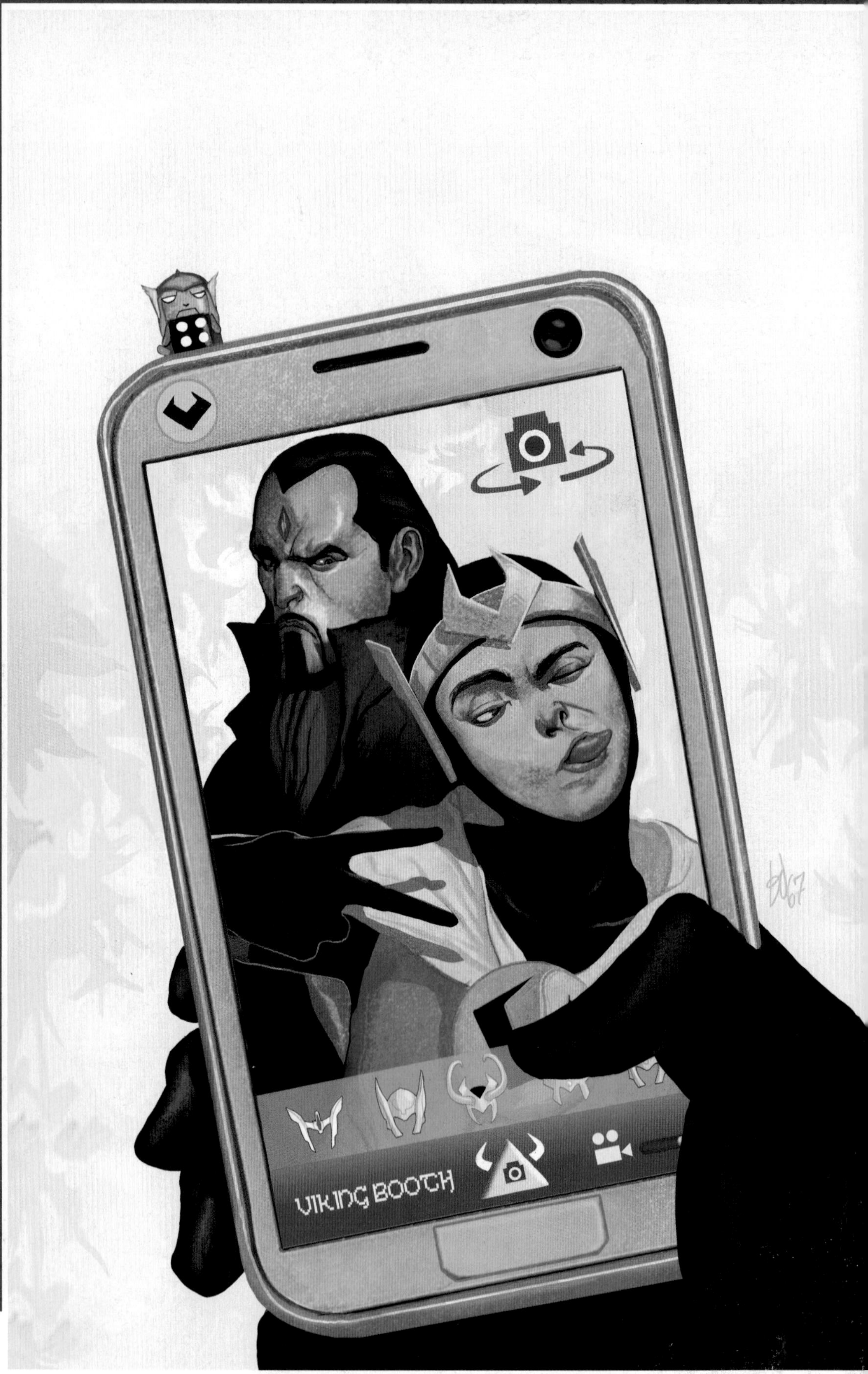
VIKING BOOTH

**A+X #5** VARIANT BY MIKE DEL MUNDO

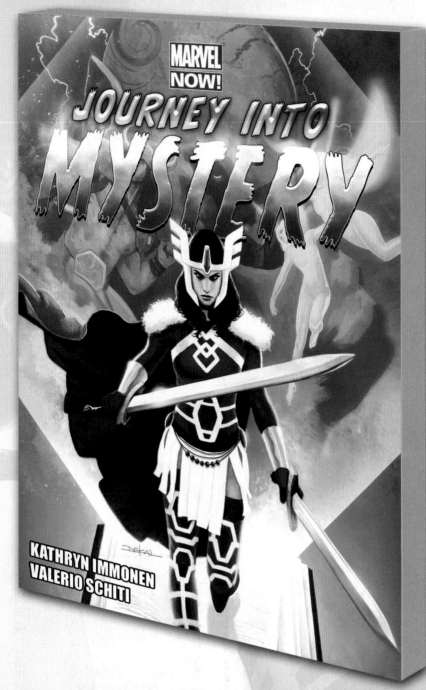

## AR INDEX

### A+X FUN FACTS

**Issue #1**
Page 1, Panel 2
Page 6, Panel 1
Page 8, Panel 1
Page 12, Panel 1
Pages 13-14, Panel 1
Page 19, Panel 1

**Issue #2**
Page 4, Panel 1
Page 5, Panel 4
Page 11, Panel 1
Page 16, Panel 1

**Issue #3**
Page 2, Panel 1
Page 7, Panel 2
Page 15, Panel 2
Page 20, Panel 4

**Issue #4**
Page 1, Panel 4
Page 8, Panel 2
Page 11, Panel 4
Page 16, Panel 5

**Issue #5**
Page 3, Panel 3
Page 7, Panel 4
Page 15, Panel 5
Page 18, Panel 3

**Issue #6**
Page 2, Panel 6
Page 10, Panel 3
Page 12, Panel 2
Page 17, Panel 3